W9-CTH-707

CIRCUMPOLAR PEOPLES: AN ANTHROPOLOGICAL PERSPECTIVE

GOODYEAR REGIONAL ANTHROPOLOGY SERIES

Edward Norbeck, Editor

ANTHROPOLOGICAL PERSPECTIVES OF:

MODERN EUROPE
Robert T. Anderson

INDIA
Stephen A. Tyler

INDONESIA
James L. Peacock

CIRCUMPOLAR PEOPLES
Nelson H. H. Graburn and B. Stephen Strong

ABORIGINAL NORTH AMERICA
William W. Newcomb, Jr.

Additional Volumes Forthcoming:

Southeast Asia

China

Africa

Philippines

Polynesia and Micronesia

Middle East

Latin America

CIRCUMPOLAR PEOPLES: AN ANTHROPOLOGICAL PERSPECTIVE

NELSON H. H. GRABURN

B. STEPHEN STRONG

GOODYEAR PUBLISHING COMPANY, INC.
Pacific Palisades, California

Library of Congress
Catalog Card Number:
72-91155
(Paper) Y-1834-4
(Cloth) Y-1842-7
ISBN: 0-87620-183-4
         (Paper)
         0-87620-184-2
         (Cloth)
Current printing (last
digit)
10 9 8 7 6 5 4 3 2 1
Printed in the
United States of America

TO SCHOLARS REPRESENTING
THREE GENERATIONS OF RESEARCH
AMONG NORTHERN PEOPLES:

WALDEMAR BOGORAS
DIAMOND JENNESS
ROBERT PEHRSON

MAPS

CONTENTS

PREFACE

This book is an introduction to the peoples of the
North in both Eurasia and America. These peoples
inhabit an area stretching over ten thousand miles
east to west and encompassing more than one-tenth
of the land surface of the whole world.
Representative peoples of many areas and a wide
range of cultures are included, many of which will
be unfamiliar to most readers. This book contains
some general ethnographic sketches, as well as
specific anthropological problems—kinship, ecology,
culture history—which together form a mosaic of
cultural description and analysis.

Both of us have major interests in the
anthropology of the North and have worked
together previously. For this book we collaborated in
writing the introductory chapter and the one on
"Modern Conditions." Although the other chapters
were individually written, we have reviewed all of
them and together bear responsibility for the
presentation. The chapters on the Athabascan and
Siberian peoples were written by Strong and those
on the Samek, Aleuts, Eskimos, and Naskapi by
Graburn.

We acknowledge our great debt to all the
ethnographers of the North, as well as to all those
others whose accounts we have used so freely. We
especially wish to thank the native peoples of the
North who have so patiently taken their time to
teach their thoughts and lifeways to generations of
anthropologists on three continents—particularly
those with whom we have worked in Alaska and
northern Canada.

Stephen Strong is indebted to and would like
to thank Jerry Dankoff, Harvey Feit, Robert R. Gill,
Ann Marie and Jean Claude Hocquenghem, Fumiko
Ikawa-Smith, Ignatius La Rusic, Richard Salisbury,
Peter S. Sindell, and Steve Talbot for aid and

discussions which have been helpful in formulating
these essays.

Nelson Graburn would like to extend his
thanks to Robert T. Anderson, Gerald Berreman,
June Helm, Karl Heider, John Honigmann, Juha
Pentikäinen, and Lucy Turner for their help and
expertise in the preparation of particular parts of
this book.

We both feel a deep gratitude to those persons
who have helped us in the preparation of this
manuscript, particularly to Judy Kleinberg and Ann
Brower of the University of California, Berkeley.

Nelson H. H. Graburn
B. Stephen Strong

CIRCUMPOLAR PEOPLES: AN ANTHROPOLOGICAL PERSPECTIVE

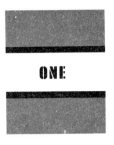

ONE

INTRODUCTION

This book provides a broad guide to the anthropology of the wide circumpolar regions by focusing on particular problems and providing brief but holistic sketches of the lifeways and history of a number of peoples of the North. This work is not intended, however, to be encyclopedic. The material presented is necessarily limited by the brevity of this book, and is further influenced by our particular interests and the lack of good comparative literature. We have selected the peoples described on the basis of the literature available and the unique or representative features of their culture. Some sections concentrate on certain anthropological problems, in which data on northern cultures have played an important part. It has been impossible to handle every problem involving the anthropology of these regions, but a number of problems—for which no solution has yet been offered—are alluded to or defined.

For readability we have omitted quotations, detailed references, and footnotes from the main text where possible. Full credit for the material and ideas is given, however, in the annotated bibliographies at the end of each chapter. These bibliographies, plus the guides to further literature, also include references to other more extensive bibliographies and provide the reader with a guide to the entire literature on the North.

THE NATURE OF THE NORTH

For the purposes of this book our area of concern includes those regions of the northern hemisphere whose lands are characterized by tundra and taiga and the seas surrounding them. These areas are commonly called the Arctic and the Subarctic, respectively. The tundra ecozone, characterized by scanty or absent vegetation, occurs in the cold areas of northern Eurasia and North America; it is kept cold by its northern latitude and proximity to the frozen arctic Ocean. Taiga is largely coniferous boreal forest, predominantly pine, fir, and spruce, with localized occurrences of such deciduous trees as birch and willow. All these trees decrease in height farther north where the taiga merges with the tundra.

These two zones are characterized by permafrost, usually continuous in the tundra and discontinuous or sporadic in the taiga. Permafrost is ground which remains below 0° C for years on end; it reaches depths of over 1,000 feet in its continuous zone and a few hundred feet in the discontinuous area. In both areas permafrost retards or prevents the growth of trees. The tree line (the northern limit of growth of trees) represents an important ecological and cultural boundary dividing the tundra from the taiga. This boundary varies where the two zones merge, with trees growing in some sheltered valleys within the tundra, and alpine vegetation growing in exposed or elevated areas within the taiga.

The climate of the North exhibits seasonal extremes. Winters are long and very cold, especially away from the coasts; temperatures reach 60–90 degrees below 0° F inland and 40–60 degrees below 0° F near the sea which freezes. The snowfall is light but the snow remains on the ground and builds up through the six- to seven-month winter. Summers are short but hot in the inland "continental" areas. Although total annual precipitation is low, when the snows melt in late spring the flat land areas usually become very swampy because of poor drainage and underlying permafrost. High winds, especially in the coastal areas, make it difficult for trees to grow; they also harden the snow on the tundra, whereas the snow remains soft and fluffy on the more protected forest floor. Farther north there is progressively longer daylight in summer (twenty-four hours above the Arctic Circle) and longer darkness in the winter.

ECOLOGY AND DEMOGRAPHY

The various chapters on human ecology demonstrate that natural production of foodstuffs for livestock kept and game hunted by circumpolar peoples and of direct sources of human food such as sea mammals, land mammals, fish, and edible vegetation is low compared to most other areas of the world. This restriction on natural production results from a number of factors common to the circumpolar regions: long winter seasons, vast sections of continuous and discontinuous permafrost which retard vegetable growth, less energy received from the sun compared to more temperate regions, and other factors. In other words, because of the special circumpolar conditions, there is less energy from the sun for the energy-fixing cycle of vegetation to transform into food and there is less time during the year for this process to take place (mainly during the short summer season). Thus less vegetable food is available for natural production of animal products upon which the circumpolar populations mainly depend.

It should also be pointed out that a number of the migratory resources on which northern peoples depend, such as salmon, waterfowl,

3

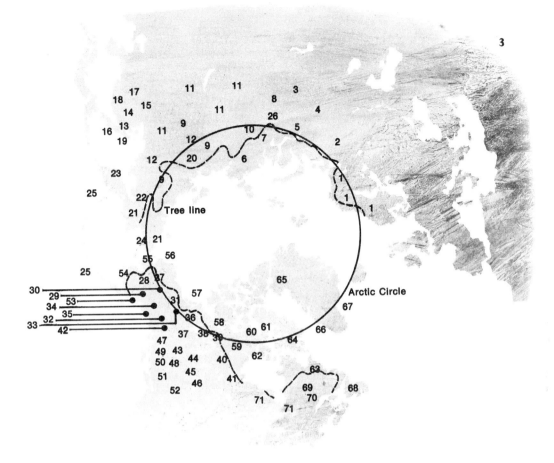

Old World
1 Samek (Lapps)
2 Komi
3 Khants
4 Mansi
5 Nentsy
6 Nganasans
7 Entsy
8 Sel'kups
9 Yakuts
10 Dolgans
11 Evenks (Tungus)
12 Evens (Lamuts)
13 Negidals
14 Nanays
15 Ul'chi
16 Oroks
17 Udegeys
18 Orochi
19 Nivkhi
20 Yukagirs
21 Chukchi
22 Koryaks
23 Itel'mens
24 Asiatic Eskimo
25 Aleuts
26 Kets

New World
27 Koyukon
28 Ingalik
29 Tanaina
30 Tanana
31 Kutchin
32 Upper Tanana (Nabesna)
33 Han
34 Copper River (Ahtena)
35 Eyak
36 Hare
37 Mountain
38 Bear Lake
39 Dogrib
40 Yellowknife
41 Chipewyan
42 Tutchone
43 Kaska
44 Slave
45 Beaver
46 Sarsi
47 Tahltan

48 Sekani
49 Tsetsaut
50 Carrier
51 Chilcotin
52 Nicola
53 Chugach Eskimo
54 West Alaskan Eskimo
55 Bering Strait Eskimo
56 North Alaskan Eskimo
57 Mackenzie Eskimo
58 Copper Eskimo
59 Caribou Eskimo
60 Netsilik Eskimo
61 Iglulik Eskimo
62 Southampton Island Eskimo
63 Labrador Eskimo
64 Baffinland Eskimo
65 Polar Eskimo
66 West Greenland Eskimo
67 East Greenland Eskimo
68 Beothuk
69 Naskapi
70 Montagnais
71 Cree

Figure 1.1   Circumpolar peoples of Eurasia and North America.

some seals, and most whales, primarily derive their food from other, warmer ecozones. The natural production of the land areas is particularly low, whereas the seas are relatively rich in plankton and differ less from other marine areas and are, in fact, connected to them through massive currents.

A particularly convincing argument on the limitations of natural production in the circumpolar areas is the small human populations found there. A rough estimate of the various aboriginal populations of the Arctic and Subarctic reveals rather scanty populations compared to other regions: Lapp, 32,000; Aleut, 16,000; Eskimo, 71,000; Montagnais-Naskapi, 5,000; Cree, 32,000; northern Athabascan, 35,000; and northern Siberian, 381,000 (of these Siberians 236,000 are Yakut, an intrusive southern group). These figures are very crude as we have no way of knowing the true population of the northern regions in aboriginal times before native populations were greatly reduced by epidemics and other influences through contact with Europeans. The figures given here show, however, that the total population of the northern Arctic and Subarctic regions of the world—580,000—was less than a quarter of the present population of Montreal and less than one-sixth the present population of Leningrad. This demonstrates in a dramatic way the limitations of hunting, fishing, and reindeer-breeding patterns of subsistence in circumpolar regions in terms of gross demography.

PHYSICAL ANTHROPOLOGY

The concept of race as defined by modern physical anthropologists is that of relative frequencies of genes of a breeding population compared to other breeding populations. Genetic differentiation in human populations results mainly from natural selection, migration, and in small populations from genetic drift. Physical anthropologists such as Washburn stress that race is of extremely minor biological importance and he further argues against the concept that certain "races" have made significant genetic adaptation to the Arctic. Thus to understand a people's life in a certain region it is much more fruitful to consider factors such as cultural adaptation than to give racial explanations.

Variations in gene frequency between breeding populations occur throughout the circumpolar regions. As the genetic causation of a series of blood types is understood, blood typing and comparing the relative frequencies of the various blood types (ABO, Rh, etc.) of different breeding populations has become a major tool for modern physical anthropologists in defining racial variation. We can mention a number of distinctions made on the basis of blood typing: Lapps generally differ from neighboring European and Siberian populations; Eskimos differ from Indians in North America; and a number of variations are found among various Siberian groups. With the exception of the Lapps, all the peoples of the North are usually classified as belonging to the Mongoloid race.

= −30°C (−24°F) January isotherm

= −10°C (+14°F) January isotherm

= less than 10″ annual precipitation

= more than 40″ annual precipitation

= major ocean currents

Figure 1.2   Circumpolar climatic features.

COMMON CULTURAL
CHARACTERISTICS

Although the peoples of the North are usually divided into "culture areas," we would like to point out some of their common features which make them a unit for study. As we pointed out earlier, the extreme seasonality of the area and the contrasting resource zones give rise to movements connected with the necessities of subsistence. The major modes of livelihood include land hunting, sea-mammal hunting, fishing, and, in Eurasia, the herding of reindeer. Throughout the area there is an emphasis on water resources which are relatively richer than those of the land. Very few northern peoples depend solely on one mode of subsistence; most combine two or even three and this reinforces the seasonality of their lives and their chances of survival. Life in the tundra, without recourse to major marine resources, is the most precarious of all; essential fuel is almost absent.

The natural resources including even the animal species of each major ecozone are common to both Eurasia and North America and are reflected in remarkably similar technologies. Tailored skin clothing and footgear are found throughout the region, semisubterranean housing and skin-covered tents are almost universal, and skin- and bark-covered boats are common to nearly all riverine and maritime areas. Other forms of transportation technology include, in the taiga, toboggans and skis or snowshoes and, in the tundra, sleds. Dogs are used to carry goods and to pull sleds in both hemispheres, and domesticated reindeer for riding, packing, and pulling sleds are found throughout Eurasia.

Traps, leisters, and weirs for fishing, and large game corrals and bows and arrows are used widely, and various forms of animal traps and snares are of great importance. In general there is an emphasis on bone and antler in the technology, but the use of metal was widespread—native copper in North America and iron and other metals in Eurasia—long before European contacts. Archeologists have pointed out similarities in worked stone throughout much of the circumpolar region. Considerable archeological literature on the North exists though there are no overall syntheses; our interests, however, center on immediately pre- and postcontact cultures. It should be noted that the archeological record shows us that differential resources were often traded over long distances and, along with technological innovations, were shared through an extensive network of native trade routes.

The extreme seasonal ecology and the variability of resources are similarly reflected in common features of social organization. All these peoples, whether they depend on hunting and fishing or on domesticated animals, have to move during the year. The demands of this transhumant and nomadic movement have precluded the formation of rigid descent groups, class structures, and permanent large-scale aggregations of population. Social groups generally split and reform throughout the annual cycle and membership is often in flux. These flexible groups are kin-based but economic considerations also determine membership. Within these social groups sharing of food is universal and economic cooperation is a major feature. Prestigious descent groups are common but leadership roles are as much achieved as ascribed.

Animism—the belief that spiritual beings inhabit or are part of all components of the natural and human universe—is universal in the North. Since interaction with these spirits determines much of one's life and fate, they must be controlled or placated. Within this religious system shamans always become the key figures. Common characteristics of the northern shamanistic complex are ability to communicate with the spirits, usually through trance and soul-flight, use of spirit assistants, belief in multiple human souls, together with a belief in other worlds. Use of the shaman's tambourine drum occurs throughout the North, usually accompanied by magic songs. Owing to his special powers the shaman often holds a position of high rank in the society, approaching that of the secular leadership. Among the spiritual relationships to animal species, the bear has an outstanding place; this widespread "bear cult" involves special deferent treatment of the bear and his remains. Songs and folklore are elaborate throughout the North, and motifs of artistic and oral traditions are often shared over wide areas, across cultural and linguistic boundaries. This suggests that intercultural contacts and diffusion, in addition to ecological imperatives, have led to some of the uniformities of the whole circumpolar region.

LINGUISTICS

Peoples of the North represent at least six entirely separate linguistic families, and cultures from five of these are discussed in the text. Linguistic differences and affinities often indicate peoples' prehistoric and historic relations, as shown in the following divisions:

Old World
I.   *Paleo-Asiatic* (probably several independent language families): Nivkhi; Yukagir; Chukchi; Koryak; Itel'mens (Kamchadal)
II. *Ural-Altaic*
     A. Finno-Ugric (including Finnish and Hungarian): Lapps; Khants; Mansi; Nentsy; Nganasans; Sel'kups; Entsy
     B. Turko-Tartar: Yakuts; Dolgans (present)
     C. Tungus-Manchu: Evenks (Tungus); Evens; Negidals; Nanays; Ul'chi; Udegeys; Orochi; Oroks; Dolgans (ancient)
III. *Ket* (not discussed in this book): Ket; Kott (extinct); Arin (extinct)
New World
IV. *Algonquian:* Montagnais-Naskapi; Cree; Ojibwa-Saltaux
V.   *NaDene*
     A. Eyak; Tlingit; Haida
     B. Athabascan (northern): Copper River (Ahtena); Beaver; Carrier; Chilcotin; Chipewyan; Koyukon; Dogrib; Hare; Han; Ingalik;

Kaska; Kutchin; Mountain; Upper Tanana (Nabesna); Sarsi;
Great Bear Lake (Satudene); Sekani; Slave; Tahltan; Tanana;
Tanaina; Tsetsaut; Tutchone; Yellowknife; Nicola (extinct)

VI. *Eskimo-Aleut*
   A. Aleut
   B. Eskimo: Yupik; Inupik

These linguistic divisions and classifications are often used as ethnic (cultural) divisions for the purposes of description. This is particularly true of the North because (*a*) the ethnic groups rarely form neat
or unified tribal or political entities, and (*b*) within major culture areas,
ethnic divisions merge gradually into each other culturally and territorially whereas dialects and languages are easier to map. The reader
should remember, however, that linguistic identity does not always
mean cultural similarity and vice versa. Further gross connections between the language families listed above have been attempted—for instance Eskimo-Aleut has been related to Paleo-Siberian, Finno-Ugric,
Indo-European, Japanese, and Sumerian from time to time—but so far,
none of these hypotheses is accepted.

RECENT HISTORY

The native peoples of the North have had, in many cases, a long period
of contact with European and Asian societies. Intrusive colonizing
groups have come from societies with an agricultural base supporting
much larger populations than that of the native northern peoples. Generally through European-native contact the aboriginal populations were
much reduced, the traditional technology mainly replaced by European
manufacture, and the native social organization altered and destroyed.
Cultural exchange was not unidirectional since many of the colonial
peoples gained much of the knowledge necessary to living in the North
from the native peoples, including crucial survival techniques and material items such as sleeping bags, skis, snowshoes, toboggans, and dog
sleds to name a few.

Generally the intruders represented imperialistic and mercantilist
powers. Prime movers were the fur trade and, later, territorial expansion
itself, both of which were destructive of aboriginal life and resources.
All of the circumpolar areas have become part of larger political states.
After varying periods of abject domination, these northern peoples have
been able only in the past few decades to reassert their rights and ethnic
identities.

ANNOTATED BIBLIOGRAPHY

Ecology and Demography

References to ecological characteristics of northern areas are to be found
in the individual chapter bibliographies. For taiga ecology see especially
Chapter 7; for marine ecology see particularly Chapter 12.

Population figures for the section on demography were taken from: Roberto Bosi, *The Lapps* (London: Thames and Hudson, 1960); Diamond Jenness, *The Indians of Canada* (Ottawa: National Museum of Canada, Bulletin 65, Anthropological Series No. 15, 1963); A. L. Kroeber, *Cultural and Natural Areas of Native North America* (Berkeley: University of California, 1939); from relevant sections of M. G. Levin and L. P. Potapov (eds.), *The Peoples of Siberia* (Chicago: University of Chicago Press, 1964); and James Mooney, *The Aboriginal Populations of America North of Mexico* (Washington, D. C.: Smithsonian Miscellaneous Collection, Vol. 80, No. 7, 1928).

Physical Anthropology

For a statement on the concept of race and a discussion of race in the Arctic, see Sherwood Washburn, "The Study of Race," in Yehudi A. Cohen (ed.), *Man in Adaptation: The Biosocial Background*, (Chicago: Aldine, 1968). Some sources of primary data on race in the circumpolar regions are A. E. Mourant, *The Distribution of the Human Blood Groups* (Oxford: Blackwell, 1954); William S. Laughlin, *Bering Strait to Puget Sound: Dichotomy and Affinity between Eskimo-Aleuts and American Indians* (Arctic Institute of North America Technical Paper No. 11, 1962); M. G. Levin, "New Blood Group Data from Siberia," *Arctic Anthropology*, 1, (1962); I. M. Zolotareva, *Blood Group Distribution of the Peoples of Northern Siberia* (Moscow: "Nauka" Publishing House, 1964); and David R. Hughes, "An Eclectic Review of the Physical Anthropology of the Eskimo," in Victor F. Valentine and Frank G. Vallee (eds.), *Eskimo of the Canadian Arctic*, (Toronto: Carleton, 1968). Further literature on the physical anthropology of particular Northern groups is given in the chapter bibliographies.

Common Cultural Characteristics

Works dealing with commonalities in the cultural history of northern peoples include: V. N. Chernetsov, *On the Problem of Ancient Substratum in the Cultures of the Circumpolar Region* (Moscow: "Nauka" Publishing House—VII International Congress of Anthropological and Ethnological Sciences, 1964); W. Bogoras, "Elements of Culture of the Circumpolar Zone," *American Anthropologist*, 31:579–601 (1929); H. B. Collins, *Arctic Area* (Instituto Pan Americano de Geografica y Historia, No. 68, 1954); A. Irving Hallowel, "Bear Ceremonialism in the Northern Hemisphere," *American Anthropologist*, 28:1 (1926). For some excellent articles on contemporary topics, see R. St. J. MacDonald (ed.), *The Arctic Frontier* (Toronto: University of Toronto Press, 1966); and G. Berg (ed.), *Circumpolar Problems* (Oxford: Pergamon Press, 1973).

Linguistics

In our classification of the languages of northern peoples, we have followed the listings in Levin and Potapov, 1964, *op. cit.* (especially pp.

2–3, 5, and map); D. Jenness, *The Indians of Canada*, 6th ed. (Ottawa: National Museum of Canada, Bulletin 65, 1963), especially pp. 17–28 and map; and R. F. Spencer and E. Johnson, *Atlas for Anthropology*, 2nd ed. (Dubuque, Iowa: Brown, 1969), especially maps VI and IX. For more recent work on the classification of NaDene languages, see Michael E. Kraus, "Na-Dene" (in press). In the literature concerning possible cross-continental affiliations of linguistic groups, see Morris Swadesh, "On Interhemisphere Linguistic Connections," pp. 884–924 in S. Diamond (ed.), *Culture in History* (New York: Columbia University Press, 1960); and L. L. Hammerich, "Some Linguistic Problems in the Arctic," pp. 83–89 in H. Larson (ed.), *Circumpolar Conference in Copenhagen, 1958* (*Acta Arctica*, 13, 1960).

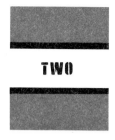

TWO

THE SAMEK (LAPPS)

The Samek[1] or Lapps have long been one of the most fascinating peoples known to the European world, and they still represent one of the most complex and enigmatic for anthropologists. Among all the peoples discussed in this book, they are unique for several reasons. The common mental picture of Lapps as smiling little Mongoloid peoples herding reindeer in the northern lands of the tall blond Scandinavians is a simplistic distortion of the very complex truth.

These people, who now number fewer than 35,000, still pursue a number of different life styles, of which extensive reindeer herding is only one and at present a minor one. They are, or were, also hunters, trappers, fishermen, boatbuilders, farmers, etc., though it is true that in recent decades those who have nothing to do with reindeer are less likely to identify themselves as "Lapps," as they are assimilated into Scandinavian national society. The two features of Samek culture that the outside world has latched upon, often to the neglect of others, have been (*a*) the invention and use of skis and (*b*) the extensive reindeer herding of the Mountain Samek. Although these features are important we shall try to give a more balanced account, including a discussion of the Coastal Samek of Norway, the Forest Samek, and the fishermen or Eastern Samek of northern Finland and Russia.

Their language is one of the Finno-Ugric branch of the Ural-Altaic stock, found in Hungary and through northern and central Russia. It is most closely related to Finnish, but less so than German is to English. There are a number of dialects, and those distant from each other are nearly mutually unintelligible. The Samek language contains many loan

[1] Though they are generally known as Lapps, they call themselves Samek or Samealbmug throughout the four countries they now inhabit. The word "Lapp," of unknown origin, first appeared in the Scandinavian literature more than seven hundred years ago. Before that they were known as Fenni, Scrithifini, or variations of these. The use of the word and root *Same-* is increasing in currency throughout Scandinavia, particularly because the foreign word "Lapp" has gathered insulting connotations.

words, some from Old Norse—showing a long history of contact—many from Finnish, and more recently from other Scandinavian vocabularies. Perhaps more than half the present-day Samek now claim one of the national languages as their mother tongue.

Physically the Samek race is more enigmatic. Older writers and laymen have regarded them as a kind of Mongoloid, like the Samoyeds, because of their short stature, dark eyes and hair, and broad heads, but they are not. Physical measurements and considerable blood-group and serum research show that they have some characteristics in common with the Mongoloids, and with the Finns and the other Scandinavians, but by other crucial measures they differ from all of these. They probably represent a separate northern European race who exhibit traces of two millennia of admixture with their neighbors (cf. the Basques). Though they share language-group identity with the Finns, this goes far back in time and does not mean that they were ever physically one group.

The archeological record shows Samek-like peoples in the same area for nearly 4,000 years. The history of contact with the many surrounding peoples and ephemeral nationhoods is extensive, including relations and interactions with the Vikings, Finns, Russians, Swedes, Norwegians, and Karelians. Culturally the Samek have taken much from these agricultural and seafaring peoples, but in other ways they resemble more closely the Samoyeds to the east, especially in their ecological adaptations and world view. The literature on the Samek is probably more extensive than that on any other small-scale peoples in the world, save the Eskimos and the Navajo, and it is undoubtedly more complex than either of those. A description of the Samek, then, involves unprecedented problems of cultural differentiation, a variety of ethnographic presents, and the question of the maintenance of Samek ethnic identity in spite of a long history of contact. The reader should be warned that no one source is by any means adequate.

The lands of the Samek (see Figure 2.1) stretch approximately 1,000 miles east to west, from the tip of the Kola Peninsula in Russia through the top of Finland and Sweden, and more than half way down the Atlantic coast of Norway. This area, now shared by four nations, is called northern Fennoscandia, and its varied physical and climatic features are of great importance in understanding the history and adaptation of Samek culture. The major feature is the high mountain chain running close to the Atlantic coast into the Arctic Ocean at the northernmost tip of Norway. In the west the sea pierces the highlands in a series of complex fjords ending in steep, wooded valleys. East of the mountains the more gradual slope to the Gulf of Bothnia is laced with many river valleys running down from the mountains. The eastern part of Fennoscandia, in Finland and Russia, is characterized by more rolling hills dotted with many lakes.

The Gulf Stream warms the western part of Fennoscandia and brings a lot of rain, whereas the east is colder and less rainy. The altitude

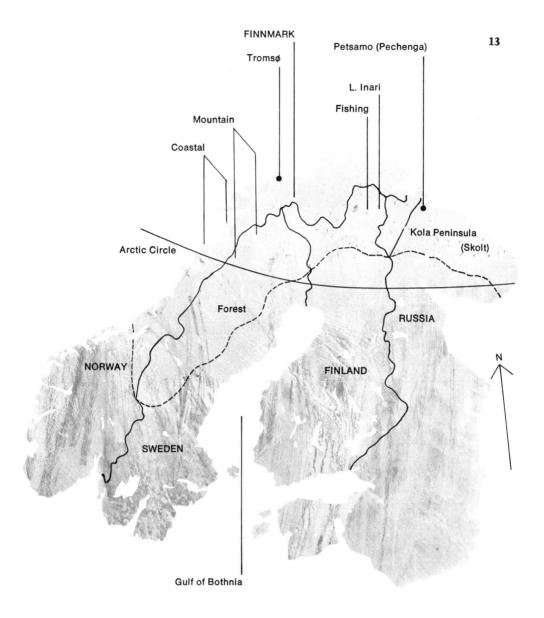

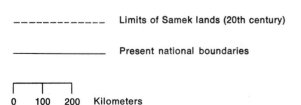

--------------- Limits of Samek lands (20th century)

_____ Present national boundaries

```
┌──┬──┬──┐
0   100  200   Kilometers
```

Figure 2.1 Samek distribution in northern Fennoscandia.

of the mountains in the west also produces a cold climate, however, with temperatures dipping below 0° F above 3,000–4,000 feet in the winters; the very highest parts, above 5,000–6,000 feet, remain snow covered during the summer. All the low-lying and foothill areas are part of the large Fennoscandian forest, consisting of pine, spruce, and birch, whereas the highlands are alpine. These higher parts, and some of the north coast of the Kola Peninsula, are tundra, and form part of the true Arctic.

EARLY HISTORY

Excavated Stone Age sites show the presence of a considerable population in this area 8,000 years ago. The remains of wooden skis, of a type used by the Samek, date back to 1500 B.C. Although the point is still argued, it is probable that the ancestors of the present population have been there for more than 4,000 years.

The earliest accounts of the Samek and Finnish peoples are the secondhand and rather ethnocentric descriptions by Tacitus (A.D. 98), who called them Fenni, and by Procopius (A.D. 550), a Byzantine scholar, who called them Scrithifini (Ski Samek). Both these accounts tell of men and women wearing skin clothes sewn with sinews, engaged solely in hunting and gathering in the forests. The wild animals in this area included caribou, bear, fox, wolverine, beaver, and, of course, fish in the lakes and rivers.

Indications of the domestication of the reindeer do not appear until the ninth century, when King Alfred of England in A.D. 893 recorded an account given to him by the Norwegian noble Ohthere. The Samek were described as hunters, fishers, and gatherers, but Ohthere claimed to own six hundred reindeer, of which six were decoys used by the Samek for attracting wild deer in the hunt. There have been many published arguments about just how domesticated the six hundred reindeer were, and it is suggested that they were herded by subject Samek. It is also important to note in Ohthere's account that the Samek had to pay taxes in the form of animal skins, bird feathers (down), whale teeth, and the hides of sea mammals, indicating considerable cross-cultural intercourse and possible modifications to Samek culture. The matter of the domesticated reindeer has been questioned because none of the other reports, either before or for hundreds of years after this time, mentioned domesticated reindeer. For all intents and purposes the majority of the Samek at this time were still hunters, fishers, and trappers.

Numerous accounts, such as those of Adam of Bremen (A.D. 1066) and Saxo Grammaticus (A.D. 1200), describe the Samek as mobile hunters using bows and arrows, fishing in the summer and hunting and trapping in the winter. These scholars remarked on the Samek's speed on skis, on which they were able to overtake wild animals, and on their incantations (hunting magic) and worship of stones (animism). Up to this point in time the Samek were probably relatively undifferentiated, adapting their common culture and technology to the local mix of resources.

15

LATER SAMEK ETHNOGRAPHY

The best accounts of the still relatively independent Samek were written after the fifteenth century by Olaus Magnus (1539, 1555), Stephen Borough (1557), Anthony Jenkinson (late sixteenth century), and Peder Claussøn (1632); much of the ethnography was summarized by Johannes Schefferus in his *Lapponia* (1673). These accounts are supplemented by remarkably good descriptions by a number of missionaries who went north to convert the Samek in the seventeenth century.

From the foregoing accounts we may reconstruct what was happening fairly clearly. As early as 1496 the Samek were described as using tame reindeer to pull sleds. We can be certain that domesticated reindeer were kept by most Samek during the 1500s and that they were used extensively by many in the 1600s, always in addition to other modes of livelihood. It is probable that the numbers of wild game were gradually diminishing and that the Samek, who had originally used a few female reindeer as decoys in the rutting season, began to depend on them more and more for milk, meat, transportation, and, most importantly, skins.

It is also apparent in these accounts that increasing differentiation had already developed among different Samek groups (see Figure 2.2). On the coast of Norway, where most of the Samek were and are found,

SWEDEN Norway	SWEDEN Norway	FINLAND Russia	NORWAY	Predominant and secondary nations
"Mountain"[b]	"Forest"[b]	"Inland fishing"[b]	"Coast fishing"[b]	Differentiation
3,000	7,000	4,500	18,000	Approx. populations[a]

	Time scale
	20th century
PARTIAL ASSIMILATION, LANGUAGE LOSS	19th century
COLONIZATION	18th century
MISSIONIZATION	17th century
(Farming and stock breeding)	16th century
INCURSIONS FROM THE SOUTH	15th century
TAXATION AND TRADE[d]	8th–14th centuries[c]
DOMESTICATION OF REINDEER?	1st–8th centuries[c]
HUNTERS AND GATHERERS (Invention of skis)	2,000 B.C.–A.D. 1

Figure 2.2 Diagrammatic representation of Samek history and differential adaptation.

the chief livelihood was sea fishing in Samek-constructed boats during the summer, and hunting, trapping, and some herding in the winter. In the forested valleys of Sweden some herding was combined with extensive hunting, trapping, and fishing. In northern Finland (which was then part of Sweden) and the Kola Peninsula of Russia, the same mix was found but with greater emphasis on inland fishing. Only on the mountainous northern borders of Norway-Sweden had extensive pastoralism begun, and here the Samek became (and some still are) primarily dependent on large herds of domestic reindeer for their livelihood. It should be emphasized that only this last group had more than a very few animals per family, and hence only that group practiced extensive transhumance (nomadism involving a set route between different ecozones every year). The other groups were more sedentary, as reflected in both their material culture and their social organization. Much, however, was still common among all groups of Samek, as we shall describe.[2]

SOCIAL ORGANIZATION

The basic unit of Samek sociopolitical organization was the cooperative group known as the *sii'da* in the west and *sit* in the east. There might be one or more of these organized groups in each *cael'de* (community district). The *sii'da* consisted of a number of families, some or all of whom were related, often through sibling links, who cooperated for various purposes, including migrating together, joint owning of land and of certain resources, building weirs, providing for the poor and sick, and exerting social control. The leader, through descent or election, called the *sii'da-ised*, was a mature and trustworthy man (more recently a rich man) who was assisted in making community decisions and maintaining order by a "sheriff" and two "jurors." These men were *primi inter pares* members of the council of all the family heads, the *norraz*. The earlier accounts stress the structured nature of this organization and the later ones the informal aspects. It is probable that as extensive herding and monetization of the economy increased, individualization became more marked. Possibly in its traditional forms the *sii'da* communally owned land and shared some of the products of hunting and trapping; later individual property in the form of large herds or plots of land became more important for inheritance purposes.

The *sii'da* was the largest permanent political unit, but members had frequent relations with people in other *sii'da* both within and outside the local *cael'de*, especially during their travels. The members of the *sii'da* were mostly kinsmen and the unit was usually exogamous, forming affinal ties between all contiguous groups.

---

[2] The following descriptions are taken from a large number of sources concerning different areas and different ethnographic presents. It is intended here to give a synthetic account of sixteenth- to nineteenth-century Samek society in its various forms, but much of the data and many of the sources are from the twentieth century; and some of the more important features had begun to disappear during the former period, as we shall describe later.

The basic kinship unit was the nuclear family household; kinsmen were reckoned bilaterally, allowing for a degree of flexibility as with most other circumpolar peoples. Women had a relatively high status among the Samek, as is apparent from the older accounts of their hunting activities and more recently in their individual inheritance of reindeer and other property. Generally, however, there was considerable division of labor, with the men undertaking the more mobile and hazardous occupations—and constituting the *norraz*—and the women being involved more with household activities, milking, and transportation of the family possessions.

RELIGION

Our accounts of aboriginal Samek religion are more fragmentary, for they were usually written by the early missionaries who were trying to eradicate the former beliefs, and from whom much was hidden. At this period (the sixteenth and seventeenth centuries) Samek religion was based on the animism and shamanism characteristic of all northern peoples, plus other beliefs derived from long Norse and Finno-Ugric contacts. Though there was a belief in a great spirit, Ibmel, and more down-to-earth deities connected with features in the natural environment, the actual religious practices resembled those of many Siberian, Eskimo, and American Indian peoples.

The basic belief was that all natural features and living beings had souls or spirits whose behavior affected human lives. Thus the animal spirits and weather deities were placated for successful hunting and taboos were observed so as not to upset them. At various places in the landscape certain natural phenomena were thought to be focal points of spirit power and these were marked with stones or effigies called *seide*. Here the Samek offered prayers and sacrificed live reindeer or presented other animals or fish, in order to ensure against disaster or to thank the spirit for fortunate events. Often these "altars"—both natural and man-made—became the repository of the horns of sacrificed deer and other remains.

The shaman (*noaide*) was a man most skillful at communicating with the supernatural. Like other circumpolar shamans he had the assistance of a magic drum, and the drum cult was probably more important here than elsewhere. All family heads had and used these tambourinelike drums, but the shaman was the most efficacious for he could engage in soul flight. Playing the drums led to ecstasy (*likkatusak*) and, for the shaman, trance, during which time his soul could leave his body and travel with the aid of a familiar spirit to the underworld (*Saivo*) where the dead and other beings could aid him. Thus he was able to cure diseases, make predictions, avert disasters, and the like. Another form of divination was practiced with the drum, on the skin head of which were painted representations of objects of Samek life as well as many spirits and deities. A small stick was placed on the skin head and the drum was shaken: the path taken by the indicator and its stopping place were "read" as messages from the spirit world.

In Samek religion, unlike that of some other pastoral peoples, the reindeer themselves did not seem to play a large part, possibly indicating the relative newness of intensive concern with owned reindeer.

The Samek held the bear in a special relationship and the hunting and killing of bears resembled aspects of the "bear cult" known throughout northern Asia, North America, and among the Ainu. Bears were hunted in their winter lairs with the aid of the shaman. The bear was aroused from its sleep and one hunter moved forward and dispatched it with a heavy spear, while the others and the shaman stood around and watched. The bear was then ceremonially hauled back to camp in a sled pulled by a reindeer, after which the women had to avoid both this sled and the reindeer for a year. There was a ritual entry into the camp and the household, followed by a ceremonial feast and a special disposition of the bones and skin. The hunters avoided intercourse with their wives for three days after the hunt, during which time they had to placate the soul of the bear. It has been suggested that the bear not only was the awe-inspiring king of the forest, but also was thought to be the most human of beasts and a repository of "male power."

ECOLOGY AND LIVELIHOOD

We have already mentioned the diversity of Samek strategic resources and the growing economic differentiation and dependence on herding during the fifteenth and sixteenth centuries. Hunting, trapping, and fishing were common to all groups.

The hunting of the bear has just been described, but however awe-inspiring the bear, the most important resource for the Samek was the wild reindeer, or caribou, and in a few areas these animals continued to be hunted until they disappeared in the nineteenth century. The image of the lone hunter chasing caribou through the forests on his skis is false for this early period, for such methods only became at all common after the advent of firearms. Early Samek hunting methods included strategic hunting, the object of which was to get as many animals together as possible, to dispatch them with the least effort, and then to distribute the products equitably among the member families of the *sii'da*. Many strategic-hunting methods involved the construction of extensive wooden or stone fences along migration routes, to concentrate the animals and guide them to the kill. The Samek used various methods. For instance, at a convenient place they built a large corral and drove the animals between converging fences, then killed them with spears. In other areas they built long fences across migration routes, with gaps at various points where they placed pitfalls or snares. In the winter's thick snow, groups of deer were surrounded and then the small Samek dogs were sent in, muzzled, scattering the deer toward the hunters who could spear them straightaway or easily catch them on skis. At other times, especially during the fall rutting season, decoys were used: a man would hide in the middle of his small herd of tame does, which would attract the buck reindeer which were then shot or speared. A man might also follow his tame male deer in whose antlers he had placed snares and when the wild bucks came to fight it they got entangled and were killed.

Other animals, including foxes, otters, ermine, and squirrels, were commonly trapped, snared, or shot with arrows. The Samek devised special traps appropriate to the habits of each species. From the time of the earliest historical records skins were used for trade and for paying taxes, and the Samek often used blunt arrows in hunting to avoid damaging pelts. The beaver, which lived in the many rivers and lakes, was the most important furbearer. The Samek placed cages at the entrance of beaver lodges or constructed nets near the lodges in the winter to trap the beaver under the ice. Beaver pelts were divided among the members of the community and were used to pay taxes or to trade; castor (the beaver's perineal glandular secretion) was also valuable in trade and was used medicinally.

Birds such as grouse and ptarmigan were very common and together with their eggs formed a major portion of the spring and summer diet. Bird skins and down were also used for trade and for taxes. A large number of birds were snared with long brush fences directing them to the kill. Many other birds—for example, ducks, geese, and other waterfowl—were shot with bow and arrow, and their eggs were also taken.

In all areas fishing was and is important; fish included salmon, trout, grayling, perch, and pike, and, on the coast, cod and herring. On the coast and on lakes the Samek often fished from small wooden boats with seine nets or with hooks and lines. Gill nets have also been used by the Samek for a long time. In the late fall nets were placed under the ice and occasionally fish would be clubbed right through thin ice. In winter and spring under-ice nets were used and also hook-and-line fishing through holes kept open with ice chisels. In winter fish might be stored frozen, and at other times they were eaten or dried and stored for later consumption, trade, or taxes.

The Samek had very little vegetable food; in the late summer they gathered berries, and used other plants for medicines. In general they had to subsist on the products of hunting and fishing, and the milk, butter, and cheese of domestic reindeer. In the last few centuries their diet has included more agricultural and imported products, including coffee and tea.

COASTAL, FOREST, MOUNTAIN, AND EASTERN SAMEK

Samek (Sea Finns or Sea Lapps)

Inhabiting the many fjords of the Norwegian coast these most numerous of the Samek have been seminomadic for a thousand years or more. From the earliest accounts they were described as excellent boat builders and seafarers. There is no evidence of their having used skin boats, as did other Arctic peoples. Their craft were made of planks sewn together with sinews or plant roots, and they were so good that, until recently, neighboring Norwegians often bought them.

Though the Norwegians were good fishermen, it was the Samek who were traditionally expert whale and seal hunters, using the typical circumpolar harpoons and other equipment. For centuries they used these skills to obtain pelts and make rawhide ropes, which they used in their dealings with the immigrant Scandinavians as trade and tax items.

The Samek usually established their base camp near the head of a long fjord, where they spent the winter in turf-covered huts *(kata)*, the basic construction of which resembled the skin-covered tents of more nomadic peoples. During the winter they hunted, trapped, fished, and, probably within the last thousand years, most of them maintained small domestic reindeer herds. In the spring and summer they moved down the fjord toward the sea, where they would spend the summer hunting and fishing from their boats. The small reindeer herds would be freed to run in the fjord valleys, often encircled by extensive fences to prevent them from escaping or mixing with wild animals. In the fall the people would move inland up the steep valleys to hunt and trap. At this time some of them would have to control the deer during the rutting season when the bucks fight; castration of animals also took place at this time.

For centuries the Samek carried on this life, side by side with the Norwegian fishermen, and both traded their fish to the Russian Pomor traders who sailed round the Kola Peninsula from the White Sea. As Norwegian fishing equipment and business acumen improved, the Lapps fared less well and came to depend more on their land-based activities. Some took up supplementary stock farming and, as wild animals to hunt and trap became fewer, the size of domestic herds and the dependence on them increased in some areas. Some of the coast Samek therefore became more fully nomadic, "typical" "Mountain Lapps." In general, however, the coastal peoples remained in the valleys, but maintained their kin and social relationships with the pastoralists from both Norway and Sweden, who often herded the deer of the settled peoples for a small fee and established long-term *verdi* (partnership/exchange) relationships.

Forest Samek

The Forest Samek inhabited the wooded valleys on the east side of the main mountain range. It is probably this group, along with some Eastern Samek, that maintained the aboriginal life style longest. Their seminomadic annual cycle was determined by the movements of the animals they hunted and trapped, and, to a lesser extent, by the needs of their few domesticated reindeer. Their winter-base villages were in the lower regions of the river valleys not far from the coastal plain, or in the river valleys of the more rolling forest area to the east in Finland. There they lived in tents (also called *kàta*) constructed from many straight poles leaning together and covered with skins or, later, with woolen cloth; they also had a pyramidal timber hut (another form of *kàta*), made of planks of wood on a log base and covered with birch bark. In addition these Samek had log storehouses *(aite)* raised on stilts and, like other Samek groups, smaller storage huts on the tree trunks or on top of wooden posts *(njalla)*; these huts were used to store meat and to protect it against the voracious wolverines.

The annual cycle was a response to the need to hunt for food, to trap high-quality furs for trade and taxes, and to fish the lakes and rivers in season. In the winter the Samek trapped beaver, fished through the ice, hunted locally, and intensively herded their few tame deer. In late winter the hunting of animals in the thick forest snow on skis was a major occupation. In April or May the Samek let the reindeer loose to roam up the valley sides, enclosed by miles of fences. Other deer were kept close by for transportation and decoys. In summer the people moved upstream and lived in tents, fishing intensively, gathering eggs, and hunting a little. In late summer they milked the doe reindeer, and in the fall they hunted the wild deer with decoys, snares, and pitfalls. Then they rounded up their tame reindeer and made their way back to their winter quarters.

This kind of life depended on adequate lichen in the forests for the reindeer to feed on and a large supply of wild game. In Finland the peasants moved north and burned the forests for farmland, causing the Lapps either to move farther north or to take up another mode of existence. This happened also in Sweden but at a much later date.

Mountain Samek (Reindeer or Fell Lapps)

At higher elevations the trees are replaced by scrub and alpine tundra, and it is in these areas that some of the wild reindeer herds used to spend their summers away from the bothersome insects of the lower regions. The aboriginal hunting Samek followed these herds, but extensive use of these areas probably came about only after the fifteenth century, when both the forest and the coastal peoples had come to depend more and more on tame deer. With the diminution of wild game and encroachment from the south, some of both the Forest and Coastal Samek derived a larger and larger proportion of their subsistence from domesticated deer. This meant that the herds had to be much larger, for it takes one hundred to two hundred animals to support a family of five, whereas before this each family had owned only about five to twenty. Based originally in the upper regions of the valleys, these Samek began to follow and herd the deer[3] throughout their yearly migrations up the mountains and north onto the treeless tundra. They

[3] The reindeer of these areas are probably a slightly different subspecies than the forest reindeer, and follow different and longer migration routes.

adapted their life style to this full nomadism, spending more time in protecting the herds (e.g., from wolves and wolverines) and less and less time in hunting and fishing. Thus evolved the familiar pastoral "Reindeer Lapps" who, though usually described as "typical," have probably never constituted more than 10 to 20 percent of the total Samek population.

The winter camp was built in the forested areas at the head of the river valleys, so that the herd could feed on lichen that grew under the snow and on the trees. These Samek lived in portable tents (*kåta*), with a frame of two pairs of curved branches joined at the upper end to each other and to a single crosspiece. On this were laid many straight poles in "tipi" fashion and the whole was covered with skins or, later, textiles. An opening at the top allowed smoke to escape from the centrally placed hearth, above which the family cooking pot was hung from the crosspiece. In many wintering areas somewhat similar dwellings were erected, but birch bark overlaid with turf covered the poles and the poles or logs were heavier. Recently these dwellings have been used along the migration routes at spring and fall stopping places, and Western-style houses have been built in the winter villages.

During the winter the herd had to be tended and moved from place to place as each area was grazed. There was also some hunting and fishing. In the spring (April–May) the herds began to move to higher ground and the Samek packed their belongings and followed the herd, trying to keep it under control. Tent materials, clothing, and the like were carried on reindeer backpacks, and the boatlike wooden sled, *pulka* or *akja*, could carry both people and belongings. These short sleds, often with a deck and a V-shaped keel, are unique to the Samek, though they were often built for them by the peasants settled in the same areas. The more open, two-runner, Samoyed-type sled was also used, increasingly replacing the *pulka* in the last hundred years.

The whole migrant groups quickly climbed to higher elevations or went north beyond the tree line to the calving grounds, where tundra and new grass fed the deer, which were intensively watched and herded twenty-four hours a day in open areas; of course, it is light all the time in summer at those latitudes. Along headlands and between arms of the sea or lakes, fences were built and herding could be less intensive. Like their coastal and forest brothers, the Mountain Samek used these devices as much as possible to reduce the manpower needed to look after the large herds. Many of the migration routes led over the mountain chain down to the Norwegian coast, where the herd would be driven across the sea onto the many islands where herding was simplified. During the summer sleds and skis were abandoned and everything had to be carried or packed. The winter equipment was often left at a convenient place along the route, to be picked up again on the fall migration.

During the summer the does and calves were protected and kept separate from the bucks, the does being milked frequently. In recent

decades more and more fencing has been erected to minimize super-
vision and allow larger herds for each family's small labor force, and
the amount of milking done has decreased. The calves were marked
by cutting patterns on the ear to indicate individual and family ownership. At the end of the summer the deer started to return to the winter
pastures. During the early fall the rutting season brought disorder as
the bucks fought for does, and in the past many deer tended to run
off to join the wild herds. At a convenient place during the fall migration, often at the point where the winter equipment was stowed, the
herds were stopped for the rutting season and corralled in huge enclo-
sures that resembled the earlier hunting corrals. Here the animals were
milked and sorted with the aid of lassos, to be returned to their proper
owners. For meat, the Samek killed reindeer by stabbing them in the
heart, and they castrated many males by biting off their testicles—these
geldings were much more tractable for transportation or for use as
decoys. After a stay at this site, the herds and their owners moved
back down to their winter villages, using their winter equipment over
what was by then snowy ground and frozen lakes and rivers.

Eastern Samek

The Eastern Samek include those who live around the lakes of Finland,
especially Lake Inari, and who concentrate on fishing; they also include
the dialectically different "Skolt Lapps" and those of the Kola Peninsula.
These peoples' mode of existence has probably been more varied and has
changed more than that of the other three groups described. They have
also been subject to the incursions of more different peoples than have
the others, especially the encroachment of the Finnish farmers who
moved north many centuries ago and with whom there has been extensive cultural interchange and marriage. The Russians also moved into
the area from the east, along with the Samoyeds, Karelians, and Syren-
ians.

In general, fishing was important throughout the year, along the
shore, under the ice, and on the lakes from boats. Originally these
peoples were hunters and trappers but, as elsewhere, wild animals diminished and subsistence and earning power had to be supported otherwise. Small herds of domesticated reindeer were kept by most families
and the annual cycle resembled that of the Forest Samek, except that
instead of going up the valleys in the summer, these people went away
from the rivers that run along the valley bottoms. The extent of reindeer
breeding has been limited not only by the incursions of Finnish farmers,
but also by those of pastoral Samek from the west and Samoyeds, Russians, and other herders from the east.

As a response to these pressures, fishing has become intensified
and a large proportion of the original inhabitants have practiced farming
and stock breeding for hundreds of years now. Except for the groups
around Lake Inari, their life style has been barely distinguishable from
that of their neighbors the Finns and the Russians. A further complica-

tion has been the changing national borders between Finland and Sweden and, more recently, between Finland and Russia. After 1945 many reindeer-herders as well as fishing Skolt Samek had to move into the already inhabited area around Lake Inari, because the Russians took over some Finnish territory.

MATERIAL CULTURE

The various types of housing and storage places have already been briefly described. Within the circular or rectangular house, the central hearth burned wood or brush for heat and for cooking, and the smoke kept away the many insects in the summer. The hearth was also symbolically important as the focal point of the home. Around the edges sat and slept the inhabitants and the floor was usually covered with twigs, pine needles, or sand, which could be changed easily for cleaning. In this century the majority of the Samek have moved into more regular Scandinavian-style houses as they have tended to live a more settled life.

Samek clothing was distinctive, at least until recently. The earlier skin clothes of the hunters and trappers, and to some extent of the herders as well, has given way to equally distinctive woven clothes, which are still used in some areas. The footwear consisted of a large ankle-length skin boot with an upturned toe, usually worn with sedge grass which could be changed when it became damp or dirty. The trousers, of leather and later of textiles, were tied low on the waist and hung around the outside of the boot tops. The upper garments, originally two layers of skin, have given way to textile clothes, sometimes supplemented by a skin coat, poncho, or scarf. The knee-length "frock coat" had no hood but was tight around the neck, at least in the North, and was always belted low on the waist. These coats were made of wool cloth, often woven by the Samek themselves or obtained in trade, and they were colorfully decorated with stitchwork and often with finely beaten tin appliqué. In the winter long gloves were worn, sometimes also packed with sedge. The Samek hat was (and is) most distinctive, and the different types indicated which area or village a person came from. These hats are large and fit tightly around the head but are loose and full on top, being cut to form a cone with a colored woolen pompon or with two, three, or four points. They have changed over time, in imitation of outsiders' styles of headgear, and most are decorated with ribbons or sometimes with tin-embroidered cloth. Young children were wrapped in fawn skins.

The very young, the old, and the infirm were carried in the *pulkas* during migrations, and babies were tied to a frame slung on the pack animals. This ingenious frame was made to carry many objects and was hung from the two pommels of the animal's packsaddle. Reindeer were rarely ridden by adults. The deer themselves were sometimes decorated with ribbons and originally were guided by a single rein. Lassos were made of leather, and the Samek were skillful at tying knots and using thong ropes.

For the last thousand years or more much of Samek material culture has been obtained in trade. Brass and iron were common for utilitarian and ritual purposes; the Samek used metal knives and weapon points, and cooking was usually done in an iron pot or kettle suspended by a chain above the fire. Of course, the Samek themselves decorated many of these items, such as knife scabbards, and they have always been skillful workers of wood, horn, and bone, making ladles, boxes, flasks, bow drills, and the like.

Samek wooden skis, bent in frames, have become narrower and longer throughout the centuries. Originally they were backed with fur for gripping. Traditionally a hunter used one ski pole in the left hand and carried the bow (or gun) in the right, with the quiver of arrows slung on his back. More recently the Samek have used manufactured skis, but apparently they have never used snowshoes.

THE SAMEK'S RELATIONS WITH
OTHER PEOPLES

Unlike many other peoples described in this book, for two millennia the Samek have had relationships with powerful outsiders and have maintained their identity in spite of a number of changes in their life style and their colonial status.

Early Contacts

The early hunters and fishers were subject to taxation and plundering by the earliest Scandinavian "war lords," and the Samek have been pushed north out of most of Finland in the past 1,800 years. Until recently, the majority of the Samek have moved or have changed their means of livelihood rather than be completely absorbed by the conquering agriculturalists, but the limit of their independent adaptation was probably reached during the last century, when European colonization became intensive all over the world.

Until the fourteenth or fifteenth centuries the Samek were subject to exploitation only along the edges of their domain. Trade and cultural interchange were undoubtedly common, but we do not have good accounts of the intercultural social relationships. A few themes are important: (1) From prehistoric times non-Samek peoples have inhabited or visited even the northernmost areas and have had contacts with the Samek. (2) The Samek have generally been the subjects of exploitation but (a) trade has usually been mutually beneficial, and (b) the Samek have very rarely fought back in any organized or violent way. (3) Until the last century or so the Samek have shared much of technology of the invaders and have often had the upper hand or even been the more prosperous, with their superior knowledge of how to adapt to the socioecological environment. (4) The national boundaries in northern Fennoscandia have been unclear until very recently, sometimes leading to wars and disputes over this territory.

Archeologists have excavated sites in northern Fennoscandia that were inhabited during the first millennium A.D. Not only do these sites yield skeletons showing Samek-Scandinavian admixture, but also many of them contain hoards of precious metals and jewelry, suggesting that some early Samek must have grown prosperous in their trade with the Vikings. Though the accounts of Ohthere and others lead us to believe that the Samek were subject peoples, they were probably economically and politically nearly on a par with the invading southerners. We are by no means certain of the nature of the trade and the taxation that took place at that time, but it was probably not too onerous for the Samek, who wanted access to imported manufactures and had plenty of skins to spare for trade.

We have historical accounts of further incursions that took place from A.D. 1000 on. Both the Norwegians and the Russians sailed round the coast, trading with and taxing the Samek, and, landward, the Finns and Karelians made advances from the south and east. There are a few accounts of battles, which probably took place in the east, but generally the Samek adapted or withdrew. During this period both Norwegians and Finns "converted" the Samek to Catholicism, sometimes hundreds at a time, but shamanism and animism continued without much alteration once the Samek were away from the meeting places.

From at least the fourteenth century, taxation and exploitation became more oppressive as the nomadic traders called Birkals (Finnish, *pirkalla*) roamed north from their base at Birkalla in Finland and were empowered to collect "taxes" for the Crown. From this time until 1809 Finland was part of the kingdom of Sweden. Although a treaty was signed in 1323 fixing the border between Russia and Finland, the Russians still claimed the right to tax and trade along the northern coast as far as Tromsø in Norway, and the Norwegians also taxed and traded as far east along the coast as they could. Thus many of the Samek were taxed annually by representatives of three nations and were even fined by one for paying taxes to the other two! Taxes were usually paid in beaver, marten, fox, wolverine, and less valuable reindeer skins, as well as in fish and occasionally in labor or valuables. This heavy dependence on pelts sharply decreased the number of wild animals, which may have moved the Samek to increase their dependence on tame deer. Nevertheless, the country was fairly sparsely populated and the crisis in resources did not come until later.

On the west coast the Samek regularly participated in Norwegian trade fairs and lived in mutual adaptation with the Norwegian fishing settlements. As has been mentioned, the Samek made boats for the Scandinavians and were more adept than they at sea-mammal hunting. In times of prosperity the Norwegians made further incursions into Samek fjord territory. In periods when the fish market collapsed, however, the settlers, who depended on suppliers in southern Norway, emigrated; if they remained they did so at a disadvantage compared with the adaptable Samek, who made better use of inland resources.

As early as the fourteenth century the Swedish Crown demarcated Samek territory within the kingdom, but this probably did nothing to hamper the plunderings of the Birkals. In 1557 King Gustaf I withdrew the privileges of the Birkals and instituted direct taxation, which was probably more equitable, and in 1584 his successor once more redefined the territory of "Lapland" within which the Samek were supposed to have traditional ownership rights. In 1520 the Russians opened a salt mine and a monastery at Petsamo on the Kola Peninsula, and converted the Samek to Orthodoxy. At the same time, slightly farther south, the Samek were subject to further Karelian incursions.

In the seventeenth century Finno-Swedish Samek land was further encroached upon by settlement from the south; Sweden pushed through to the Arctic Ocean, but the Swedes, under Carl IX, were repulsed by Norway and Russia. The State Lutheran Church began an intensive mission campaign and by the 1670s the Samek villages were ringed by churches, though the most intensive proselytizing did not occur until the 1700s. A more serious threat was the Swedish discovery of minerals within Lapland and the opening of mines there in the seventeenth century. This brought many settlers, who trampled on the Samek rights and pastures, in spite of the token legal protection the traditional territory nominally had. The settlers established farms on Samek lands, burned the forests that were the reindeer's winter grazing, forced the Samek to pay one-tenth of their herds in taxes, and required each family to provide reindeer *pulka* transportation to the coasts for the mined ore. In reaction to this, the Swedish Samek turned to more extensive herding and greater dependence on the reindeer that grazed in the tundra during the summers. Many followed their reindeer's migration routes into Norway as far as the coast, pressing on the lands of the Coastal Samek. Others moved with their extensive herds to the southern mountain regions, pressing on other Forest Samek, and some undoubtedly settled down to become farmers and mingled with the Swedes and Finns. In the late seventeenth century, pressures on the Samek throughout the North made it necessary once more to define the traditional lands of the Samek in northern Finland. In 1680 Peter the Great defined their lands in Russia and at the same time reduced the monopolistic powers of the Orthodox monasteries. In general one might say that the early and middle seventeenth and the nineteenth centuries were the periods of the greatest disregard for and expropriation of the Samek traditional rights to land ownership and herding territory.

By the 1700s the amount of wild game was seriously diminished, not only because the Samek hunted to secure furs for trade and taxes, but also because other Scandinavians also hunted and trapped and because farming changed the ecology. As early as the 1680s the Samek used guns and by 1751 beaver conservation had to be enforced and wild reindeer became rare. As other sources of livelihood diminished, more and more extensive herding was recorded from the Kola Peninsula to Norwegian Finnmark. In Finnmark the Norwegian settlers moved inland from the fjords, and all along the coast farming and stock breeding became a major livelihood of Norwegians and Samek, leading to further conflict with herders. In Finland there were border wars with Russia that led to Finnish expansion into northern Sweden. But the greatest changes were wrought by the zealous preachers. As early as 1619 a prayer book was printed in the Samek language and for a hundred years or more the missions tried to eradicate "heathen" beliefs. *Noaides* became illegal and magic drums were collected and burned by the hundreds. Some writers claim that shamanism "went underground" and was practiced into the nineteenth century, and we know that the Samek hid some of their drums and disguised worship at their *seides*.

In 1723 in Finland-Sweden the churches were enjoined to run Christian schools for conversion and literacy; in 1752 in Norway a Lapp Mission College was founded to train Samek to become priests. The College had some success, and from this period on there have been constant attempts to impose formal education on the Samek. Though the earlier priests and settlers spoke the Samek language, in the last one hundred fifty years the positions have been reversed, with the often consciously intended effect that the Samek have become a minority group within their own land, having to learn a second language and to assimilate the patterns of the national society.

With the great ecological and demographic changes, and the imposed external institutions and economy, the power and cohesion of the *sii'da* (*sit*) was broken. During the seventeenth and eighteenth centuries individual ownership and inheritance probably increased, and monetization of trade and taxation abetted this trend. In the nineteenth century the same trends were even more apparent. More settlers arrived, and friction led to some murders by both sides. In 1809 Sweden lost control of Finland, which became a Grand Duchy of Moscow, and in 1826 Russia and Norway settled their border dispute. In Finland-Russia more Samek were subject to formal education and tended to assimilate Russian life styles and to join the Orthodox Church. In Finland forestry became big business, threatening herding and hunting lands, and road construction brought more southern influences. In Norway the settlers encroached on the Samek territories, and, as Norwegian business skills and fishing technology improved, the Samek played an ever lesser role on the coast, though both groups still benefited from the Russian Pomor trade. More Samek were forced into farming or into disadvantageous positions in the markets controlled by Norwegian traders. In response to these and other pressures some Samek were described as indulging increasingly in drinking, petty crime, and reindeer rustling.

In 1845 a Swedish Lutheran minister, Lars Laevi, brought up in the Samek land and language, began a revivalist reform movement in the parish of Karasuando (Swedish Finnmark). Preaching hellfire, brimstone, and moral rebirth, and raging against immorality and drunkenness, he made many converts. His work was carried on by Johan Traatamaa, and the movement spread to 20,000 in Sweden, Finland, and Norway—of whom less than half must have been Samek. The sect, known as Laestadianism, emphasized personal statements and actions by the congregation, and the Samek adherents exhibited speaking in tongues, dancing, and trance during the services. The religious ecstasy resembled *likkatusak*, as in the old, supposedly eradicated, shamanistic performances. Some authorities have cited this to show that the old *noaide* religion was by no means dead, whereas others have pointed out that such behavior is characteristic of extreme Protestant sects all over the world. In any case, the movement did much to curtail Samek disintegration and crime, created a sense of identity and community, and led to an ethnic pride that muted the worst excesses of exploitation at the hands of unscrupulous Scandinavian traders. The movement did not spread to all the Samek populations, nor did it confine itself to this group, and in the nineteenth and twentieth centuries branches of this sect spread to other countries, even across the Atlantic to the United States.

Modern Contacts

The late nineteenth and early twentieth centuries constituted a period of intensive colonization of the North and great difficulties for the Samek. At various times the borders between Finland-Russia and Sweden, and later Russia and Norway, were closed during boundary disputes. This wrought hardship on the reindeer Samek, who had to follow certain annual migrations for the grazing of their herds. There were large population movements, some friction and murders, and in some places readjustment to more settled ecological niches. In 1869 Sweden once more redefined Samek territory and granted exclusive right to herd reindeer to the Samek, and other countries followed suit in later decades. At the same time, monetization became universal and the Samek—whether fishermen, farmers, or herders—had to pursue a livelihood that provided profit rather than self-sufficient subsistence. Herds grew larger and overgrazing became a problem; some Finnmark herders were transferred to southern Lapland, where they encroached on the already present Forest Samek. In Norway commercial fishing was taken over more and more by the Norwegians and, with the end of the Russian Pomor trade after the Revolution of 1917, the Samek economy suffered greatly, resulting in more settlement, farming, and assimilation. Education was enforced more universally in Sweden and Norway, and the dropping of instruction in Samek was part of a conscious policy of assimilation. Finland gained its freedom from Russia in 1917–1920, and new roads and mines were opened in the Samek lands. In the Kola Peninsula the Orthodox Church was dispossessed, and most Samek became collectivized herders, fishermen, and lumbermen. The new government, however, offered instruction in the native language and emphasized education.

After World War I, arguments about special versus universal education for the Samek led to vacillating policies in the three major homelands, and in the south romantic "leave-the-happy-natives-alone" adherents vied with those advocating vocational training and advanced education in formulating "minority" policy. There have been national and international pro-Samek movements and publications in all three countries in the past century, but few of these have lasted long or gained adherence from the majority of Samek within their borders. These movements, usually·led by sympathetic liberals and educated Samek, have found little following among the poorer members of the Samek population to date.

A major blow was World War II, during which the Germans invaded Fennoscandia, opened roads, brought machinery, razed houses and forests, and fought with the Finns against the Norwegians and Russians. In Finland and Sweden many Samek were evacuated to the south until 1945. Others joined the Underground and fought well alongside the Scandinavians, toward whom they previously had been hostile. A new unity and mutual understanding developed but disappeared soon after the war. Now because the ubiquitous roads and tourists have made the "Reindeer Lapps" objects of romantic inspection and interference, most of the other Samek try to carry on their various and hardy livelihoods as inconspicuously as possible.

ANNOTATED BIBLIOGRAPHY

Abundant literature exists on nearly all aspects of Samek culture, and luckily for the English-speaking world, much of it has been written in or translated into English. Most standard ethnographies and lay writing have sections on the physical and racial identity of the Samek, but the reader is advised to consult the more specialized works such as B. Lundman's "Publications of the Physical Anthropology of the Lapps," pp. 277–284 in Arne Furumark (ed.), *Arctica, Studia Ethnographica Upsaliensia*, XI (Uppsala, 1956) and Lars Beckman's "On the Anthropology of the Swedish Lapps," pp. 35–44 in Arne Furumark et al. (eds.), *Lapponica, Essays Presented to Israel Ruong, Studia Ethnographica Upsaliensia*, XXI (Uppsala, 1964). Additional accounts of recent physical anthropological research can be found in the special issue of *Arctic Anthropology*, 7:1 (1970), entitled "Health and Biology of Circumpolar Human Populations."

Given two millennia of contact with the literate world, writings on the archeology, origins, and culture history of the Samek are often identical with one another and, of course, with the earlier ethnographies. A few articles in the two collections (1956 and 1964) mentioned above concern detailed aspects of these topics, and more information is summarized in the general ethnographies (see below). A major ethnohistorical problem has been the origin of reindeer domestication and particularly the spread of extensive pastoralism. The lawyer Erik Solem has argued at length for relative recency of both in his monumental reconstruction *Lappiske Rettsstudier* (Institutet for Sammenlignende Kulturforskining, Ser. B, XXIV, Oslo 1933), which was well summarized in Robert H. Lowie's "A Note on Lapp Culture History," *Southwestern*

Journal of Anthropology, 1:447–454 (1945). Ernst Manker has expressed the opposite view, maintaining more ancient origins in his *De Svenska Fjallapparna* (Stockholm: Svenska Turistforeningens Forlag, 1947) and his useful summary article, "Swedish Contributions to Lapp Ethnography," *Journal of the Royal Anthropological Institute*, 82:39–54 (1952). Additional arguments have been published by Robert T. Anderson in his "Dating Reindeer Pastoralism in Lapland," *Ethnohistory*, 5:361–391 (1958a); and, for northern Norway, by Gutorm Gjessing in his excellent monograph, *The Changing Lapps*, London School of Economics Monographs in Social Anthropology, No. 13 (1954). A novel approach to Samek cultural divisions is J. Pentikäinen, "The Division of Lapps into Cultural Areas," pp. 135–152 in G. Berg (ed.), *Circumpolar Problems* (Oxford & New York: Pergamon Press, 1973).

Samek ethnography perforce includes much on culture history and acculturation. We are fortunate that of the earliest sources, Tacitus' *Treatise on the Situation, Manners, and Inhabitants of Germany*, Vol. II (London: Oxford University Press, 1901), and Johannes Sheffer's *History of Lapland* (Frankfurt, 1673; London, 1701) have both been published in English, but sadly, Olaus Magnus' *Historia de Gentibus Septentrionalibus* (Antwerp, 1558) has not. Although the accounts of the many early Lutheran missionaries have not been translated *in toto*, we have the interesting "ethnography" by the Samek Johan O. Turi, *Turi's Book of Lapland* (*Muittalus Samid Birra*), ed. and trans. by Emilie D. Hatt, published in English (New York: Harper, 1910). This account, ostensibly written to counteract false Scandinavian notions of Lapp life, tends to reinforce the "noble savage" tradition of the last century.

It was not until 1949 that a general summary account of Samek ethnography and culture history appeared, in the form of Bjorn Collinder's *The Lapps* (Princeton: Princeton University Press, 1949); however, this tended to emphasize the atypical Reindeer Samek, as did the synthetic accounts that followed by R. Bosi, *The Lapps*, trans. from the Italian (London: Thames and Hudson, 1960), and by E. K. Minns, *The Lapps* (New Haven: Human Relations Area Files, 1955). Ernst Manker's beautifully illustrated *People of Eight Seasons*, trans. from the Swedish (New York: Viking Press, 1963) also concerns the Swedish Mountain Samek, but concentrates mostly on their material culture. Ørnulv Vorren and E. Manker's *Lapp Life and Customs*, trans. from the Norwegian (London: Oxford University Press, 1962) is probably the best rounded account, based on the extensive historical and field researches of these two senior "Lappologists."

Since World War II a number of excellent field studies on Samek culture and history have appeared, many of them published in English. Robert N. Pehrson made the Könkämä Samek famous, along with the concept of bilateralism as a social structural type, in his "The Lappish Herding Leader: A Structural Analysis," *American Anthropologist*, 56:1076–1080 (1954); "Bilateral Kin Groupings as a Structural Type,"

Journal of East Asiatic Studies (Manila), 3:199–202 (1954); and *Bilateral Network of Social Relations in Könkämä Lapp District* (Indiana University, Research Center in Anthropology, Folklore and Linguistics, No. 3, 1957). The works of Robert Paine on "Lapp Betrothal" (pp. 234–263 in Furumark et al., 1964, *op. cit.*), of Vorren on Reindeer nomadism (*ibid.*, pp. 304–320), of Itkonen on the Finnish Lapps, and of Ruong, Gjessing, and Eskeröd in Furumark, 1956, *op. cit.*, are important contributions to limited aspects of Samek culture, as are the following works, which particularly concern socioeconomic problems.

Traditional Samek religion of course has to be reconstructed and good accounts appear in Rafael Karsten's *The Religion of the Samek* (Leiden: E. J. Brill, 1955); D. Strömbäck's "The Realm of the Dead on the Lappish Magic Drums" (pp. 216–220 in Furumark, 1956, *op. cit.*); C. Nooteboom's "Sketch of the Former Religious Concepts of the Atele Lapps" (*Anthropologica* II, *Tot de Taal-, Land-, and Volkenkunde*, 117:118–140, The Hague); and in the general ethnographies listed above.

Many recent works concern contemporary Samek ethnography and consider the changes brought about by acculturation and colonization. Papers by Nickul and Whitaker in Furumark, 1956, *op. cit.*, and in Pehrson's rather romantic "Cultural Contact without Conflict in Lapland," (*Man*, 50:157–160, 1950) discuss certain recent aspects. Ian Whitaker's longer *Social Relations in a Nomadic Lappish Community* (Oslo: Norsk Folkemuseum, 1955), Paine's excellent *Coast Lapp Society* (Tromsø Universitetsforlaget, I, 1957; II, 1965), and Gjessing's *Changing Lapps* (*vide supra*) present detailed case studies of intercultural relations in communities in both coastal and inland Finnmark. Shorter papers on the same subject area include those of Paine ("Changes in the Ecological and Economic Bases in a Coast Lappish District," *Southwestern Journal of Anthropology*, 14:168–188, 1958; "The Emergence of the Village as a Social Unit in a Coast Lappish Fjord," *American Anthropologist*, 62:1004–1007, 1960) and H. Eidheim's "Lappish Guest Relationship under Conditions of Cultural Change" (*American Anthropologist*, 68:426–437, 1966), which note the strain on and decline of *verdi*. More specialized works worth perusal include Tomas Cramer's excellent account of the "Right of the *Same* to Land and Water" (pp. 55–62 in Furumark et. al., 1964, *op. cit.*), illustrating the history of broken and subverted treaties of protection; K. Lundström's short article on "Swedish Nomad-Schools" (*ibid.*, pp. 182–185); and S. Porsanger's "The Sense of Solidarity among the Lapps" (*ibid.*, pp. 264–266). Rowland Hill's edited version of two conferences of the Nordic Lapp Council appear as the rather haphazard volume, *The Lapps Today: In Finland, Norway, and Sweden*, partially in French (Paris: Mouton, 1960); this book contains many useful papers on such topics as economics, education, reindeer, welfare, pan-Lappism, and the like by experts from diverse fields. A more recent case study of Samek acculturation is E. Asp, "The Finnicization of the Lapps," *Annales Universitatis Turkuensis* B. 100.

THREE

A CHIEFDOM OF THE NORTHERN YAKUTS

The Yakuts, the most numerous of all the peoples of the circumpolar regions (the census of 1926 listed their number at 235,926), are intrusive to the North. A Turkic-speaking people, they migrated centuries ago from more southern regions of Asia to a new homeland centered on the middle section of the Lena River, bringing with them their pastoral economy based on horse and cattle breeding. The main theme of this chapter shall be to examine the political structure of the Yakut, the chiefdom—a form of organization unique in the North, although former-ly common in more southern regions. Chiefdoms are characterized as centralized political-military organizations leading to wars of conquest, and approaching the limits of kin-based society.

This chapter is based on the works of Sieroshevski and Jochelson, who, as political exiles in Siberia, conducted fieldwork among the Yakut around the turn of this century. Material is also drawn from the essay of the Soviet scholars Tokarev and Gurvich. The main source for this chapter, however, is the classic work of Okladnikov, who reconstructed the history of the Yakut in a masterful synthesis of data drawn from the historical, folkloric, linguistic, ethnographic, and archeological record. The time period dealt with here includes the sixteenth through the eighteenth centuries, and especially the decades before contact with the Russians in the 1630s.

ECOLOGICAL ADAPTATIONS

Much of the Yakut region lies in an area of permafrost (see Figure 3.1), and the low natural production of fodder and the long severe winters made it necessary for the Yakut to adapt their pastoral economy. Hay was cut in summer for winter fodder for livestock, and when no fodder was available cattle were sometimes fed fish. (Some of the early Russian travelers complained of the taste of milk from cows fed on fish.) In winter horses foraged for themselves and cattle were housed under the same roof as the people. Both horses and cattle were exploited

34

Figure 3.1 The peoples of eastern Siberia.

for milk, meat, and transportation, and some of the more northern Yakut kept reindeer.

The Yakut diet varied from area to area depending on the natural resources available; its major components, in order of importance, were dairy foods, fish, sapwood from pine trees, and meat. A number of special foods were prepared from milk: sour milk was stored frozen in great slabs during the winter; butter was made; kumys, a mildly alcoholic drink of ritual significance, was prepared from mare's milk; and there were other varieties of dairy foods. Fishing, an important subsistence activity for many Yakut, was done in summer with horsehair nets. The Yakut also hunted and trapped in the surrounding taiga.

Sieroshevski estimated that the average Yakut household required ten cattle to meet its needs and that more were required in areas where resources such as fish were not readily available. The diet of each household depended on its economic position—that is, on the number of livestock it kept. The richer sections of Yakut society had comparatively large portions of dairy products and meat in their diet, whereas families with few livestock depended more upon fish and the sapwood of pine. The ethnographers of the Yakut note that periods of hunger and starvation, particularly in late winter and early spring, were part of the normal condition for the majority of the people. Thus part of the "adaptation" of these pastoral people to conditions in the North includes the enduring of hunger.

Yakut dwellings consisted of two types, the winter yurt, made of poles or boards covered with sod and clay, and the summer conical birch-bark tents. The Yakut settled in scattered villages and had a dual pattern of residence, following an annual cycle of winter and summer camps. Winter camps were generally composed of three or fewer yurts; summer camps were somewhat larger. Excavated Yakut sites show a pattern of settlement near rivers or lakes with communities enclosed by stockade structures, indicating Yakut dependence on littoral resources and the presence of warfare. Other aspects of Yakut material culture include a long tradition of smelting and working iron and other metals and of working in ceramics.

SOCIAL STRUCTURE

The basic economic and social unit of the Yakut was the household. Some Yakuts of high status practiced polygyny, having as many as five wives and maintaining a separate household for each. A bride price was paid in livestock, and sometimes a dowry was paid when the social status of the bride was higher. The clan organization of the Yakut did not continue into this century, and there has been some controversy about its nature and about the related problem of residence after marriage. It now seems established, however, that postmarital residence was patrilocal and that the Yakut social structure consisted of a number of tribes made up of patriclans. Although the general outlines of the social structure have been established, little detail is known of the nature and workings of the patriclan. Livestock was not held in common by members of the clan, but there is some evidence that meadow land was periodically redistributed to equalize access to land. Clan or tribal leaders were called *toyons* or *darkhani*—the head of the clan might also be a leader in the Yakut raiding wars. Clan functions extended to a pattern of food sharing and of caring for clan members without livestock. The preferred mode of inheritance, after direct male and female descendants, was by male members of the clan.

In the Yakut social structure a number of positions were more sharply differentiated than they were for any other peoples of the North. Sieroshevski emphasizes the subjection of women to men and the subjection of the weak to the strong: Apparently Yakut women were more inferior to men than were women in other societies in the circumpolar regions. Other positions in Yakut society included slaves, servants, young people adopted for their labor, and the poor—that is, people without livestock and those dependent on the rich whom they served —and finally a class of men rich in homesteads, livestock, and helpers, who were often clan leaders and chiefs. There were two additional social positions, those of the shaman and the blacksmith; shamans had the high social rank common to them in the Arctic, and blacksmiths held a magical position similar to that of the shaman—a social theme common in Siberia.

POLITICAL-MILITARY
ORGANIZATION

Various scholars of the Yakut describe an ancient pattern of raiding wars carried on against other Yakut groups by clan or tribal chiefs, who were rich in cattle and horses and were surrounded and aided by dependent kinsmen and slaves. Of particular interest in Okladnikov's analysis of the Yakut tradition is the chiefdom of Tygyn. Tygyn plays a dominant role in Yakut legend and folklore, which picture him as carrying on a war of conquest against other Yakut clans and tribes, in time bringing almost all the Yakut nation into subjection, sometimes killing entire clans and acquiring farmsteads, great herds of horses and cattle, and slaves. Tygyn ruled autocratically over the subjected Yakut clans, but, according to the Yakut oral history, when he tried to enforce the same rule over his own clansmen against their communal sentiment, his kinsmen rebelled. In the resulting conflict some of Tygyn's kinsmen broke away from his political influence and moved to regions not under his control. Apparently Tygyn lived until the coming of the Cossacks and the building of the Russian fortress at Iakutsk (established in the 1630s), so Tygyn, who was a famous figure illustrating the cyclical nature of the Yakut chiefdoms, lived to see the beginning of a new era for the Yakut.

Although the formation of the chiefdom is rare for the circumpolar regions, it occurs in many other parts of the world—for example, in Polynesia (Hawaii and Tahiti), in Africa (the Zulu), and also among the herdsmen of central Asia. An important feature of these chiefdoms is their cyclical nature; each individual chiefdom usually lasts for several generations at most, breaks up, and is followed by reformation. In the absence of formation of the state, the chiefdom can be seen as following a repetitive social dynamic of formation, breakdown, and reformation under new heirs.

Okladnikov examines the theoretical implications of the chiefdom of Tygyn. He points out that, although the Yakut kept slaves, slavery was not a dominant mode of production, nor were the Yakut at a developed feudal stage—their society was still kin based rather than territorial and there was no centralized state expropriation as is characteristic of the Asiatic mode of production. Okladnikov, citing the works of Morgan and Engels, considers the Yakut to have been at a stage in which the foundations of kin-based society were pushed to the limits. We recall that Tygyn was successful in establishing dominance over other clans, raiding them of cattle and slaves, but that when he tried to subject his own clan his kinsmen rebelled. On the basis of the works of such scholars as Service, we suggest that pre-Russian Yakut society constituted a chiefdom. It is not that of Okladnikov, although it falls within the criteria he defines for the political organization of the Yakut. In the past decades inquiry into social evolution has assumed a new respectability in the West, and of all the stages in man's historical movement that of the chiefdom—midway between kin-based society and the formation of the state based on territory—is the least well defined in both the ethnographic and theoretical literature.

ANNOTATED BIBLIOGRAPHY

For two prerevolutionary ethnographies of the Yakut, see V. L. Sieroshevski, "The Yakuts," *Journal of the Royal Anthropological Institute of Great Britain and Ireland*, 4:65–110 (1901); and Waldemar Jochelson, *The Yakut* (New York: Anthropological Papers of the American Museum of Natural History, Vol. 32, Part II, 1933). For a summary of Yakut culture, see S. A. Tokarev and I. S. Gurvich, "The Yakuts," pp. 243–304 in M. G. Levin and L. P. Potapov (eds.), *The Peoples of Siberia* (Chicago: University of Chicago Press, 1964). The major portion of this chapter was based on the classic in the Soviet tradition of anthropological scholarship of A. P. Okladnikov, *Yakutia before Its Incorporation into the Russian State*, ed. by Henry N. Michael (Montreal: McGill—Queen's University Press—Arctic Institute of North America, Anthropology of the North, Translations from Russian Sources, No. 8). For an additional source of information, see the chapter on the Yakut, pp. 87–99 in Valentin A. Riasanovsky, *Customary Law of the Nomadic Tribes of Siberia* (Bloomington: Indiana University Publications, Uralic and Altaic Series, Vol. 48, 1965). For a theoretical discussion of the chiefdom as a stage in social evolution, see Elman R. Service, *Primitive Social Organization: An Evolutionary Perspective* (New York: Random House, 1962).

FOUR

THE DECLINE OF THE YUKAGIRS

This chapter on a small group of inland Arctic hunters in northeast Asia has two main aims: to document the decline—physical and cultural—of the Yukagirs as a people, and to briefly describe the lives of these hunters to provide a basis for an implicit comparison with other groups, especially with the Subarctic Indian of North America. We depend here mainly on the ethnography of Waldemar Jochelson, who carried out fieldwork among the Yukagirs in 1895–1896 and in 1901–1902. Jochelson was a Russian revolutionary who, as an exile in Siberia, made ethnographic studies of a number of Siberian groups. The account of Jochelson is the most complete extant and the period in which he did his fieldwork is taken as the ethnographic present for this study of the Yukagirs.

HISTORY OF THE DECLINE

The Yukagirs have been selected as an illustration of cultural decline brought about through contact with Europeans, but this process of physical and cultural extinction, or near extinction, has occurred in many areas throughout the North; the Beothuk of Newfoundland, the Eyak Athabascans of the south Alaska coast, or the North McKenzie Delta Eskimo could have been used equally well as examples of this historical movement. In ancient times the Yukagirs and an ethnic subbranch of the Yukagirs, the Chuvantzy,[1] ranged from the Lena to the Anadyr rivers and were bounded in the south by the Verkhoyansk Range (see Figure 4.1). By their traditions and by those of their neighbors they were a numerous people before the days of the Russians. By the time of the ethnographic present, however, the Yukagirs had suffered the most drastic decline of any of the tribes of the Siberian northeast and existed as small, scattered groups surrounded by alien peoples, new-

[1] There also were a number of other small ethnic subdivisions of the Yukagirs of which little is known.

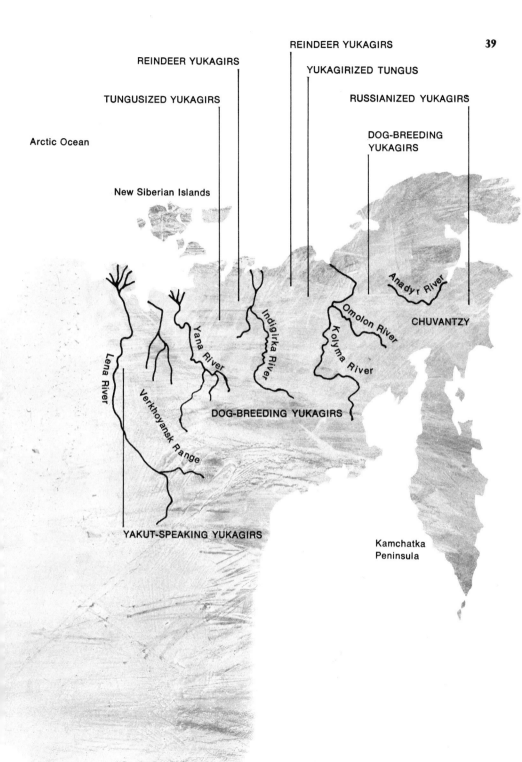

Figure 4.1 Distribution of the Yukagirs, 1895 (after Jochelson).

comers to the Yukagir country: the Yakut, Tungus (the Tungus considered in this chapter are of the Lamut/Evens subdivision), Chukchi, and Russians.

Before the coming of the Russians the Yukagirs fought raiding wars against the reindeer Tungus, and during this same time some Yukagir groups merged with the Tungus. The Yukagir pattern of tending small herds of reindeer, used mainly as draft animals, was probably introduced at this time. Following the first contact, in 1633, the Russians established trade with the Yukagirs, formed administrative clans for the purposes of taxation, and exacted tribute from these people. Census for the purpose of taxation was taken infrequently and the amount of tribute was calculated on the basis of numbers shown on the census, so the rapidly declining Yukagirs often found themselves paying taxes for dead men who had not been taken off the tax list. Trade was highly unfavorable to the Yukagirs, the Russian traders taking advantage of their ignorance of financial matters. In the 1700s the Yukagirs and the Chuvantzy fought a series of wars with their neighbors to the east, the Chukchi, and the Russians fought by the side of the tribute-paying Yukagirs; however, the expanding Chukchi won the first series of these battles.

More disastrous to the Yukagirs than these raiding wars was the introduction of diseases by the Russians. A series of smallpox epidemics caused numerous deaths among the Yukagirs between 1691 and 1885, and in some areas more than half the Yukagir population died. There were also epidemics of measles, which killed both adults and children. Syphilis reached epidemic proportions and was responsible not only for deaths, but also for reducing the birthrate through sterile unions and congenital syphilis. Jochelson mentions that the people living in this harsh climate were "poorly clad," and adds numerous respiratory diseases to the list of diseases just given.

With the introduction of firearms and the fur trade, the number of many important game animals was greatly reduced in the Yukagir country. During the nineteenth century the migrations of wild reindeer ceased in widespread areas. At times when the fish-spawning runs were low, this reduction in game often resulted in starvation, and, as in many other areas in the Arctic, starvation sometimes forced people to cannibalism.

War, epidemic, and starvation greatly reduced the Yukagir population in a period of three centuries. Jochelson estimates the population of Yukagirs and Chuvantzy in the 1750s, after they had begun their decline, at around 5,000. The census of 1859 gives a population of 2,350 and the census of 1897 shows 1,500. The Yukagir population continued its decline, until the 1920s—the census of 1926–1927 showing 443 Yukagirs.

The past centuries were not only a time of physical decline for the Yukagirs but also of assimilation into neighboring ethnic groups. The sketch map after Jochelson (Figure 4.1) showing the distribution of the Yukagirs indicates directions of assimilation, using Jochelson's terms "Tungusized," "Yukagirized," and "Russianized." The picture presented by Jochelson, however, is somewhat more complex than this map indicates. At the time of the ethnographic present the greatest assimilation movement for the Yukagirs was toward the Tungus, with these Yukagirs speaking Tungus as a native language. This movement was two-directional, however, approximately three hundred Tungus having assimilated into the Yukagirs and speaking Yukagir as a native language; there is sometimes a question as to which groups were originally Yukagirs and which originally Tungus. A number of Yukagirs assimilated toward the Yakut, and some Yukagirs and Chuvantzy assimilated toward the Russians. In addition, a number of Chuvantzy assimilated toward the Chukchi and Koryak.[2] At the time of the ethnographic present Jochelson lists only one hundred twenty-six Yukagirs who speak Yukagir as their native language. The foregoing sketch indicates that the paths of assimilation taken by the Yukagirs were many and complex and, it is interesting to note, oriented at the time of the ethnographic present more toward other native Siberian groups than toward the Europeans.

LIVELIHOOD AND NATURAL PRODUCTION

At the time of the ethnographic present, the Yukagirs were divided into a number of bands, ranging in population from 13 to 191 individuals, many of which had been formed by the merging of several depopulated clans. There were three main modes of life. Some groups herded reindeer, keeping small herds for transportation—generally about eight to fifteen reindeer per family; they lived as nomads, hunting and fishing and following a seasonal pattern of movement, often spending the summer in the tundra and the winter in the taiga. An alternate mode of life was followed by groups who kept dogs rather than reindeer for transportation; these people also followed a seasonal pattern of movement, fishing in the summer and fall, hunting in the spring, and spending the most severe part of the winter in small settlements. A third group had given up a nomadic life to stay in Russian settlements, and they lived mainly from fishing. The first two groups of Yukagirs depended chiefly on food from the land; domesticated reindeer provided a negligible part of diet even for the reindeer herdsmen, who used them mainly as a means of transportation, for riding in the summer and for drawing sleds in winter. A brief overview of the natural production in the Yukagir area provides the setting for their way of life.

The Yukagir country lies in the coldest area in the world (the Northern Hemisphere record temperature of $-90.4°$ F was taken there). The climate is extreme continental in an area of continuous permafrost.

---

[2] Jochelson (1910:59–60) lists the population of each mutually exclusive native-language group of the Yukagirs in 1897. However, the sum of these groups (1.904) is higher by 449 individuals than the total (1,455) given by Jochelson.

The number of days without frost ranges from about 41 to 84 according to place. For a time, the Verkhoyansk Range acted as a barrier to keep the more southern Siberian tribes out of Yukagir country as well as being the southern boundary for the Yukagirs. The major rivers—Lena, Yana, Indigirka, Kolyma, and Omolon—form avenues of communication and in the warmer seasons of the year are sites of great migrations of fish. The river basins are tundra plains with many lakes; in the summer large parts of the tundra become bogs, making travel very difficult. The irregular tree line extends across the southern part of the Yukagir country and follows the rivers into the tundra. On the tundra and the taiga grow mosses that support various species of lichens, which in turn form the main fodder for reindeer. Where trees grow, they consist mainly of several species of Siberian conifers and deciduous trees such as poplar, aspen, birch, alder, and willow.

The fish migrating up the rivers are mainly species of whitefish, sturgeon, and dog salmon, but apparently their numbers fluctuate greatly. In addition, several species of nonanadromous lake and river fish are present. Ptarmigan and other species of birds are found throughout the year, and swans, geese, and ducks migrate to the Yukagir country during the warm seasons. There are also wild reindeer and elk, and in the mountains musk deer and mountain sheep. Animals, once numerous but at the time of the ethnographic present close to extinction owing to overhunting, include wolverine, sable, and lynx. Black bear, wolves, fox, and ermine are present, and hares are common in the tundra. Squirrels occur frequently in the taiga, along with a number of other tundra and taiga rodents.

The most important component of the diet of all groups of Yukagirs is fish. Fish often have the role in the Arctic diet that vegetable foods have as a staple in the diet of more southern hunting bands. The Yukagirs relied mainly on the great migrations of whitefish that run up the rivers in the spring and summer and return to the sea in the fall. Other species of fish making similar migrations were also exploited by the Yukagirs. In addition, Arctic char, Arctic grayling, pike, and other fish are native to the lakes and streams. The Yukagirs caught fish in a number of ways—with nets (often made of horsehair traded from the Yakuts), with hook and line, and with fish weirs built across streams and used in conjunction with basket traps. In using these weirs, the Yukagirs practiced a native conservation, letting a number of fish pass the weir to spawn before closing the stream. The principal fishing occurred at the time of the autumn run to lay in food stores in preparation for winter.

The Yukagirs followed the principle of strategic hunting of Arctic hunters, making their greatest harvest when the animals were massed together and especially vulnerable. Thus the greatest amount of food (energy input) could be obtained with the least amount of work (energy output). We have already noted that the Yukagirs derived their main subsistence from fish, massed for their spawning migrations and vulnerable to nets and weirs blocking their path of migration. Similarly, the wild reindeer, also an important food staple for the Yukagirs, usually were hunted at periods when they were massed for their spring and autumn migrations and at places where they were especially vulnerable, such as river crossings where they could be killed by pikemen in boats. They were also hunted by means of large surrounds or corrals, which were placed at strategic places with respect to land formations and migration paths; the Yukagirs drove the reindeer into the corrals or into nets set up in conjunction with corrals, where they were killed by another group of hunters. Elk, before they were nearly exterminated through the use of firearms in hunting, played an important part in the subsistence of the Yukagirs; they were large animals and provided great amounts of meat. They were hunted when the snow was soft, which impeded the elk so that the hunters could easily overtake them on snowshoes.

The concept of strategic hunting also extended to the exploitation of waterfowl, which formed a large part of the Yukagir diet in the warmer seasons of the year. Ducks and geese gathered together during their moulting season in autumn; they could not fly at this time and the Yukagirs harvested large quantities by driving them into nets. The Yukagirs also ate squirrels, depending upon them especially in periods of food shortages. It should be noted that many of the Yukagir hunting methods—such as the reindeer surround—required communal hunts with the band acting as a unit.

The Yukagirs preserved food by drying it in the summer and freezing it in the winter. In the winter they often ate raw fish. Like most Arctic people, the Yukagirs valued fat as a food, which is indicated by the number of names in their language for different types of reindeer fat. Tea and tobacco obtained in trade were frequently used, the latter by men, women, and children—as it is by many other Arctic peoples; Jochelson refers to the Yukagirs as "constant smokers." Supplementing their diet of animal foods, the Yukagirs ate various berries and other vegetable foods, including the contents of reindeer stomachs. In times of starvation they ate the inner bark of scrub willow.

In addition to hunting animals for food, the Yukagirs hunted and trapped for the fur trade, using a wide variety of snares and deadfalls. The two most important animals for the fur trade were the fox and the squirrel; other furbearers were either unimportant or, like the sable, nearly exterminated. Mammoth ivory formed another article of trade, and fur was exchanged for such items as tobacco, guns, gunpowder, tea, sugar, articles of clothing and cloth, brandy, beads, cord for fish nets, knives, axes, copper kettles and teapots, and other items common to the fur trade in the circumpolar regions. The Russian and Yakut traders took advantage of the Yukagirs in this traffic and through various means entangled them in debt. In addition, the Russians benefited from the labor and services of the Yukagirs without paying them in return.

A short account of the items of Yukagir material culture and its processes will indicate the function and extent of their technology. Yukagir clothing, apparently adopted from the Tungus, suited the harsh Arctic environment less well than their previous style of clothing. Clothes for men and women were essentially the same, consisting in winter of a long coat, tight trousers, and an apron. Winter mittens and boots were made from reindeer leg skins—the warmest and most waterproof part of the skin. Snow goggles, worn when there was a bright glare off the snow, were made of leather, wood, or birch bark.

By the time of the ethnographic present the Yukagirs were constructing a wide variety of dwellings, including winter and summer models of skin tents, semisubterranean houses of logs and other materials, and the Russian log cabin. At night sleeping tents were put over the beds of couples or individuals to give some measure of privacy.

Two types of boats were used—dugouts made from logs and canoes built of thin, shaped boards and sewn with sinew. For winter transportation the Yukagirs made various types of reindeer and dog sleds. They used snowshoes and covered the bottoms of their broad skis with reindeer skin, the hair pointing back.

Other items of their material culture included metal lamps with moss wicks that burned reindeer fat or fish oil, wooden bowls, baskets of birch bark, bags made of fish and reindeer skins, spoons of wood and of reindeer antlers, and the ancient stone axes which they found and used. The Yukagirs tanned skins using alder bark and urine. Most of this catalog of material culture could be extended to other circumpolar groups.

The Yukagirs made both compound and simple bows; they constructed compound bows with a layer each of birch and larch, reinforced with fish glue and sinew. They tipped arrows with points of wood, ivory, or iron, using both blunt and sharp arrowheads. After the introduction of firearms the bow was little used. Yukagir warriors, before the coming of the Russians, used compound bows made especially for war, spears pointed with an elk rib, armor of reindeer antler rings strung on sinew, daggers, and bone-tipped arrows. The Yukagirs made and used a number of iron tools and weapons, including axes, knives, lances, and scrapers. The iron was always imported, probably formerly reaching the Yukagirs by way of native Siberian trade routes. Yukagir smiths used a kit of tools that included bellows, tongs, anvil, and hammer, but they did not know how to temper iron. The acquaintance of the Yukagirs with the use and working of iron apparently is ancient, possibly originally from China and the Yakut and Mongol tribes. It is interesting to note that although the Yukagirs worked iron (they did not smelt it), their technology remained at a rather simple level (comparable to the non-iron-working Eskimo, for example). Further, the level of production was low as indicated by the periods of starvation that were common in Yukagir history.

There is some question as to the nature of the aboriginal Yukagir clan.[3] Apparently the clan formed a unit for the nomadic travels of the Yukagirs—at least for certain parts of the year. There is no record of all the Yukagir clans acting together as a single political unit. The aboriginal clan should not be confused with the "clan" which the old Russian government imposed as an administrative aid upon the native Siberian peoples—whether they had clans or not. The old Yukagir clan had neither clan territory, such as exists for the Tungus, nor other concepts of property in land. Strangers could freely join the clan, and thus a Yukagir "clan" comprised two groups: kinsmen by blood and members by virtue of the fact that they lived and traveled with the group.

The Yukagir pattern of property was that common to hunting-group societies. The concept of individual ownership extended only to personal items such as clothing, weapons, hunting gear, and such women's gear as sewing kits; it did not include food, boats, dwellings, fish nets, and larger articles made by group labor, all of which were held in common. The Yukagirs extended hospitality to visitors so generously that it was sometimes abused by neighboring Yakuts, who visited the Yukagirs at the autumn fishing sites and consumed their winter fish supply. All members of the band shared the products of the land and rivers through a system of distribution and redistribution. The ideal pattern was for one of the older women of the band to carry out this distribution, although there are variations of this theme. Little specific data exist on the internal Yukagir economy and pattern of distribution, but clearly it is similar in general to that of other Arctic societies.

The Yukagir social structure was organized by division of labor according to sex and age. There were also a number of special positions. In aboriginal times a clan elder or "old man" supervised the everyday affairs of the band as well as war and hunting trips. He was usually either the oldest man of the group or the most able of the old men, and it was most often his wife who saw to the redistribution of the products of the hunt. With the coming of the Russians the aboriginal clan elder was replaced by a person responsible to the Russians for taxes. The replacement of aboriginal leaders by leaders responsible to Europeans was common in the history of the contact of band and tribal peoples with whites in the Arctic.

In addition to the "old man," the clan had a "strong man," distinguished by training and personal qualities as the chief warrior. Often this "strong man" was a stranger to the clan. Young men were more-or-less formally trained as warriors. In ancient times the Yukagirs raided the Tungus and Koryaks for their reindeer, and in these raiding wars took captives who became slaves, giving rise to another "class." After the coming of the Russians the roles of "strong man" and warriors

---

[3] For a further discussion of the Yukagir kinship and social structure, see Chapter 8.

disappeared. The clan also had a chief hunter, a man who distinguished himself in the hunt and who, through his great powers of endurance, usually managed to reach and kill game before any other hunter. Young men were physically trained and otherwise prepared for the hunt.

The Yukagir blacksmith held a position of high respect and a status somewhat similar to the shaman, his craft being regarded as something related to the supernatural. His economic relation to the clan was one of easy exchange—people gave the blacksmith what they could in return for his services and when he bought iron from the traders the people of the clan aided him in his purchases. (The position of the clan shaman will be considered later.) Thus in the Yukagir social structure there was some emphasis on ranking and a degree of differentiation in division of labor.

The young Yukagirs were sexually free before marriage. When a girl reached puberty she received her own sleeping tent in her father's dwelling and she was free to receive young men during the night; according to Jochelson the young men seldom slept in their own beds. The Yukagirs practiced a form of what older ethnographers called "hospitality prostitution" (a bad term since no prostitution is involved), in which men visiting a Yukagir camp were offered the bed of a young girl for the night; the explanation was that it was the bed and not the girl that was offered to the visitor—the girl could do as she pleased. It must be noted that after a period of sexual experimentation many Yukagirs remained together as couples and that faithfulness was a Yukagir ideal. (This pattern of sexual experimentation in youth and subsequent pairing with a marriage partner is a common one for people at the band and tribal level and is perhaps more realistic, in a human sense, than many other forms of courtship and marriage.)

Rules on marriage and incest have become somewhat confused since the coming of the Russians. On the one hand, there is an ideal discouraging marriage to relatives by blood of the same generation, and, on the other hand, there is a tendency toward marriage of closer kinsmen—probably resulting from such demographic factors as a sparse population spread over a wide area—and most marriages occur within the clan. The Russian Orthodox Church has influenced Yukagir marriage patterns as it forbids second-cousin marriage, whereas many Yukagir marriages formerly were to second cousins. Jochelson gives an example of Church interference with a marriage of this type. The Yukagir customs of avoidance also have had an effect on the number of marriages between kinsmen falling in this class. There is a single cover term, as well as more specific kin terms, for a number of close relatives including sisters, brothers, cousins, aunts, and uncles. For kinsmen in this category certain forms of avoidance are prescribed, including speaking directly to each other, showing sexual organs, speaking of sexual matters, and sharing of a sexual partner. This custom of avoidance probably functioned to minimize conflict among kinsmen, especially in sexual matters. It must be remembered that this avoidance pattern was an ideal, and there were most likely many variations in actual practice.

A prospective groom provided service to the bride's family for a period, working for them and giving them all the game he killed. This could also be regarded as a period of testing in which the young man proved his worth and ability to the father of the bride. The ideal was for the groom to live initially with the bride's family after marriage —although there were variations in this pattern of residence—and to obey the bride's father, mother, and older kinsmen without speaking or looking at them. Again the probable function of this custom was to minimize conflict. The groom continued to give products of his labor to the father of the bride until the groom himself became a father. Toward the bride's younger relatives the groom might assume a role of authority. No specific statements describe the position of women in Yukagir society, but in the absence of statements to the contrary it would seem that they had much more "freedom" than their sisters in many societies materially more advanced.

The study of the position of the shaman and of shamanism leads to insight not only into the social structure of the people concerned, but also into their view of the world. Jochelson says that "nervous" people were likely to become shamans. Because psychological explanations are sometimes advanced for shamanism and the phenomena connected with it, it should be stressed that, although a man may in some ways have been predisposed toward becoming a shaman, a Yukagir became a shaman by training. Usually a shaman taught his art to one of his sons. The shaman provided protection for the clan in the realm of the supernatural at certain critical times. Each clan had its own shaman who was of the same blood—the clan shaman could not be a stranger but had to be a kinsmen to the core group of the clan. Thus the Yukagir shaman had an "office" or position defined in relation to his clan. In addition to the living shaman, the Yukagirs had dead shamans as spirit protectors of the clan. When a clan shaman died, his flesh was removed from his bones and dried, and the flesh and bones were divided among his kinsmen as amulets. The ancient Yukagir shamans played a role in the hunt by influencing the spirits that controlled the animals; but with the coming of the Russians and the consequent destructive influences on Yukagir life, the relations of the shaman to the hunt and to the clan were destroyed, and his major function became the curing of sickness. In the Yukagir belief system, sickness can be caused either by evil spirits or by a displacement of one of the three souls in the Yukagir soul complex. The shaman cured sickness by acting on the causes. In effecting a cure the shaman was aided by his helping spirits—mainly the souls of animals and birds and those of dead shamans who were kin to the living one, who were in communication with him, and who stood in a special relationship to him.

A shaman's performance to cure a patient proceeded as follows. In the company of the band, the shaman puts on a special coat, unties his long hair, and beats his drum, giving the calls of his spirit helpers to gather them to him. He then asks the spirit helpers the cause of the patient's illness and they reply, speaking through the shaman, that a soul of the patient has gone to the land of the dead and is staying with its ancestors. The shaman goes into a motionless trance; his soul, together with his helping spirits, makes the journey to the land of the dead. The shaman finds the soul and asks the spirits of the dead to return it; they refuse and with the aid of his helping spirits the shaman takes the soul by force and brings it back to earth. The shaman then comes out of trance and returns the soul to the patient, effecting the cure. The main points of a Yukagir shaman's performance included trance and the alternate side of trance, soul flight—the journey to a spirit world in which the ancestors and dead kinsmen of the clan live in a setting similar to the real world. Also important was the belief that sickness was caused by a missing soul or by evil spirits and that the removal of the causes effected the cure, through the aid of the shaman and a group of helping spirits in special communication with him.

The shaman's costume symbolized various aspects of his art. His coat represented a bird and aided the shaman in soul flight; various metal pendants represented his spirit helpers. His drum was of the tambourine type used throughout the Arctic. Yukagir shamans practiced divination with bone. Among the Yukagirs, as elsewhere in the Arctic, a spirit of competition prevailed among shamans, who sometimes vied to demonstrate superior powers. Yukagirs and alien tribes sought the services of each other's shamans and this interaction may in part explain the uniformity of many features in the shamanism of northern Siberian peoples. The Yukagirs had neither women shamans nor transformed shamans (that is, shamans who took the role of women), as did some of the neighboring Siberian tribes. In addition to shamans, there was a class of wizards among the Yukagirs who worked through incantations and charms rather than through helping spirits; wizards were considered evil beacuse their magic could harm or kill men.

Perhaps the most difficult part of an ethnological reconstruction of a people's life is to describe and reconstruct their unique way of seeing the world. By the time of the ethnographic present much of the ancient Yukagir belief system had been changed and destroyed through contact with Europeans, and thus it is forever lost to us. Jochelson describes his account of the Yukagir belief system as a "vague shadow" of what once existed. Some fragments of this original belief system can be described. There was some sort of a concept of reincarnation in which a soul of a dead ancestor entered a child. The Yukagirs practiced a form of bear ceremonialism in which the bear was regarded as being kin to humans, and they took special care of the bones of bears and avoided killing them or eating their flesh. In times past the Yukagirs ate fly-agaric mushrooms, which induced hallucinations and otherwise altered perception.

CONCLUSION

The preceding account is a one-dimensional outline of a people's life. Although in our judgment Jochelson gave a good description of the Yukagirs, given all the conditions under which he worked, we do not have a holistic picture of these people much beyond what has been presented here. Historical work, of course, could result in a more complete picture of the Yukagirs. The Yukagirs are a classical example of a tribal grouping almost destroyed through European contact, and they offer an interesting instance of assimilation of a tribal grouping into other societies at the tribal level. Apart from this, a study of the Yukagirs is rewarding because they share many cultural features with other circumpolar groups.[4]

ANNOTATED BIBLIOGRAPHY

Little has been published on the Yukagirs in English. The basic ethnography is Waldemar Jochelson, *The Yukaghir and the Yukaghirized Tungus*, Part I (1910), and Parts II and III (1926) (Memoirs of the American Museum of Natural History). Another very useful work on the Yukagirs is by M. V. Stepanova, I. S. Gurvich, and V. V. Khramova, "The Yukagirs," pp. 788–798 in M. G. Levin and L. P. Potapov (eds.), *The Peoples of Siberia* (Chicago: University of Chicago Press, 1964). A. P. Okladnikov also gives scattered bits of information on the Yukagirs in his "Ancient Population of Siberia and Its Culture," in *The Peoples of Siberia, op. cit.*, pp. 13–98. For a brief sketch of Yukagir reindeer hunting, see N. B. Simchenko, *Main Features Pertaining to the Culture of the Hunters of Wild Reindeer in Northern Eurasia* (Moscow: "Nauka" Publishing House, 1964). A secondary source is the relevant section of C. Daryll Forde, *Habitat, Economy and Society* (New York: Dutton, 1963).

[4] For a consideration of the Yukagir in modern times, see Chapter 13.

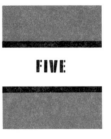

FIVE

SHAMANISM AND WORLD VIEW
OF THE NORTHERN EVENKS
(TUNGUS)

The Evenks are a taiga people scattered throughout one-quarter of the land mass of Siberia, ranging from the Ob to the Amur River and Sakhalin Island and extending south into Manchuria (see map in Figure 3.1). This chapter deals mainly with the Evenks in the regions east and northwest of Lake Baikal. Around the turn of this century, the Tungus groupings of Evenks and Evens[1] in Siberia and Manchuria numbered about 75,000, of which somewhat less than half were taiga reindeer herdsmen and hunters. These people kept small herds of reindeer, which they used mainly for transportation but also for food when no other sources of food were available, and which they milked in the summer. For food the Evenks depended on elk, wild reindeer, bear, other species of large and small game, and fish. We are concerned here chiefly with the northern reindeer-breeding and hunting Evenks; in the more southern regions of their territory, through historical influences, alternative modes of subsistence—horse and cattle breeding and agriculture—have been adopted.

Throughout a long history the Evenks have had contact with many Asian cultures and been influenced by them; these include Mongol tribes, Manchu, Yakut, Chinese, and, in the last centuries, the Russians. At one time some Evenk groups served as bannermen in the military of the Manchu rulers of China. The ethnographic record of the Evenks is fairly extensive and they are among the best documented of all northern groups in the areas of religion and world view. This discussion emphasizes the least acculturated of the Evenks and draws from sources based mainly on fieldwork done from 1910 to the 1930s. These sources include the extensive descriptive writings of Shirokogoroff, who worked with the Evenks east of Lake Baikal in the prerevolutionary period;

---

[1] In the older literature the culturally related Evenks and Evens were called Tungus and Lamuts, respectively, or were lumped together under the term "Tungus." The word "Evenks," used here to distinguish these people from other Tungus ethnic groups, is the term they apply to themselves and is also generally used in modern Soviet literature.

the series of articles by Vasilevich, the Soviet specialist on the Evenks; and the masterful essays on the Evenk religion by the Soviet scholar Anisimov, whose essay on the shaman's tent is perhaps the most brilliant synthesis in the literature on shamanism. A good part of this chapter is based on Anisimov's work.

SOCIAL ORGANIZATION

The Evenks were organized into patriclans, which dominated and permeated the social organization. Land was occupied and controlled by the clan as a corporate unit. Since residence was patrilocal and clan exogamy was practiced, an Evenk patriclan included kinsmen (blood members of the clan), wives of clan members who came from other clans, and people adopted into the clan. Clan membership was emphasized in the Evenk kin terminology; kin terms distinguish Ego's (any hypothetical speaker's) clan, his mother's clan, his wife's clan and the clans into which Ego's kinswomen marry. Generally a clan numbered from twenty to two hundred individuals.

When it was necessary to act on clan problems, clan meetings were called. Clan leaders or war leaders were sometimes selected in these meetings, but apparently the position of clan leader most often was not formalized. The clan governed its members; it settled conflicts between clan members and directed interclan relations. When epidemics destroyed reindeer, the clan acted as a unit in redividing the reindeer among clan members.

Exchange of sisters was the preferred mode for the Evenk to obtain wives. When two Evenk clans entered into a close relationship, sharing the same territory but each remaining an exogamous unit, women were exchanged between such clans as wives.

The family or household was the basic economic unit. Each household had its own hunting territory, within land controlled by the clan, through which it wandered during its seasonal migrations.

SHAMANISM AND WORLD VIEW

In his classic work *The Elementary Forms of the Religious Life*, Durkheim makes a fundamental inquiry into the bases of human knowledge. He notes the connection between religion and cosmology in that each religion sets forth a particular view of the world. Durkheim also points out that basic categories of knowledge and religion are socially defined and that, in consequence, these categories vary among cultures (for instance, other anthropologists have noted that the color spectrum is divided in different ways by peoples of different cultures); thus the particular way in which a people sees the world is molded and influenced by social factors. Durkheim stresses the social character of world view, in particular pointing to the fact that certain tribes divided by clans and moieties also divide the external world in a way that reproduces their social structure; that is, the social organization by clan and moiety becomes a model for the organization of space, in which the world is divided into corresponding halves and sections. In this chapter the main theme will be to show, following Durkheim, how the social factor of strict clan organization influences Evenk world view.

As in all circumpolar societies, the shaman plays the central role in Evenk religious life—in fact the word "shaman" came from the Tungus language. Czaplicka defines a shaman as a man who has contact with one or more spirits who act as his helpers. Also the shaman is a specialist in trance and in the alternate side of trance, soul flight. With the aid of his spirits and through magical means, the shaman protects the clan against human or supernatural enemies, cures disease and heals injuries, and attracts game animals.

The ultimate problem in the study of shamanism is an epistemological one: Does the shaman do the things he claims to do? The question is not as facetious as it may appear; an impressive list of witnesses could be compiled if it would prove the point, but science proceeds differently from law and accounts of witnesses cannot be accepted as proof in these matters. In this study the question is not asked because it is unanswerable, and science is the art of asking those questions that can be answered. For that reason we ask here not what is true, but what do men believe to be true. In his study of primitive religion, Lowie best sums up this problem by pointing out that by its very nature the subjective religious experience is incommunicable. Accounts of the wonders of the shaman's performances are given here without the use of qualifiers, which would be tedious to use throughout, and it must be remembered that the accounts are indeed factual in the sense that men believe these events to be true.

Shamans were historically recruited in two ways. In one way the novice went alone into the taiga, fasted and carried on other activities until a patron spirit appeared and provided instruction in shamanism and the necessary spirit helpers. In the other method the spirits themselves chose the novice, and the novice was harmed if he disregarded this call. Only shamans recruited by the second method could assume the office of clan shaman, and they were regarded as being more effective than those who *sought* to become shamans. The position of clan shaman was generally hereditary, the usual pattern of inheritance being to skip alternate generations, the position going from grandfather to grandson; consequently clan shamans usually came from one family within the clan.

The clan shaman's function was to protect the clan against anything that threatened it, human or spiritual enemies, disease, and misfortunes of any kind. He also served to attract game and to make predictions concerning hunting and other matters. When the clan shaman died, it was believed that the magical fence of spirit protectors he had erected around the clan territory also died or went away; thus the death of the clan shaman was seen as a catastrophe in which the clan was left completely unprotected.

Clan shamans received no direct payments for their services to their kinsmen, although they did receive economic support from their clan; clan members hunted, herded reindeer, and built fish weirs for the clan shaman, and the best and most productive areas of the clan territory were assigned to him. Because of the spiritual demands placed upon them, clan shamans did not do the same amount of work as other men, and the reason for the inheritance pattern of the office was economic at least in part. Within the shaman's family members of the intermediate generations often could not become shamans because they had to support their fathers.

The clan shaman had one of the highest social positions in the clan. The welfare and very existence of the clan was seen to be in his control and he was treated by other members of the clan with great and elaborate deference. His position would be compared somewhat to that of the clan leader, and in fact sometimes shamans acted as clan leaders and as leaders of military campaigns.

Several other ranks of Evenk shamans existed; women could sometimes become minor shamans and there was also a "neurotic" type of petty shaman. In the twentieth century a class of shamans arose who were not integrated in the clan and who, as Vasilevich suggests, became shamans solely to receive payments from people of other clans; these shamans fought against socialist reconstruction. Some petty shamans were eligible to become clan shamans, and this was confirmed in a rite of consecration held by the clan shaman, which established in the eyes of the clan that the novice was officially recognized as a shaman, had undergone instruction by the clan shaman, and had been selected by the spirits. In this rite of consecration the novice and the clan shaman traveled through the other worlds and the clan shaman showed the novice all the mysteries. Subsequent rites over a period of years advanced the new shaman through the several degrees of shamanism, and he received items of equipment until he had the complete shaman's costume. Thus shamans were seen as having different degrees of supernatural power which could grow stronger in time.

The shaman's performance took place in the shaman's tent, which was a model of the Evenk view of the universe. In that view the world is seen as divided into three parts: an upper world of the high lords of nature and of the souls of those who are yet to be born, a middle world of the earth of the living, and a lower world containing the souls of the deceased. The clan territory is seen as extending to the upper world, the earth, and the lower world; therefore each clan has its own land on earth and its own slice of the upper and lower worlds. In the shaman's tent, going through the smoke hole, stood a tree which served as a magical ladder for the shaman to use in going to the upper and lower worlds. Another magical pathway to the upper and lower worlds, the shamanistic river, was represented in the shaman's tent by a model of a raft. Fences made of young trees around the tent served as representatives of guardian spirits and protected the whole clan and its territory. A number of wooden figures of men, animals, and other shapes also symbolized spirits, acting as guards in this and in other worlds.

The mythical clan river, which runs through all three clan worlds, forms a closed cycle upon which the clan's souls travel in their journey through the time before birth, the time of living, and the time after death. The Evenks believe in reincarnation and also that each human has three souls corresponding to various personal, spiritual, and physical characteristics; just how souls complete the cycle is not clear.

The clan territory, with its complement of unborn, living, and dead souls, is seen as standing in isolation from all other clans except when a hostile alien shaman sent evil spirits to cause misfortune. To prevent their entrance the shaman placed assistant spirits as guards and set snares and barriers of all kinds in the model of the clan's mythical universe, the shaman's tent. The clan shaman thus waged magical war and defended against other clans in the shaman's tent where, in this model of the universe, he performed, surrounded by members of the clan. By manipulating the model he manipulated the world—a most powerful idea common to the magical thinking of many peoples.

To cure sickness the shaman began by calling the spirits, beating his drum, and singing special songs. (His shaman's drum was thought of, among other ways, as a boat for soul travel and his drumstick as a paddle.) After calling the spirits, the shaman gave them directions, and his soul, accompanied by the helping spirits, began its travels to the other worlds. The shaman gave a running account of his journey as he entered a state of trance and ecstasy—talking in the voices of spirits, making other sounds, and leaping about the tent screaming. He fell to the ground and was received by an assistant; then the shaman performed the dance of the return of his soul from the other world with advice from the clan ancestor shaman on how the spirit causing the disease should be fought. The disease-causing spirit was seized, taken to the lower world, and thrown into an abyss. This was done by one of the shaman's spirit helpers who, in the form of a bird, swallowed the disease spirit and expelled it through its anus. The clan shaman avenged the clan by sending a group of evil spirits to the clan whose shaman had made the clan member sick. At the conclusion of the shaman's performance, a reindeer was sacrificed and the sick man's soul was sent to a guardian in the upper world for safekeeping.

Thus the Evenk patriclan social organization permeates their world view in the concepts of a closed circuit of clan souls, of clan territory extending to other worlds, of the fence of spirit protectors around the clan territory, and in the office of clan shaman. The Evenks, with their lineal structure of rigid clan territory, rules of residence, clan exogamy, and clan membership, define the social position or office of shaman more clearly than do northern bilateral bands. In bilateral bands such as the Chukchi, Lapps, Montagnais-Naskapi, and in many Eskimo societies, the social position of the shaman, as that of the bilateral band, is of an *ad hoc* nature. In bilateral bands, although there is a role of shaman in the social network, the position depends not at all on the assumption of office but entirely on the attitudes of the people. In clan societies like the Evenks a more rigid hierarchy of professional shamans serves a wide circle of people, which indicates a new dimension in the social position of shaman as compared to that in bilateral societies. Anisimov comments on this tendency of lineal clan societies to differentiate the social position of shaman and notes that this practice may be seen as a historical stage in the development of a hereditary priesthood based on class.

The rise of a class of "false" shamans among the Evenks in more recent historical times has already been mentioned. Anisimov says that these shamans allied themselves to the *kulak* class in the struggle carried on for socialist reconstruction and that the decline of the *kulaks* resulted in the destruction of shamanism as a social institution. In some respects the dominance of shamans is unique to kin-based societies —although shamanlike figures are found in class society, and often there appears to be an undercurrent of shamanism in the beliefs held by followers of the classical religions. Even a brief review of the history of the peoples of the Arctic shows that the shaman was among the first to come in conflict with representatives of European culture, whether missionaries or atheists, or socialists, capitalists, or members of a feudal state. In this sense the shaman can be seen as the prime holder of culture of these band and tribal societies. Like many other peoples of the North, the Evenks in pre-Soviet times accepted a thin veneer of Christianity from the Russian Orthodox Church. One of the main spiritual inducements these representatives of Christ on earth offered the Evenks was a three-year moratorium on taxes in return for their accepting baptism.

CONCLUSION

We have touched here, mainly through the insights of Anisimov, upon a small part of the world view of the Evenks. Of all the aspects of culture, world view is perhaps the most difficult for an alien to define, so we have concentrated on those aspects of shamanism and world view which could be connected or synthesized. Shirokogoroff's works are a treasure house of descriptive information on the Evenk world view in which he records such facts as their love for their children and reindeer, their sound naturalistic explanations for many phenomena, and their preference for trading for small amounts of well-made goods rather than for larger amounts of cheap goods. We realize the value of such facts for our understanding of Evenk life, but it is difficult to incorporate them into a holistic synthesis.

An inquiry of this type into a particular society can establish factors connected with shamanism and world view that are held in common by many groups throughout the circumpolar regions. Aspects shared by the Evenks with many other Arctic groups include: the shamanistic complex of trance and soul flight to multiple worlds; the idea of multiple souls for each individual; the belief that sickness is caused by evil spirits stealing one of the souls and that the cure is effected when the shaman, aided by his spirit helpers, regains the soul. The idea of a special shaman's costume occurs commonly throughout Siberia, and the shaman's tambourine drum is common throughout the circumpolar regions. Additional widespread points of world view include a belief in reincarnation, in the concept of bear ceremonialism (in which parts of the bear's body are treated with special regard), and in the idea of spiritual danger from menstrual blood.

ANNOTATED BIBLIOGRAPHY

For a main theoretical basis of this chapter, see Emile Durkheim, *The Elementary Forms of the Religious Life*, especially pp. 9–13 (Glencoe: Free Press, 1954). For a definition of shamanism, consult M. A. Czaplicka, *Aboriginal Siberia: A Study in Social Anthropology*, especially p. 172 (Oxford: Clarendon Press, 1914). For an intelligent statement on the subjective nature of religious experiences, refer to Robert H. Lowie, *Primitive Religion*, especially p. v (New York: Grosset and Dunlap, 1952).

The factual basis of this chapter draws from the following works of Glafira Makarevna Vasilevich: "Early Concepts about the Universe among the Evenks," pp. 46–83 in Henry N. Michael (ed.), *Studies in Siberian Shamanism* (Toronto: University of Toronto Press, 1963—Anthropology of the North, Translations from Russian Sources, No. 4); *Tungus Types of Reindeer-Breeding* (Moscow: "Nauka" Publishing House, 1964); "The Acquisition of Shamanistic Ability among the Evenki (Tungus)," pp. 339–349 in V. Dioszegi (ed.), *Popular Beliefs and Folklore Tradition in Siberia* (Bloomington: Indiana University Publications, Uralic and Altaic Series, Vol. 57, 1968); and from G. M. Vasilevich and A. V. Smolyak, "The Evenks," pp. 620–654 in M. G. Levin and L. P. Potapov (eds.), *The Peoples of Siberia* (Chicago: University of Chicago Press, 1964). Additional and equally important sources of information are the works of S. M. Skirokogoroff, *Social Organization of the Northern Tungus* (Oosterhout N.B., The Netherlands: Anthropological Publications, 1929, 1966) and *Psychomental Complex of the Tungus* (London: Kegan Paul, Trench, Trubner, 1935).

The major theoretical and factual basis of this chapter, however, is derived from Arkadiy Fedorovich Anisimov, "The Shaman's Tent of the Evenks," pp. 84–123, and "Cosmological Concepts of the Peoples of the North," pp. 157–229, in Henry N. Michael (ed.), *Studies in Siberian Shamanism* (Toronto: University of Toronto Press, 1963—Anthropology of the North, Translations from Russian Sources, No. 4). For a descriptive, secondary source on the Evenks, see the relevant section of C. Daryll Forde, *Habitat, Economy and Society* (New York: Dutton, 1963).

SIX

THE ARCTIC BILATERALISM OF THE CHUKCHI

A feature of social structure shared by societies in the circumpolar regions—including the Lapp, many Eskimo groups, and some Arctic drainage Athabascans—is a bilateral, nonunilineal social organization. In this chapter, after presenting some background information, we shall examine the bilateralism of the Siberian Chukchi. Arctic bilateralism has long been discussed, but what was perhaps the first scientific examination of this form of social organization was conducted by Waldemar Bogoras in his monograph on the Chukchi published in 1904–1910. Bogoras was a Russian revolutionary who, during periods of exile in Siberia in 1890–1898 and 1900–1901, carried on fieldwork among the Chukchi and other Siberian groups. His ethnography of the Chukchi may be one of the most complete conducted by one man on a people; for example, he records such details as the Chukchi way of dividing and naming the star constellations, their division of the color spectrum, and their large vocabulary of names differentiating reindeer by color pattern and by age and sex. After the Russian Revolution Bogoras remained in the Soviet Union and assisted in the formulation of the first phase of Soviet national policy concerning the peoples of the North.

Although in the early years of the revolution resources were not available for the reconstruction of the lives of these northern ethnic groups, the new national policy provided that they were to be protected from the harmful influences of some segments of the larger society and encouraged in the development of tribal and national political organizations. In this chapter we review some aspects of the work of a rather neglected founder of anthropology, a man who worked for long periods both in the field and in the university, and who turned his scientific work to practical account in the political struggle in the development of the peoples of the North.

SUBSISTENCE PATTERNS

At around the turn of this century the Chukchi numbered approximately 12,000; they inhabited the tundra section of Siberia that juts toward Alaska. The Chukchi have two major divisions: the reindeer groups of the hinterland, who derive their chief subsistence from their reindeer herds; and the maritime groups on the coast, who derive their main subsistence from sea mammals. The reindeer Chukchi keep large herds of reindeer, which often exceed one hundred animals, and depend mainly on them for meat and skins. They follow a pattern of extensive reindeer breeding, using large herds, in contrast to most Eurasian reindeer-breeding groups, which follow a pattern of intensive reindeer breeding using small herds that are exploited for dairy products and transportation and seldom slaughtered. The reindeer Chukchi also use reindeer for drawing sledges, but they do not ride them. The maritime Chukchi have a subsistence pattern similar to that of the Eskimo—in fact, there are groups of Asiatic Eskimo intermingled with the maritime Chukchi; they depend on various species of seal, walrus, and whale, which are taken from kayaks and open skin boats by harpoon, and they also exploit sea mammals by other methods including the use of the seal net. Additional sources of wild foods include the salmon, which make spawning runs up the Anadyr River and are taken in weirs, traps, and nets, and the migrating wild reindeer, taken as they cross rivers.

A constant exchange of products takes place between the two divisions of the Chukchi, reindeer meat and skins going to the maritime people and blubber and sea-mammal skins going to the reindeer people. The Chukchi live in double tents of skins and use lamps that burn either reindeer fat or blubber for their heating and cooking. After a series of wars with the Russians in the 1700s, in which the Chukchi were often the victors, trade with the Russians was established and the Chukchi visited Russian trading fairs to exchange polar furs for tea, tobacco, and other European goods.

SOCIAL STRUCTURE AND BILATERALISM

The basic social unit of the Chukchi is the family or household, which consists of a husband, one or more wives, and children; each household has its own tent. The basic social unit after the family is the *varat*, a collection of kindred families, which often centers around a group of brothers and, secondarily, a group of cousins. Paternal kin ideally are considered more important than the maternal line; however, for practical purposes the Chukchi are almost bilateral. There are no strict residence rules, and residence is a matter of convenience. The *varat* is a residential group that works together and forms a unit for blood revenge. Actual individual membership in the *varat* may change, but the *varat* itself remains a constant feature of Chukchi social structure. Kin terminology for the parental generation is of the lineal type that classifies father's sister and mother's sister together, and a common term applies also to mother's brother and father's brother.[1]

---

[1] For a discussion of the relationship between kin terminology and bilateralism, see Chapter 8.

The *varat* of the reindeer Chukchi generally comprises two to three families, who camp together and tend the herds of reindeer. In maritime villages the *varat* centers around the boat crew, usually composed of the eight men needed to operate the Chukchi skin boat and their immediate kinsmen; a maritime village might consist of several separate boat crews and their kinsmen. Bogoras points out that the *varat* of the reindeer Chukchi was of a stricter character than that of the maritime peoples because of the ecological and economic requirements. However, the main feature of Arctic bilateralism—or indeed of the bilateralism of many peoples of the world—is a social structure in which individual membership constantly changes but which retains a structure over time based on an alliance of close kinsmen, often brothers and cousins. Although the Chukchi emphasize the paternal line ideally, actually behavior often shows bilateralism in practice.

In Chukchi society the position of women is somewhat inferior to men, but the economic role of women in maintaining the household, no small task under the conditions, is of the utmost importance. The Chukchi marriage rite often requires a period of matrilocal residence before and immediately after marriage. Pairing-type marriage prevails, with frequent divorces, and networks of wife exchange often arranged by people of different camps ensure that on travels no man need sleep alone.

Chukchi society is differentiated somewhat by social rank as has been pointed out. The status of men and women differs; there is a camp master for the reindeer people and a head of the boat crew for the maritime people; assistant herdsmen help rich reindeer herders, often building up their own herds or marrying into the families of their employers in the process; captives and slaves are taken in war; and there is a class of idle wanderers, people who travel from camp to camp without material possessions. In addition there are several grades of shamans and the social position of the highest grades compare only to the leaders or strong men of the *varat*. The professional shamans serve a wide circle of clients as opposed to the more common family shamans who serve only kinsmen. The professional shaman maintains his position through competition with other shamans, and he receives payment for his services. Both the camp leaders and professional shamans hold nebulous social positions, apparently depending on personal influence and the attitudes of group members toward them rather than on established office.

CONCLUSION

The Chukchi live along the coastline and in the hinterland in scattered camps that constantly change in membership. Although their social organization can be characterized mainly by a lack of structure, Bogoras points out that certain social structures have endured, based on shamanistic powers, on the ownership of large herds of reindeer, and on personal qualities making for leadership and for success in production. Differences in social position derive from personal skills and qualities rather than from office, and the Chukchi camp is based on a kin bond of brothers and cousins. In thus defining the social structure of the Chukchi, Bogoras set a model that can be used for many other circumpolar peoples.

ANNOTATED BIBLIOGRAPHY

For a discussion of the life and work of Waldemar Bogoras, see the obituary by Franz Boas in *American Anthropologist,* n.s., 39:314–315 (1937), and see also Erich Thiel, *The Soviet Far East: A Survey of Its Physical and Economic Geography,* especially pp. 133–134 (London: Methuen, 1957). The material for this chapter was drawn mainly from the masterpiece, neglected in both the historical and ethnographic literature, of Waldemar Bogoras, *The Chukchee, Part I, Material Culture; Part II, Religion; Part III, Social Organization* (New York: Memoirs of the American Museum of Natural History, Vol. XI, 1904–1909). For an additional source on the Chukchi, consult V. V. Antropov and V. G. Kuznetsova, "The Chukchi," pp. 799–835 in M. G. Levin and L. P. Potapov (eds.), *The Peoples of Siberia* (Chicago: University of Chicago Press, 1964). For a review of the literature on Arctic bilateralism, see Joel S. Savishinsky, "Kinship and the Expression of Values in an Athabascan Bush Community," *Western Canadian Journal of Anthropology,* 1:1, 31–59 (1970), Special Issue: Athabascan Studies. For an additional source of information on Arctic bilateralism, consult Chapter 8. For an overview of everyday life of the Chukchi in historic times before the Soviet Revolution, see the work of the Yukagir novelist, Taeki Odulok (Nikolai I. Spindov), *Snow People* (London: Methuen, 1934).

SEVEN

ABORIGINAL SUBSISTENCE PATTERNS OF THE ATHABASCAN INDIANS

In this chapter an attempt will be made to define the aboriginal cultural ecology of the Alaskan Athabascans in terms of the natural resources of the various Athabascan regions by establishing the main components of diet, gross demography, band size, and degree of permanence of settlement. That is, an efficiency study will be made of these hunters' lives with emphasis on which food-getting techniques (energy output) and which types of animals—large game, fish, or small game—contribute most to these people's diet (energy input).

The theoretical orientation here follows Lee's analysis of the African Bushmen in part—that is, in the efficiency study. Lee, however, could make a direct study of a still functioning hunting group, but aboriginal Athabascan subsistence patterns can no longer be studied directly so we shall have to rely on modern ethnographies written since 1930 and on records left by the earlier explorers. The latter are particularly profitable for a study of this type; the earlier explorers often relied on the land and on the cooperation of the natives for food during their travels, and their reports give a rather good account of this one aspect of aboriginal life. The influence of European culture, however, with subsequent disturbances in aboriginal subsistence patterns, often made itself felt before literate explorers arrived to make their historical records. For example, firearms frequently reached areas through native trade routes long before the first whites arrived, and fur traders and prospectors who left no record were often in "unknown" areas long before the "official" literate explorers arrived to make their reports. Therefore what was often described, even in early records, was not an aboriginal lifeway, but a mode of life altered by contact with whites with resulting demographic changes and shifts in emphasis in subsistence patterns. Entire Indian populations were reduced by epidemics of smallpox, measles, scarlet fever, and other European diseases. Because of these problems, an indirect analysis of aboriginal Athabascan subsistence patterns through the historical record yields little significant quantitative data;

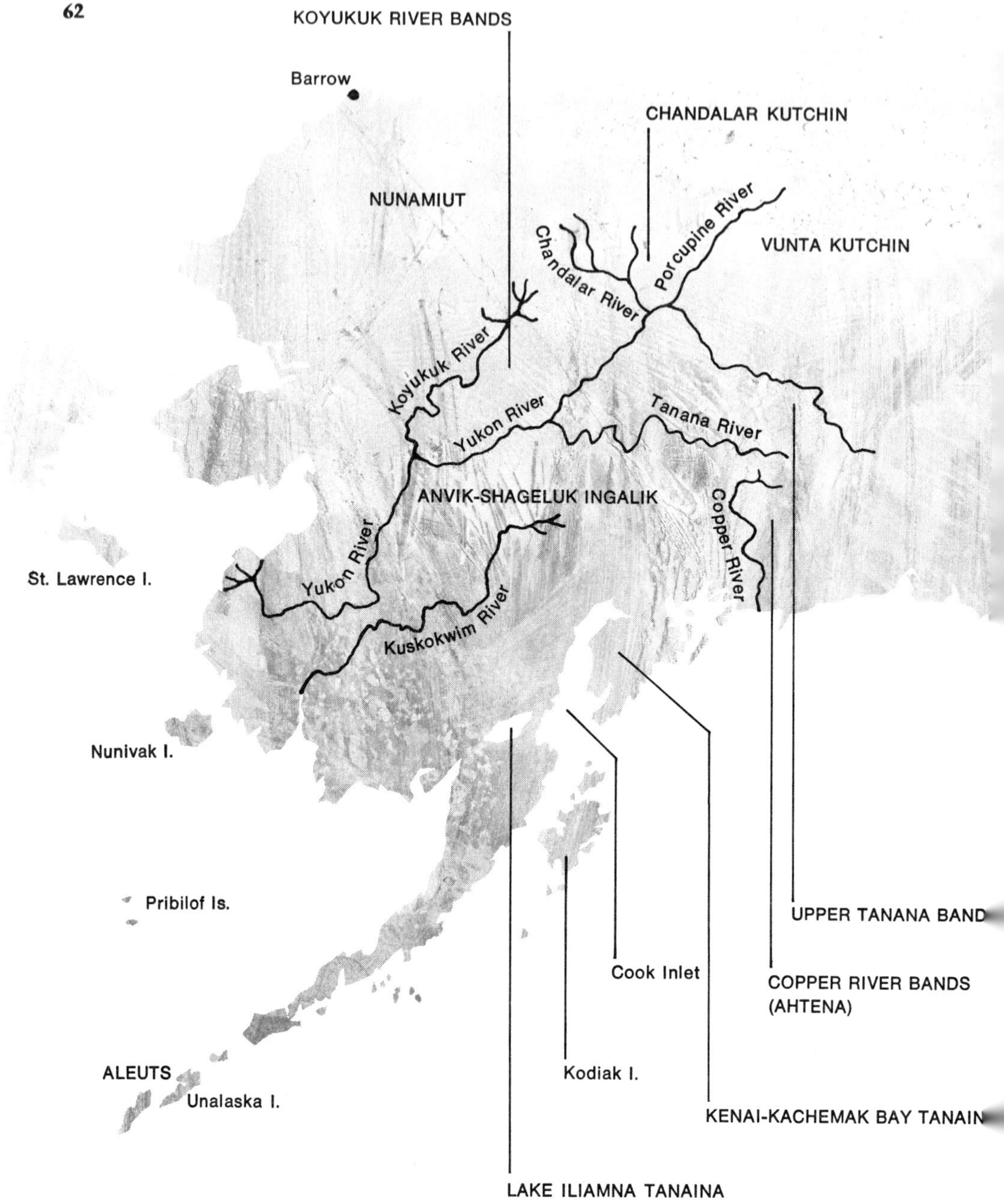

Figure 7.1   *Athabascan Indians of Alaska and Yukon.*

the early Alaska and Yukon explorers did not make diet studies of
the native peoples and the information on demography, viewed critical-
ly, may be said to be only a rough sketch at best. Consequently it
will be necessary frequently to substitute statements of emphasis taken
from the historical record for quantitative data.

THE PEOPLE

A number of Alaskan Athabascans—the Kenai-Kachemak Bay Tanaina
and the Lake Iliamna Tanaina, the Anvik-Shageluk Ingalik, the Copper
River grouping, the Koyukuk-Yukon rivers grouping, the Chandalar Kutchin and Upper Tanana grouping, and one northern Yukon Athabascan
group, the Vunta Kutchin—have been selected as case studies for this
inquiry. They illustrate the range of variations in Alaskan Athabascan
subsistence patterns, and they are groups for which some of the best
aboriginal population estimates and ethnographic descriptions are available, either from the historical record or from the work of modern
ethnographers.

A common cultural division made by ethnographers of the northern
Athabascans is between those bands living in the Pacific drainage and
those living in the Arctic drainage. Although this division is perhaps
not useful for many purposes, we hold a number of factors common
by restricting our areas of concern to the northernmost tribes of the
Pacific drainage area.

Describing groupings of Athabascans is difficult because each village
or microband differs a bit from neighboring villages in culture and
speech, and these differentiations between groups are likely to be gradual rather than sharp. Of all groups under consideration here the Kutchin
probably form the most discrete larger unity—both in their own view
and in their language and culture. Athabascan groups are usually named
after the macrobands inhabiting a river valley or a section of a river
valley; thus macrobands share names with the main rivers in their
areas—for example: Copper, Upper Tanana, Koyukuk-Yukon (Koyukon), and Chandalar. A problem also occurs in deciding what designation to apply to the various Athabascan groupings. If we use the word
"tribe" for the bands found in one river valley, it would not have its
usual implications of political unity. If we use the word "band," the
larger grouping would have to be distinguished from the number of
distinct smaller bands that usually make up the larger unity. Hence
we use the terms "macro-" and "microband."

NATURAL PRODUCTION OF THE LAND

Like other circumpolar peoples, the Alaskan Athabascans depend mainly on animals for subsistence. Limitations on the amount and variety
of natural production of vegetation in the Athabascan regions restricts
the animal population, which in turn limits the human population
living under aboriginal conditions. To understand the nature of these

societies, we must examine the environmental factors that influence and restrict their formation.

The Athabascan Subarctic region receives less energy from the sun than do more temperate regions (approximately a quarter of the energy of tropical areas), and this retards the growth of energy-fixing plants, thus limiting the amount of vegetable food capable of sustaining animal life. The climate of the interior is a continental one of long, cold winters and short, hot summers, which, of course, limits the season of vegetable growth. Moreover, the interior receives little precipitation—generally from four to twenty inches annually. The Alaskan Athabascan region is bounded to the north by a line of continuous permafrost and tundra, and to the west by tundra. Most Athabascans live within the taiga, the tundra zones being inhabited chiefly by Eskimos and Aleuts. Much of the Athabascan region lies within the zone of discontinuous permafrost, which, together with other soil conditions, retards the decomposition of vegetable material by fungus and bacteria, thus preventing the return of nitrogen and other plant and mineral nutrients to the soil. These factors contribute toward keeping the natural production of vegetation below the level found in most other areas of the world.

Farther north the number of plant and animal species progressively decreases. Only a couple of hundred land plant species occur in the Arctic—as against more than a hundred thousand in the tropics—and less than 1 per cent of the world's species of mammals, birds, and fishes are found there. South of the Arctic in the taiga a number of species of conifers flourish, including spruce, fir, pine, and larch; the boreal forest also includes some deciduous trees, such as willow, poplar, aspen, alder, and birch. Many of these broadleaf trees grow along streams and many taiga animals (e.g., moose, hare) depend on their leaves for fodder. Between the tundra and the climax boreal coniferous forest, a transition zone of sparse trees occurs and the tree line is not always sharp. The development of seed and other life processes of these Subarctic plants frequently extend over several years. Although little is known of the basic productivity of the taiga, it is certainly lower than forests in warmer areas.

Animals generally characteristic of the Alaskan Athabascan region include moose, caribou (in most areas), black, brown, and grizzly bear, Dall sheep (in certain mountain areas), beaver, land otter, muskrat, mink, weasel, marten, lynx, snowshoe hare, red fox, wolf, ptarmigan, and grouse. Before the coming of Europeans, musk-ox had a wider range than they do now, and it has been suggested that not only was their range far vaster but also their population was much larger than today.

Arctic and Subarctic animal populations vary greatly over time and space as a result of migrations and gross population cycles. The caribou herds in Alaska and the Yukon generally keep to mountain areas, some massed groups migrating to the tundra in the summer and returning to the taiga in the winter. The hard-packed tundra snow prevents them from obtaining feed, but the taiga snow is fluffier and softer; the caribou winter in areas with the least and softest snow cover, moving on if the snow becomes too hard. In the spring various migrating waterfowl, including swans, geese, and ducks, arrive in the Athabascan areas. Species of freshwater fish make spawning migrations from the lakes and large rivers to the smaller streams; these migrations include the July-early winter runs of whitefish and the spring-June run of grayling. Salmon ascend freshwater rivers and streams from the sea. The most important spawning runs for salmon in this region are the runs of Chinook/king salmon (May to June), Chum/dog salmon (June to September), Coho/silver salmon (late June to August), and Sockeye/red salmon (August to September). The snowshoe hare and lynx have a seven- to ten-year peak population cycle and snowshoe hare almost disappear during the low period of the cycle. The massings of animals and fish for migrations and the population cycles have important implications for the aboriginal patterns of subsistence.

Finally, it should be noted in this overview of Alaskan Athabascan ecology that although other Athabascan macrobands are within the Subarctic taiga ecozone, two groupings, the Kenai-Kachemak Tanaina and the Lake Iliamna Tanaina, live within the most northern part of the Northwest Coast temperate rain-forest ecozone. Characterized by a milder climate, higher annual precipitation (up to sixty inches), and a preponderance of hemlock, cedar, and Sitka spruce, this ecozone is one of the most abundant in natural food resources in the world—that is, in food obtained mainly from the rivers and sea.

STRATEGIC AND EXTENSIVE EXPLOITATION OF ANIMAL RESOURCES

The concept of strategic hunting, discussed earlier in Chapter 4, plays an important role in the consideration of how the Athabascans provided for their subsistence and thus defined large areas of their life. The Athabascan hunters, like the Yukagirs, make their greatest harvest of animal resources at periods when the animals are massed together and especially vulnerable. Examples of strategic exploitation include: (a) fish massed for spawning migrations and vulnerable to nets and weirs blocking their path, especially in smaller tributary streams; (b) caribou massed for migration taken either in caribou surrounds placed in mountain passes or from boats when the caribou herds are crossing rivers; and (c) the exploitation of migrating waterfowl when they are massed in breeding areas and are especially vulnerable due to molt. Examples of subsistence techniques that partially fulfill the criteria of strategic hunting of animals (when they are particularly vulnerable but not massed) include the practice of hunting moose from boats when they are swimming in the rivers and thus helpless or the running down of moose in the deep, crusted snow of late winter which supports the

Figure 7.2   A Koyukon deer corral. (From Frederick Whymper, Travel and Adventure in the Territory of Alaska, *New York: Harper, 1869, p. 210.)*

weight of a man on snowshoes but breaks and retards the movements of the heavier moose.

Animals that are scattered and not particularly vulnerable require different harvesting methods. Extensive hunting techniques are used to harvest animals such as moose, bear, hare, and ptarmigan, which do not generally mass together for migrations. These methods include the snaring of snowshoe hare and ptarmigan, and the tracking and shooting of a moose by a lone hunter with bow and arrow.

In large areas of the Athabascan region there are few game animals. Early explorers traveled entire river valleys and recorded only as many large game animals as could be counted on the fingers of one hand. Changes in animal populations (in salmon runs, the hare cycle, and in caribou migration routes) often had drastic effects on aboriginal populations. Many of the earlier explorers in the Athabascan regions recorded instances of starvation and of cannibalism induced by starvation—indeed, the literature on the northern Athabascans reports cannibalism due to starvation as a common theme. In attempting to define the major components of Athabascan diet we will emphasize those food items that may have strategic importance during parts of the year when there is danger of starvation. The demographic data on the aboriginal and early historical Athabascans are crude, and of necessity the treatment of demography here will be crude, establishing only a gross relationship between the natural resources of the land and numbers of people, band or village size, and degree of mobility. The major subsistence activity will be defined in the discussion of techniques for obtaining the major food items in the diet and those food items that are important in a strategic sense during a particular time of the year.

The case studies that follow form the basis for a comparison of various Athabascan macroband patterns of subsistence, made in terms of the major natural resources of the respective areas, demography, village or microband size, degree of mobility throughout the annual cycle, major components of diet, and technology connected with subsistence.[1]

Intensive Riverine and Maritime Emphasis

Kenai-Kachemak Bay Tanaina. The Kenai-Kachemak Bay Tanaina live in a maritime region on the eastern part of Cook Inlet, probably the richest in food resources of the entire northern Athabascan areas. These Tanaina groups exploit not only the vast maritime resources of the sea but also the large game of the mountain hinterland. The major part of the Kenai Tanaina diet is salmon, and it is probable that sea mammals, particularly the hair seal, constitute the chief items of diet for the Kachemak Bay Tanaina. Five species of salmon make spawning runs in this area, and they are trapped in weirs and taken with dip nets or dragnets. Osgood describes the fishing and preparation of fish for drying as a cooperative effort in which all sex and age groups participate in some aspect. In addition to salmon a number of other fish and sea foods are eaten; the sea mammals hunted in the Kachemak Bay area include hair seal, fur seal, sea otter, sea lion, porpoise, and beluga (white whales). Beluga and hair seals are common in Kenai and are exploited there.

The Tanaina use spears to hunt large game, especially the commonly found black bear. They take caribou with the aid of small hunting dogs and bow and arrow, and also with snares used in conjunction with long fences. The big-game fence used by many Athabascan groups consists of a long row of logs and brush built with a number of openings, each covered with a snare. The fence obstructs the animal, which then goes through the opening to be caught in the snare.

The Tanaina also exploit a number of other land animals, but it is difficult to define the roles of large and small game in the Kenai-Kachemak Bay Tanaina subsistence from the historical and ethnographic record. Osgood notes, however, that they are probably important for their hides as well as for their meat. Hunting techniques, as we have said, include use of bow and arrow, spears, hunting dogs, fences used in conjunction with snares, and snares, but again it is difficult to evaluate the contribution each technique makes to total subsistence. As salmon is the major food for the Kenai Tanaina, however, we can

---

[1] For a further consideration of the social structure of several groups considered in this case study, see Chapter 8.

be sure the salmon-fishing technology—weirs and nets—contributed most.

Captain Cook's voyage of 1778 brought the first European contact with these groups. After this there followed a period of contact—including wars—with the Russians. The Tanaina were greatly reduced in population during the smallpox epidemic of 1838. Lisiansky, writing in the first decade of the nineteenth century, records the entire population of the Cook Inlet Tanaina as 3,000 individuals, settled in fourteen villages, and Osgood, the major ethnographer of these Tanaina, agrees with this estimate. There is little information on the population size of aboriginal settlement in the literature, but the figures given above would give 214 as the arithmetical mean for village size. Because the Kenai-Kachemak Bay region is superior in food resources to the Upper Cook Inlet Tanaina region, it would be reasonable to expect larger settlements to fall in Kenai-Kachemak Bay areas. The villages consisted of winter semisubterranean houses, and there was a pattern of dual residence throughout the annual cycle, winter being spent in villages and summer in fishing camps.

Lake Iliamna Tanaina. The Lake Iliamna Tanaina live in a region similar to their relatives at Kenai-Kachemak Bay except that they depend more on freshwater than on maritime resources for subsistence. Salmon, especially the red salmon, form the main staple of their diet, and are taken as they ascend the streams in spawning runs by fish spears and by fish weirs used in conjunction with traps. Hare and ptarmigan form important food staples in winter. Large game such as caribou and bear are taken by a variety of methods including the use of spears, sinew-backed bows, deadfalls, surrounds, and tracking dogs. Trips are made to Cook Inlet for fish, sea mammals, seals, and sea foods.

A brief explanation of some of the subsistence technology follows. Deadfalls are a type of trap in which a large weight, usually a log, falls on the animal touching the trigger. The surround, resembling the big-game fence, consists of two long wing fences built into a V-shape with an opening at the point of the V which leads into a smaller circular fence. Large game animals, usually caribou, are driven into the wings by a group of drivers and forced into a corral at the end, where they are killed by another party of hunters. Usually this technique requires a communal effort. Surrounds are often placed at passes and other strategic places in regard to the land formation on paths of the migrating caribou. Fish weirs, consisting of fences of sticks blocking the paths of migrating fish, are placed across streams with spaces left for dip nets or cylindrical, wicker fish traps with funnel-shaped openings. This subsistence technology occurs generally throughout the entire Alaskan Athabascan area.

The Russians made contact with the Lake Iliamna Tanaina in the last two decades of the eighteenth century. There followed a brief period

Figure 7.3 Fish traps on the Yukon. (From Whymper, op. cit., p. 195.)

of contact with the Russian traders and missionaries and then a period of wars brought about by mistreatment of the people. Father Juvenal,[2] writing in 1796 in the village of Ilymna, estimates the total population at between six hundred and eight hundred individuals. Although this estimate cannot be accepted uncritically, it suggests that at least one village in the region had a comparatively high population. Various trips were made away from the village during the annual cycle for hunting or for establishing fishing camps, but the village, composed of a number of semisubterranean houses, formed a base for large parts of the year.

Anvik-Shageluk Ingalik. Among the Athabascans living on the Yukon River, the Anvik-Shageluk Ingalik live farthest downstream, and great quantities of salmon pass their territory before branching off to the tributaries to spawn. The Anvik-Shageluk thus have an advantage over their upstream neighbors since as the salmon go up the river numbers of them divert to tributaries and also individual salmon lose weight because of the exertion of the upstream migrations. Explorers traveling in the Anvik-Shageluk area commented on the vast supplies of salmon taken by the Ingalik and spoke of river banks red with racks of drying salmon. The earlier explorers and Osgood, the major ethnographer of these people, agree that fish, especially salmon, form the major propor-

[2] A number of historians have suggested that Father Juvenal's diary was a fraud. We do not find their arguments convincing, and the journal is accepted, with minor reservations, by Townsend, the major ethnographer of the Lake Iliamna Tanaina. Therefore we are using information from Juvenal's journal here, mainly material on aboriginal population estimates. See Townsend (1965:37–38) for a more comprehensive review of this problem.

Figure 7.4 Moose hunting in the Yukon River. (From Whymper, op. cit., p. 244.)

tion of the diet. The Anvik-Shageluk catch salmon in the warmer seasons, and take whitefish and blackfish when the rivers are covered with ice. The chief means of taking fish, both when the rivers are covered with ice and when there is open water, is with fish traps used in conjunction with weirs. Dragnets made of the inner bark of willow are also used in open water, but the weir and trap remain most important in the Ingalik subsistence technology.

Osgood mentions the taking of caribou by means of fences and snares, the killing of animals as they massed to cross rivers, the running down of moose in late winter when the snow crust would support the weight of a hunter on snowshoes but not that of a moose, and the netting of geese during the August molt. Despite the rich food supply, March and April bring hunger and occasional starvation in this region. At this time the fish traps have to be taken away before the ice breaks up, and the people must depend upon snaring hare and ptarmigan until the arrival of waterfowl and king salmon in the spring break this period of fasting. As a factor limiting population in aboriginal times, Osgood notes that there were periods of starvation perhaps every ten or fifteen years when slumps in the spawning runs of fish coincided with times of little game.

Apparently the first date of contact with Europeans was 1833–1834, when the Russian explorer Glazunow reached the Anvik-Shageluk Ingalik. A period of trade with the Russians followed, and the best record of this early historical period is the journal of the explorer Zagoskin written during his travels in 1842–1844. Zagoskin gives a careful account of the demography of the areas he visits and reports the total population of the Anvik-Shageluk area as 770, settled in villages ranging from 33 to 170. These figures are of particular value as it was rare for earlier Alaskan explorers to note settlement size with such thoroughness. The pattern of residence throughout the annual cycle in this area was rather sedentary. The semisubterranean houses were occupied for the nine winter months, with occasional hunting trips (sometimes of entire families) being made away from the winter village, and summer was frequently spent in tents in scattered fish camps.

Inland Riverine Emphasis

The Copper River Bands (Ahtena). Compared to most other inland Athabascan regions the Copper River area is rich in animal resources, with large moose populations and salmon runs. Allen, the American explorer who in 1885 became the first white to travel the length of the Copper River, and Abercrombie, who made several trips on the Copper before the turn of this century, both agree that salmon formed the main part of the diet of the Copper River bands. Allen notes that hare followed next in importance in their diet, and he mentions that other animals exploited by them included large game animals such as moose, caribou, bear, and sheep, and smaller game such as beaver, muskrat, porcupine, and waterfowl. There are aboriginal large-game surrounds in this area as much as ten miles long. Although this area may have been comparatively rich in salmon and large game, from the accounts of the early explorers it would seem that the salmon stores did not last the winter and that large game was often unavailable. Early spring, especially before the first salmon runs, seems to have been a time of hunger, and Allen gives vivid accounts of the condition of some groups he met during this period of hunger.

Abercrombie, who traveled a short distance up the Copper River in 1884, gives a population estimate, based on information received from the people, of 350 to 400, and he mentions a settlement of sixty individuals. Allen, who traveled up the Copper a year later, records a population of 366 individuals and notes two settlements of 47 and 30 people, as well as a number of small groups scattered throughout the area. In 1898 Abercrombie returned to the Copper region, and he divides the river-valley grouping into four bands, giving the population of three as 150, 75, and 35. Little is specifically written on these people's pattern of movement throughout the annual cycle, but it is known that some subsistence-connected movement occurs in which small groups scatter throughout the countryside—especially in late spring—and that at other times of the year the people come together in the larger settlements.

The Koyukon River Group. The emphasis here will be on the Koyukon group of the Koyukuk River proper (Upper Koyukuk) rather than on those groups sharing the same name that are found to the west of the mouth of the Koyukuk River on the Yukon River (Lower Koyukuk). Explorers have noted the scarcity of game in the Koyukuk River valley and mention that the salmon runs are small compared to those of the Yukon. Allen, the first white to travel the length of the Koyukuk, mentions that in 1885 caribou were so scarce that the Koyukon people tried to buy caribou skins from him.

Allen says that salmon and other fish formed the main subsistence for these people, fish being caught with weir and traps, both in times of open water and of ice. The people used caribou surrounds and took the caribou either in the communal drives or in large-game snares. Waterfowl were taken in largest numbers during the molt, but seem to have had a strategic importance in the spring when other food is scarce and before the salmon runs.

Zagoskin traveled part way up the Koyukuk River in his journey of 1842–1844, and he gives the total population of this river as 165, in settlements ranging from 6 to 65 individuals. He also lists five other camps in this grouping living on the Yukon River near the Koyukuk, with a total population of 124 individuals, giving a total of 289 for Zagoskin's Koyukon grouping. Allen gives the total population on the Koyukuk River in 1885 as 276 individuals living in nineteen camps, the largest of which was inhabited by 45 people, but his figures are somewhat skewed because an epidemic reduced the population two years before his visit. About twenty years later, Stuck gives the population of the Koyukuk River as 250 individuals. Thus for a period of about sixty years, beginning at a date close to European contact, we have a series of fairly similar population estimates. Zagoskin describes a pattern of three basic movements throughout the annual cycle: to summer camps, to winter houses, and a nomadic spring hunt. From the descriptions of scattered groups throughout the Koyukuk area it would seem that they had a more extensive annual pattern of movement than did the comparatively sedentary Tanaina and Ingalik groups described previously.

Vunta Kutchin. The Vunta Kutchin live on the Lower Porcupine and Crow Rivers in the northern Yukon Territory, a region similar to areas in interior Alaska. The area around Crow River is dotted with a number of lakes and the Vunta Kutchin country is bounded to the north by the Brooks Range and to the east by other mountains. Osgood describes the livelihood of these people as borderline between fishing and hunting with a bit more emphasis on fishing. These Kutchin are in an area of comparatively small salmon runs, but salmon, whitefish, and grayling form a steady and more-or-less dependable food staple. They are taken in weirs used in conjunction with basket traps or dip nets. Caribou are numerous and make up an important proportion of diet; they were taken in surrounds until the turn of this century. Balikci notes that the caribou surround and the big-game snare were effective in securing a source of food. Caribou were also killed while crossing rivers in their migrations, but the caribou in this region followed varied migration routes and probably the Vunta Kutchin could not always be sure of being in the right place for their kills. Porcupine, muskrat, and hare were particularly important animals in the native diet. Cases of cannibalism induced by starvation are mentioned for this group, indicating periods of failure of food supplies and an ecological limit on population size.

The population estimates for the Vunta Kutchin are not very good. Murray, a fur trader at Fort Yukon in the 1840s, gives the population as "80 men." Thus if women and children were counted the total population would probably be at least 200 to 400 individuals. Although the exact patterns of aboriginal subsistence movements throughout the year are not clear, a pattern appears of small hunting bands in winter and gatherings for fishing in the warmer seasons, with the entire Vunta Kutchin apparently coming together on certain occasions.

Inland Hunting-Snaring Emphasis

Chandalar Kutchin. Few descriptions exist in the historical record of the Chandalar Kutchin, who live in the river valleys in the mountainous region of the Chandalar River. Therefore we shall rely mainly on the ethnography of McKennan, which is based on fieldwork done in 1933 and which gives a description of their pattern of subsistence. Salmon do not ascend the Chandalar River and, according to McKennan, large game animals, especially caribou, from the basis of the subsistence of these Kutchin. McKennan notes further that smaller game, including porcupine, hare, beaver, muskrat, ptarmigan, migratory waterfowl, and freshwater fish (mainly whitefish and grayling), played a role in the aboriginal subsistence. Most of the caribou were caught in surrounds in communal drives and moose were taken by means of long straight fences with openings for snares. As many as four hundred caribou at a time were taken in these communal drives into surrounds; this represented the most efficient of the aboriginal caribou-hunting techniques, although other more individualistic methods were also used. In addition, musk-oxen were driven off cliffs; moose were run down in crusted snow; and hare were snared or taken in group drives. McKennan lists the surround, snare, and deadfall as major aboriginal Chandalar Kutchin food-getting technology. They caught whitefish, grayling, and other species of freshwater fish in weirs used in conjunction with fish traps and spears, employing both these techniques in summer and in winter. It is certain that these people did not have a secure base of subsistence; from time to time periods of starvation reduced the population, and specific cases of cannibalism brought about by starvation were remembered. McKennan's account gives us some idea of the ecological factors limiting population size.

The census of 1910 gave the population of this group as 177 individuals. McKennan counted 124 Chandalar Kutchin (197, including those living out of the area). The usual problems connected with establishing the aboriginal demography exist, especially the influence of epidemics. McKennan estimates that restrictions of natural production have maintained the aboriginal population at about two hundred individuals and Hadleigh-West gives an aboriginal population estimate of from two hundred to three hundred individuals.

The Chandalar Kutchin are divided into three microbands. Although little specific information exists on patterns of movement throughout the year, it is known that the Chandalar Kutchin were a highly mobile people, making numerous movements throughout the annual cycle.

Upper Tanana (Nabesna)[3]. The Upper Tanana (Nabesna) live at the sources of the Tanana River, below the modern village of Tanacross in Alaska, in a region bounded on the southwest by the Wrangell range, which separates them from the Copper River valley. Characterized by many glacier streams, the region's climate, animal life, and vegetation are typical of interior Alaska. Contact with Europeans probably occurred around 1885, but for the following decades the Upper Tanana were relatively isolated from European influences. The historical record is very sparse for this region and we shall rely on McKennan's monograph based on fieldwork done in 1929–1930.

Salmon do not ascend the Tanana beyond the Goodpaster River and very few salmon are found in this area. Large game including sheep, moose, and especially caribou form the basis of Upper Tanana diet. Most caribou were taken during their spring and fall migrations, usually with fences used in conjunction with big-game snares in communal drives. McKennan emphasizes the importance of the large-game snare in the subsistence technology of these Athabascans; it was also used in narrow passes in the mountains to capture mountain sheep. The hare also played an important role in subsistence, especially during periods when large game was not available. Whitefish were caught during summer runs in weirs used in conjunction with the usual Athabascan cylinder-basket fish traps.

There is little information on the aboriginal population of this group, but in 1929–1930 the population figure was 152, divided into five microbands. Although the Upper Tanana may have been reduced

[3] Subsequent fieldwork conducted by W. D. Strong with a neighboring group suggests a pattern of subsistence for the Upper Tanana of an inland riverine emphasis (on freshwater fish, muskrats, and waterfowl) with larger aboriginal population estimates and more sedentary populations than suggested by McKennan.

by scarlet fever, spread by native trade routes connecting them to the

Northwest Coast before the period of white contact, McKennan, taking ecological factors into account, makes a guess that his population figures are close to the aboriginal ones. Semipermanent villages were occupied for only short periods of time and the pattern of movement throughout the annual cycle consisted of an almost constant series of moves.

CONCLUSION

The data from these examples suggest three major patterns of subsistence based on amount and kind of natural resources available: an intensive riverine and maritime subsistence emphasis; an inland riverine emphasis; and an inland hunting-snaring emphasis. A summary of the essential features of each of these three patterns follows.

I. *Intensive Riverine and Maritime Emphasis*

Characteristics are from these groups: (*a*) Kenai-Kachemak Bay Tanaina, (*b*) Lake Iliamna Tanaina, and (*c*) Anvik-Shageluk Ingalik. Major features of this pattern of subsistence include:
1. Rich riverine or maritime salmon area
2. Emphasis on salmon in diet
3. Total macroband populations of more than 500 individuals
4. A number of settlements with populations of more than 100 people
5. Emphasis on dual residence throughout the annual cycle—winter houses and summer fishing camps

II. *Inland Riverine Emphasis*

Characteristics are from these groups: (*a*) Copper River, (*b*) Koyukon, and (*c*) Vunta Kutchin (a borderline case between this and hunting-snaring emphasis). Major features of this pattern of subsistence include:
1. Inland salmon area
2. Emphasis on salmon and other fish in diet, with other animals, especially caribou and hares, playing an important role
3. Total macroband populations of more than 250 individuals (Vunta Kutchin borderline case)
4. Most microbands fewer than 100 individuals
5. At least a trilocal pattern of residence throughout the annual cycle—winter houses, spring hunts, and summer fishing camps

III. *Inland Hunting-Snaring Emphasis*

Characteristics are from these groups: (*a*) Chandalar Kutchin and (*b*) Upper Tanana. Major features of this pattern of subsistence include:
1. No salmon in area
2. Emphasis on caribou in diet with other large and small game and whitefish playing an important role

3. Macroband population between 150 and 200 individuals
4. Microband groupings fewer than 65 individuals
5. Pattern of frequent movements throughout annual cycle

In a more extensive examination of the Alaskan Athabascan region as a whole, these three suggested patterns of subsistence would merge to form a spectrum of gradual variation from area to area with significant differences over a wide region. The range of subsistence patterns has been defined for a number of Alaskan Athabascan groups not discussed in this study, and all macrobands not covered here would fit within the foregoing outline.

The major independent variable is the "richness" of an area in food resources capable of exploitation given the level of aboriginal Athabascan technology and social organization for production. Dependent variables include the major components of diet, macro- and microband populations, and the degree of mobility throughout the annual cycle, all these depending in turn on the "richness" of natural food resources. Aboriginal subsistence technology remains almost constant throughout the region. For the purposes of this discussion it would have been better if the independent variable could have been established in quantitative terms rather than in terms of emphasis drawn from statements of the early explorers and ethnographers. However, those quantitative data on the natural resources of the region that have been gathered in modern times cannot be accepted uncritically as representative of conditions in aboriginal times. The major features of natural food resources in Alaska have been in flux throughout historic times; examples in this process of alteration of the Alaskan ecology are the extinction of musk-oxen in Alaska, the great reduction of caribou herds in various regions owing to the introduction of firearms, the tremendous reduction in salmon from commercial overfishing, the destructive influence of mining dredges on the food-producing capabilities of some rivers, increased frequency of forest fires, and the impact of the increasing white population on natural food resources. Not only have the natural food resources been altered quantitatively since the time of European influence, but also the aboriginal patterns of subsistence have been influenced greatly by the introduction of European technology. The aboriginal Athabascan surrounds and fences, big-game snares, fish weirs, wicker traps, and smaller nets of willow bark or rawhide gave way to European technology: firearms, fish wheels, larger fish nets made of cotton cording, steel traps, and other items, all of which had an effect both on the ecology and on patterns of subsistence.

It seems clear from the historical and ethnographic record that salmon were the major component of diet for most Alaskan Athabascan groups, and salmon were most plentiful and in the best condition in such special spawning areas as the lower sections of Cook Inlet and the lower sections of the Yukon River. From these areas especially rich in salmon our examples of intensive maritime and riverine emphasis are taken. The dependence on salmon, where salmon are present, derives from the fact that salmon arrive in masses fairly dependably at a season of the year and provide a particularly rich source of protein, fats, and other food nutrients. They can be taken in large quantities during their migrations and are easily preserved by drying. No other animal provides such a dependable, high-quality food source that can be easily harvested in such great quantities as to support the comparatively high populations found in the intensive riverine and maritime subsistence areas. With a reduction in the amounts of salmon available inland, we find a corresponding reduction in population.

Caribou, which forms the major component of diet for the inland hunting-snaring subsistence groups, shares some qualities in common with salmon in that it has a high food value and can be harvested in large numbers during the massed migrations. It is not nearly so dependable a source of food as salmon, however, as there are variations in the paths of migrations of caribou, which introduces a factor of uncertainty into the harvesting of these animals. This is reflected in the fact that the groups that depend on caribou for a major portion of their diet have comparatively low population; when caribou fail as a food source periods of starvation limit population. The inland riverine emphasis, midrange between the two extremes, has an advantage over the inland hunting-snaring emphasis in having a dependable salmon supply, but it apparently does not have salmon resources capable of supporting the higher populations of the intensive riverine and maritime subsistence pattern.

The concept of strategic hunting, discussed in the introduction, motivated the subsistence activity of these people who exploited particular species at definite times and places, when these species were massed and/or particularly vulnerable. Given the level of technology and social organization, these methods ensured that a minimum energy input of work would result in the maximum energy output in food. Salmon and caribou, which either separately or together probably formed the basis of diet of all Alaskan Athabascans, were taken almost exclusively by strategic hunting. In the inland areas hare probably played an important role in diet; these animals are widespread during the high points of their population cycle and can be taken in late winter and early spring, when other food sources may fail. Methods of exploiting hare were extensive rather than strategic; they were generally taken individually in snares. The type of subsistence technology that contributed to the bulk of the diet—the large-game fences and surrounds, the snares for large and small game, fish weirs and wicker traps, small nets and fish spears—indicates a concern for conserving the energy of the hunter (for example, stringing out a number of snares over game trails rather than depending on killing animals with a bow and arrow with the individual hunter waiting by a game trail) while harvesting as many animals as possible.

The connection between available food supply and population has been mentioned, and the list of population figures for the three patterns of subsistence bears out this thesis. A rough comparison of population per square mile can be made, based on calculations from Mooney's figures for aboriginal American populations and from macroband areas as defined by Osgood:[4]

Macroband	Number of square miles per individual
Tanaina	12
Ingalik	16
Copper River	24
Koyukon	37
Chandalar Kutchin	40–60
Upper Tanana	63

These figures are given mainly as possible indications of relative population densities, and they bear out one thesis of this chapter. A more accurate method of assessing relative population densities would be to define the ecozones exploited within the macroband area and to base population-density calculations on those, but there are no data on this point in the ethnographic record.

In the richest food areas village population frequently exceeded one hundred individuals, and in such areas there was a dual pattern of residence, winter villages and summer fishing camps. In the areas of intensive riverine-maritime subsistence, more people could spend more time together during the year. In the more inland salmon areas microband populations generally are fewer than one hundred individuals, and the subsistence movement was at least triresident during the annual cycle. For the groups falling into the hunting-snaring pattern of subsistence, microband population most often falls under 65 individuals with frequent movements throughout the annual cycle. Thus microband size and the amount of time throughout the annual cycle that band members can remain together as a unit depend on the richness of natural resources in the area.

These residence patterns have important implications for Athabascan social organization; in general a small scattered population precludes such complex social formations as chiefdoms and class society. It would require another study to define the relation of the Athabascan social organization to the ecology, but a brief review of the ethnographic literature suggests that the most extreme Athabascan form of social ranking (something approaching a chiefdom) occurs in the areas with an intensive riverine-maritime subsistence, with a somewhat modified form found in the other two subsistence areas.

ANNOTATED BIBLIOGRAPHY

For a perceptive analysis of the cultural ecology of hunters, see Richard B. Lee, "What Hunters Do for a Living," in R. B. Lee and I. DeVore

[4] The figures for the Chandalar Kutchin are taken from Hadleigh-West (1963)—see bibliography at end of Chapter 9.

(eds.), *Man the Hunter* (Chicago: Aldine, 1968), and "!Kung Bushmen Subsistence: An Input-Output Analysis," in *Environment and Cultural Behavior* (New York: Natural History Press, 1969). For an analysis of the relation between production and social organization, refer to Marvin Harris, "The Economy Has No Surplus?" *American Anthropologist,* 61:185–199 (1959). Excellent studies of cultural ecology in other areas of the world are Clifford Geertz, *Agricultural Involution: Process of Ecological Change in Indonesia* (Berkeley: University of California Press, 1970), and Marshall D. Sahlins, *Social Stratification in Polynesia* (Seattle: University of Washington Press, 1958).

For studies of Athabascan distribution and the problem of the nature of Athabascan groupings, see Cornelius Osgood, *The Distribution of the Northern Athapaskan* (New Haven: Yale University Publications in Anthropology, No. 7, 1936), and Robert A. McKennan, "Athapaskan Grouping and Social Organization in Central Alaska," in David Damas (ed.), *Contributions to Anthropology: Band Societies* (Ottawa: National Museum of Canada, Bulletin No. 228, Anthro. Series 84, 1969). For a discussion of aboriginal Athabascan demography, see James Mooney, *The Aboriginal Populations of America North of Mexico* (Smithsonian Miscellaneous Collection, Vol. 80, No. 7, 1928).

For discussions on various aspects of Arctic and Subarctic ecology, consult the following works: L. S. Berg, *Natural Regions of the USSR* (New York: MacMillan, 1950); M. J. Dunbar, *Ecological Development in Polar Regions: A Study in Evolution* (Englewood Cliffs, N.J.: Prentice-Hall, 1968); J. D. McPhail and C. C. Lindsey, *Freshwater Fishes of Northwestern Canada and Alaska* (Ottawa: Fisheries Research Board of Canada, Bulletin 173, 1970); Eugene P. Odum, *Fundamentals of Ecology* (Philadelphia: Saunders, 1965); A. L. Rand, *Mammals of Yukon, Canada* (Ottawa: National Museum of Canada, Bulletin No. 100, 1945); Victor E. Shelford, *The Ecology of North America* (Urbana: University of Illinois Press, 1963); B. A. Tikhomirov, *Relationship of the Animal World and the Plant Cover of the Tundra,* E. Issakoff and T. W. Barry (trans.), W. A. Fuller (ed.) (Moscow and Leningrad: Botanical Institute, Academy of Science of USSR, 1959); *Alaska Natives and the Land* (Washington, D.C.: U.S. Government Printing Office, 1968); and also see various useful articles in *Ecology of the Subarctic Regions* (Paris: UNESCO, 1970). For a unique cultural ecology study (on the Cree) on the dynamic of the boreal forest, consult Harvey Allan Feit, *Mistassini Hunters of the Boreal Forest: Ecosystem Dynamics and Multiple Subsistence Patterns* (unpublished masters thesis, McGill University, Montreal, 1969).

Two important historical records on the Tanaina groupings are those of Juvenal, "A Daily Journal Kept by the Rev. Father Juvenal" [1796], in *Kroeber Anthropological Society Papers,* No. 7 (Fall 1952); and Urey Lisiansky, *A Voyage Round the World in the Years 1803–06* (London: John Booth, 1814). The two main ethnographies on the Tanaina are Cornelius Osgood, *The Ethnography of the Tanaina* (New Haven: Yale University Publications in Anthropology, No. 16; reprinted by Human Relations Area Files Press, 1966); and Joan Broom Townsend, *Ethnohistory and Cultural Change of the Iliamna Tanaina* (Ph.D. dissertation, University of California, Los Angeles, 1965; published by University Microfilms, Ann Arbor, Michigan). For other publications by Joan Broom Townsend on the Tanaina, see "Ethnographic Notes on the Pedro Bay Tanaina," in *Anthropologica*, n.s. 5:2 (1963); the "Introduction" to Bill Vaudin, *Tanaina Tales from Alaska* (Norman: University of Oklahoma Press, 1969); and "The Tanaina of Southwestern Alaska: A Historical Synopsis," in *Western Canadian Journal of Anthropology*, 1:1:2–16 (1970), Special Issue: Athabascan Studies.

The main historical records on the Ingalik include L. A. Zagoskin, *Lieutenant Zagoskin's Travels in Russian America, 1842–1844*, H. N. Michael (ed.) (Toronto: University of Toronto Press, 1967); William H. Dall, *Alaska and Its Resources* (Boston: Lee and Shepard, 1870); V. C. Cantwell, *Report of the Operations of the U.S. Revenue Steamer Nunivak on the Yukon River Station, Alaska 1899–1901* (Washington, D.C.: U.S. Government Printing Office, 1902); Hudson Stuck, *Voyages on the Yukon and Its Tributaries* (New York: Scribner, 1917); and Frederick Whymper, *Travel and Adventure in the Territory of Alaska* (London: John Murray, 1868). The main modern ethnography on the Ingalik is the series by Cornelius Osgood, *Ingalik Material Culture* (New Haven: Yale University Publications in Anthropology, No. 22, 1940); *Ingalik Social Culture* (New Haven: Yale University Publications in Anthropology, No. 53, 1958); and *Ingalik Mental Culture* (New Haven: Yale University Publications in Anthropology, No. 56, 1959).

Since there is no modern ethnography on the Copper River Athabascans, the material on this case study was taken mainly from Henry T. Allen, "Report of an Expedition to the Copper, Tanana and Koyukuk Rivers" [1885], in *Compilation of Narratives of Explorations in Alaska* (Washington, D.C.: U.S. Government Printing Office, 1900), and the two reports by W. R. Abercrombie, "A Supplementary Expedition into the Copper River Valley, 1884" and "A Military Reconnaissance of the Copper River Valley, 1898," both reports being in *Compilation of Narratives of Explorations in Alaska* (Washington, D.C.: U.S. Government Printing Office, 1900).

There is no modern ethnography on the Athabascans of the Koyukuk River proper, but the ethnography by Loyens on the Lower Koyukuk macroband makes references to the Upper Koyukuk macroband (and also includes extensive extracts from the unpublished work of the missionary J. Jette); see William John Loyens, *The Changing Culture of the Nulato Koyukon Indians* (Ph.D. dissertation, University of Wisconsin, 1966; published by University Microfilms, Ann Arbor, Michigan). The works of Zagoskin, Allen, Whymper, Dall, Cantwell, and Stuck, listed in the two preceding paragraphs, provided the basis of material for this case study.

For an extensive list of references for the Kutchin macrobands, refer to the bibliography in Chapter 9.

The case study on the Upper Tanana was based on Robert A. Mc-Kennan, *The Upper Tanana Indians* (New Haven: Yale University Publications in Anthropology, No. 55, 1959).

For a more complete list of historical sources on northern Athabascans, consult George Peter Murdock, *Ethnographic Bibliography of North America* (New Haven: Human Relations Area Files, 1960), pp. 35–47.

EIGHT

SOCIAL STRUCTURE AND KINSHIP TERMINOLOGY OF NORTH PACIFIC GROUPS

In this chapter a number of societies that have been considered in previous chapters—the Yukagirs, Kutchin, Tanaina, and Ingalik—will be discussed further with emphasis on the relationship between social structure and kin terminology systems. These groups, in common with other tribal groups in the North Pacific region, are organized at the level of ranking societies. The concept of ranking society and the place of ranking societies in historical political development is perhaps best expressed by Fried in his work *The Evolution of Political Society*, upon which we shall depend for a good part of the theoretical discussion here.

SOCIAL STRUCTURE

Ranking societies, once numerous throughout the world, have a form of social structure somewhat more complicated than that of egalitarian hunting bands. In ranking societies, however, differentiation in rank, prestige, division of labor, and economic status is not as rigid as in chiefdoms or nearly so rigid as in class society, and, as Fried points out, no individual is denied access to strategic natural resources. In social complexity and in emphasis on ranking, the groups considered here would be at the lower end of the spectrum compared to groups on the Northwest Coast and in Polynesia which put much greater emphasis on ranking.

In Yukagir and Athabascan ranking the highly ranked individual —the "chief," "clan elder," or "big man"—organizes the production and storage of goods and then distributes or redistributes these goods to the community. The whole point of wealth is to have something to give away; in the act of giving things away or in redistributing things the "big man" gains prestige. The success of a chief depends on his ability (*a*) to organize his kinsmen and other followers to produce a "surplus" of goods and (*b*) to organize the proper conditions for the redistribution of this wealth. As he depends directly on these helpers there is a limit to his authority—he can give directions but not orders. If he treats his followers too harshly they are free to attach themselves to another chief.

KINSHIP TERMINOLOGY

Following the work of Lewis Henry Morgan, beginning in the mid-nineteenth century, anthropologists have been interested in the relationship between types of kinship terminology systems and forms of social structure. In primitive societies kinship often forms the basis of social organization, and the study of kinship and of kinship terminology is necessary for the understanding of these groups. As a number of scholars (e.g., Service, Lehman, Goldman, and Damas) have pointed out, however, there is not always a direct relationship between the form or specific features of social organization and the type of kinship terminology. Societies that have many features of social organization in common may have different types of kinship terminologies.

Nevertheless, regularities have been noted in the relationship between specific features of social structure and types of kin terminology. For example, Lowie has pointed out regularities between bifurcate merging terminology (use of one term for father and father's brother, and of one term for mother and mother's sister) for the first ascending generation (generation of mother and father) and a unilineal descent group—that is, a matrilineal or patrilineal clan (see Figure 8.1). Part of the logic of this merging is that, given a unilineal descent group,

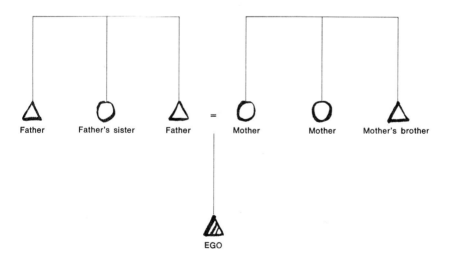

Figure 8.1 Bifurcate merging terminology for parental generation. Note that the actual terms used vary from society to society, and we have given an example using only English words. It is also important to realize that the actual native terms are not directly translatable to English kin terms, for they may have connotations wider than the English terms "father," "mother," etc.

both mother and mother's sister would be in the same clan, hence merged together in terminology as they are of the same generation and sex; the same logic applies to father and father's brother. Other features of social structure that anthropologists have considered important include type of residence—that is, whether married couples live with the relatives of the wife (matrilocal), the relatives of the husband (patrilocal), or elsewhere—and special forms of marriage (for example, cross-cousin marriage) which may also be influential in forming this specific type of kinship terminology.

Bilateral bands, common throughout the North and characteristic of many hunting groups throughout the world, are often reflected by a bilateral kinship terminology system—either a lineal or bifurcate collateral type for parental generation (see Figure 8.2). In neither of these two cases is father or mother merged with their siblings. In the lineal system both father's brother and mother's brother are called by the same term; another term applies to both father's sister and mother's sister. In the bifurcate collateral system there are separate terms for mother, mother's sister, mother's brother, father, father's sister, and father's brother.

A number of scholars have related this Arctic bilateralism in kin terminology to a flexible band that often changes membership. The first such scholar was Bogoras, who wrote around the turn of this century, and the discussion continues to the present day (for example, see Pehrson, Damas, Graburn, and Savishinsky). Bilateral kin terminology results from the demands for flexibility imposed upon small hunting or herding groups in the Arctic by the comparatively low level of production that often permits only small groups of people to exist in any given area during the year. In order to produce enough to live, the band requires a certain flexibility in membership which precludes strict residence rules. The first explanation for the lineal and bifurcate collateral kinship terminologies, then, is that the conditions—the environment, the level of technology, and so on—under which these people secure the material bases of life require flexible bands that constantly change in size and in membership, and therefore any given individual or couple is likely to change microband residence comparatively frequently.

We argue that the lineal and bifurcate collateral systems represent two possible responses to conditions in which it is not possible for the same set of kinsmen to always live together. The lineal system may be a response to conditions in which either mother's and father's brothers or mother's and father's sisters may be possible allies and co-members of Ego's band; hence they are merged. The bilateral terminology of the Chukchi, both the maritime hunters and the reindeer herders, exemplifies the lineal type. An alternate response could be the bifurcate collateral system, in which father's and mother's siblings are differentiated from each other and by sex. This system may result from the fact that these four classes of kinsmen (MoBr, MoSi, FaBr,

85

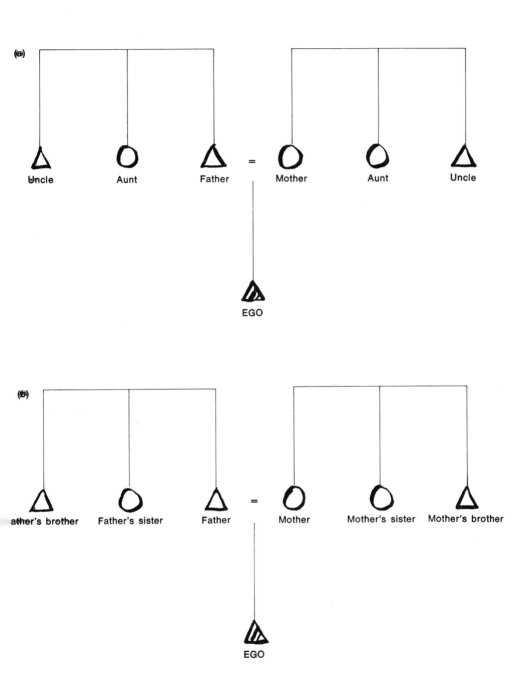

Figure 8.2   (a) *Lineal* and (b) *bifurcate collateral terminology for parental generation.*

and FaSi) are often in different groupings and may represent for Ego possible allies and comembers of his band, hence they are distinguished and called by separate terms. Many Eskimo groups illustrate the bifurcate collateral type. The explanation given above is not to be taken as inclusive—undoubtedly a number of factors come into play in determining these responses. Thus factors of marriage, residence, and alliance may have an influence on kinship terminology systems.

COMPARISONS AMONG SPECIFIC GROUPS

It has been mentioned that similar social organizations may differ in kinship terminology systems, and that a number of factors may come into play in the formation of a specific system of terminology. Here we will inquire into the relationship between a bifurcate collateral kin terminology and the ranking type of social order in the society of the Siberian Yukagirs and of some Alaskan and northern Canadian Athabascans. To keep the problem to a manageable length this inquiry will be restricted to a consideration of the terminology used for the parental generation. A consideration of cousin terminologies, with the extremely wide variation found among these groups, would require a much more complicated discussion. A number of historic events since contact with Europeans have resulted in alteration in these peoples' social organization and in their systems of terminologies, which were often distorted before they could be recorded. Therefore a study of this type often results in suggestions rather than in firm explanations. The selection of these specific groups of this chapter was based on the following factors: they live in the Arctic and Subarctic in the North Pacific region; they depend mainly upon hunting and fishing for their livelihood; and they share a general level of ranking in their social organization.

Yukagirs

In a previous chapter the differentiation on the basis of specialization in Yukagir society was pointed out, together with the fact that high status attaches to the clan elder who directs the activities of the clan, to the distinguished warriors, hunters, shamans, and blacksmiths, and to the wife of the clan elder, who sees to the division of game and its distribution among members of the clan. We have only a sketchy knowledge of Yukagir ranking in aboriginal times and very little information on the internal band economy, but it is clear that ranking did exist and that the Yukagir social organization was at a level more complex than that of the egalitarian band.

For both the Kolyma and tundra dialects of Yukagirs, the parental generation kin terminology is bifurcate collateral and differentiates further by having terms for the older and younger of each parent's siblings of both sexes (mother's older brother, father's younger sister, and so on).

Our main argument is that in societies that do not have a strict pattern of residence based on a unilineal descent group, ranking gives rise to a bifurcate collateral kin terminology for the parental generation; that is, individuals or couples select the set of kinsmen with whom they will live on the basis of a number of factors—the kinsmen's membership in the group that can best aid or support them at a given time, and so on—and they are not required to live with any specific set of kinsmen. A bifurcate collateral kin terminology ensues as these kinsmen are differentiated by Ego as possible choices for alliance and for band coresidence.

It might seem on first glance that the Yukagirs do not fit these conditions; the major ethnographers of these people (Jochelson and the Soviet ethnographers Stepanova, Gurvich, and Khramova) argue for an aboriginal unilineal descent group. We shall consider the evidence for a unilineal clan in some detail because it provides a classical problem in ethnohistory. The aboriginal clan is not to be confused with the "administrative clan" of the old Russian government.

According to Jochelson, the Yukagirs had a patriclan organization before the coming of the Russians, but by the time of the ethnographic present their social structure was destroyed and this question could not be studied directly. Jochelson does point out, however, that the clan had no clan territory—as exists for the Tungus—or other concepts of exclusive property in the land. Moreover, strangers could freely join the clan, as was related in Chapter 4, and thus a Yukagir "clan" comprised two groups: kinsmen by blood and members by virtue of the fact that they lived and traveled with the group. As to whether the aboriginal Yukagir clan was patrilineal or matrilineal (or ambilineal or just a bilateral group), the main evidence Jochelson can muster for a patriclan is that in aboriginal times the duty of blood vengeance fell on the victim's kinsmen on his father's side, and that sometimes clan ancestors on the paternal side were counted as far back as six or seven generations.

The Soviet authors on the Yukagirs (Stepanova, Gurvich, and Khramova) argue for an aboriginal matriclan (or rather for survivals of matriarchy), pointing out that the groom goes to live with the family of the bride. Indeed, it would be hard to see how a patriclan could stay together with matrilocal (uxorilocal) residence predominating, if it were not, as Jochelson reports, that at the time of his fieldwork most marriages took place within the clan. The problem is not so simple, however; the Soviet authors point out that most Yukagir clans at the ethnographic present represented the merging of depopulated clans and that, according to marriage records of the eighteenth-century archives, Yukagir marriages had usually been between people of different clans. This leads us back to the original problem: were the Yukagir matri- or patrilineal?

Jochelson gives some additional bits of evidence for some lineal emphasis in descent: each "clan" of Yukagirs had two clan shamans, one living and one dead, and the clan shaman must be of the same blood as that of the original clan group; also a common clan cult of ancestor worship existed, although there is little record of it. We review the evidence:

1. Evidence for an aboriginal patriclan (Jochelson):
   (a) Blood vengeance on father's side
   (b) Tracing of kinsmen on father's side for a number of generations (at least in some groups)
2. Evidence for aboriginal matriclan (Stepanova, Gurvich, and Khramova): Matrilocal residence together with clan exogamy would destroy bases for a localized patriclan and is evidence for matriarchal-matrilineal clans
3. Evidence for some type of lineal emphasis, as opposed to a simple bilateral grouping (Jochelson):
   (a) Office of clan shaman who must be one in blood with the clan core group
   (b) Memory of a previous clan ancestor cult

A possible answer to the question may be drawn from the following data given by the Soviet authors: ancient legends suggest that it was Yukagir custom for the oldest son and the oldest daughter to join the clan of the mother, whereas the younger offspring joined the clan of the father; the Soviet authors interpret this in terms of transition from a matrilineal clan to a patrilineal clan. Together with the evidence listed above, this would suggest that the aboriginal Yukagir clan was ambilineal (ambilateral), and that descent could be either as in the legendary ideal or, more likely, according to the situation—that is, the choice could be based on a consideration of the relative advantages and disadvantages of joining mother's or father's kinsmen, which would allow for the flexibility often necessary in Arctic band society and also for the demands of a ranking system. Such ambilineal social organizations are found in the North Pacific region—for example, the Kwakiutl, among the Northwest Coast Indians. It should be noted that the concept of ambilineal descent was introduced into anthropological literature after the time of Jochelson's fieldwork. It must be admitted that the reasoning given above is not "proof" that the Yukagirs had an ambilineal structure; reconstructions of this type require a deeper historical probe than that done here. However, we suggest this as the most probable solution, fitting all the available evidence, and we offer it not merely as a compromise solution. It can be said, in addition, that regardless of what the aboriginal Yukagir social structure was, by the time of the ethnographic present it was functionally a bilateral grouping.

Northern Athabascans

We move from the Yukagirs to a series of brief case studies of the northern Athabascans. Most of the groups reviewed here were discussed in the preceding chapter. Selection of the same groups provides a continuity between these two chapters, as level and type of social structure are often directly connected with mode of subsistence. Also, we suggest that Yukagirs and Athabascans share a similar type of ranking social structure, which may be useful for understanding the internal dynamic of these social organizations, as well as that of many other groups found throughout the circumpolar regions.

Tanaina. The matrilineal Tanaina were divided into two moieties, each of which was divided horizontally into two ranks—one of chiefs, shamans, and "big men," and the other of the people who were not particularly prestigious. The chiefs, who were older men, directed the affairs of the village; a class of younger leaders personally led war and hunting parties. Succession to the chieftainship usually fell to the son of a chief, although others could sometimes break in on the basis of wealth or shamanistic prestige. The top rank of shamans among the Tanaina, as elsewhere in the North, had a great deal of influence and prestige. In addition to formalized chiefs and shamans, a class of wealthy men had high rank and prestige. It should be noted, however, that under aboriginal conditions the amassing of wealth and the social rank and prestige derived from its proper distribution to kinsmen and members of the community depended largely upon the individual's personal qualities and not just upon the possession of wealth itself.

Beads made of a particular species of shell, the *hyqya* shell, constituted "primitive money," and ranking individuals wore large quantities of these beads as a display; products of the land and sea and various manufactures were other forms of wealth. Ranking individuals enlisted and organized nonranking individuals to work for them and thus became a focus of production and distribution. To retain his labor force the ranking person had to treat his followers well and see to their welfare, aiding them in obtaining marriage partners, organizing communal feasts, and otherwise looking after them. A means of redistribution of wealth was the potlatch for the dead, which the ranking man organized with the aid of his followers. Goods were produced and collected by the group headed by the ranking man and were distributed during the potlatch; in the Tanaina potlatch poorer individuals received more goods than the rich and thus the wealth of the community was redistributed. Since for the Athabascans the social value of wealth consisted in having something to give away, the ranking organizer of the potlatch, who gave material goods, gained in rank and prestige, one of the concomitants of which was that "big men" often had a number of wives.

The parental kin terms for the various groups of Tanaina are bifurcate collateral (with the exception of the Kamchemak Bay group who merge father's sister and mother's sister). A possible explanation is that, as the ranking system is in flux, individuals must choose the kinsmen or "big men" with whom they want to align themselves. The choice undoubtedly rests on the basis of several factors, with the individual aligning with the group that is most to his advantage. As older kinsmen are most likely to be ranking individuals, it is logical that the kinsmen of the parental generation would be distinguished in terminology and that there would be a symmetry in arrangement of the terminology of this generation because each might offer Ego a possible choice in alignment in a rank-focused grouping.

Anvik-Shageluk Ingalik. The Ingalik of the Anvik-Shageluk area are Athabascans who resemble the Tanaina in richness of natural resources and in social organization. They are also a ranking society, composed of three orders of rank: rich men, people without any particular rank or prestige, and people who do not work (*eninglani*). Prestige and rank are based on wealth, which is gained through the particular individual qualities and social ties needed to amass and distribute it in an effective way. Wealth consists of particular forms such as the highly valued dentalium shells and red ocher, the natural production of the land—fish, fish oil, hides, and so on—and also native manufactures. The rich men organize others to work for them and aid their helpers in turn. The *eninglani*, the lowest rank, do not work and, because they do not work, do not marry. Again, the whole value of wealth is to have something to give away—in this distribution and redistribution the rich man gains wealth and prestige. The Athabascan potlatch for the dead serves as one means of redistribution, and for the giver it provides a means of gaining rank.

The kin terminology of the Anvik-Shageluk Ingalik is lineal in the parental generation. Here we have an exception to the thesis argued in this chapter, an exception that is all the more striking because the Tanaina and these Ingalik have many features in common. Compared with other northern Athabascan groups, they both occupy areas rich in natural resources and maintain a level of food production sufficient to support comparatively high populations in sedentary groupings; they share a similar emphasis on ranking; and they both participate in the ceremonial potlatch for the dead. This deviation in kin terminology of the Ingalik emphasizes that although a particular sociological theory may often explain a pattern of kin terminology, a significant number of exceptions may exist.

Kutchin. The Kutchin are divided into three ranked matriclans. These clans, although theoretically exogamous, do not form territorial groups and all macrobands apparently have representatives of all three clans. The ranking of clans is not entirely clear—chiefs usually come from only two of the three clans and there is a suggestion that clan ranking order has changed over time. The Kutchin are further divided into two ranks: one of chiefs, shamans, and wealthy men, and the other of individuals without particular rank and prestige. Osgood suggests that chiefs are not sharply distinguished from wealthy men and also that the role and influence of the chiefs and the shamans are similar. A common theme in northern Athabascan society seems to be that the roles of economic organizers, political and military leaders, and religious figures are not strongly differentiated. Hence the term chief used for these peoples must have a slightly different meaning than its common usage.

A prestigious descent group headed by an influential chief or a group of highly prestigious men is a common aspect of Kutchin social organization. Such groups often work and travel together and form a social unit for production. Rank again is based on wealth. A chief displays large amounts of dentalium shell and ranking individuals organize accumulation of goods for distribution and feasting at the potlatch for the dead. Also, as among the Tanaina, a chief or wealthy man may have a number of wives.

The kin terminology of the Peel River, Chandalar, and Vunta Kutchin is bifurcate collateral for the parental generation, whereas the Yukon Flats band has a lineal terminology, providing an exception. In spite of exceptions such as this one, we argue that bifurcate collateral kin terminology reflects a society in which an individual may align himself to the group of his mother's kinsmen, his father's kinsmen, or to the kinsmen of his wife according to the situation. This gives an individual the chance to take part in a ranking unit and to choose the grouping that is most effective for him.

CONCLUSION

In societies in the Arctic and Subarctic the combination of some degree of social ranking and bifurcate kin terminology for the parental generation is common. Two possibly interconnected explanations are given here. The first is that in the circumpolar regions conditions of life make the following of strict residence rules impossible. The membership of the band changes, with resulting changes in coresidence, and kinsmen of the parental generation, who represent possible choices for coresidence, may be scattered in various microbands over the countryside. Hence Ego distinguishes between these kinsmen and a bifurcate collateral kin terminology develops. The second explanation is that in a ranking society individuals are differentiated in terms of rank and prestige, and Ego will most likely elect to join a ranking group headed by a wealthy man or chief. The decision will be made on the basis of several factors; however, as the status of "big man" usually comes later in life, "big men" are likely to be of an older generation than Ego at the time of his initial choice. As all kinsmen of the parental generation are possible choices for Ego, they have to be differentiated in his eyes, which gives rise to bifurcate collateral terminology for the parental generation. Murdock also suggests a special marriage form (nonsororal polygyny) as giving rise to a bifurcate collateral terminology. Probably some combination of these three factors could explain most instances of this kin terminology system in the circumpolar regions.

Although kin terminology systems are a rather specialized concern, we have shown how they are linked with the larger political, economic, and social organization. Bifurcate collateral terminology has been demonstrated as suitable for a flexible ranking society. By applying Fried's model of ranking society to the older, descriptive ethnographies, we can gain a better insight into the actual social dynamic of these groups under aboriginal conditions. We have also pointed out that the simple egalitarian band is not the only social formation to be found in the circumpolar area.

ANNOTATED BIBLIOGRAPHY

Perhaps the best theoretical discussion of ranking societies is Morton H. Fried, *The Evolution of Political Society: An Essay in Political Anthropology* (New York: Random House, 1967), especially pp. 109–184.

For intelligent discussions on the relationship between social structure and kinship terminologies, see Elman Service, "Kinship Terminology and Evolution," *American Anthropologist*, 62:747–763 (1960); F. K. Lehman, "Typology and the Classification of Socio-cultural Systems," pp. 376–396 in R. A. Manners (ed.), *Process and Pattern in Culture* (Chicago: Aldine, 1964); and Irving Goldman, "The Evolution of Polynesian Societies," pp. 686–712 in S. Diamond (ed.), *Culture in History* (New York: Columbia University Press, 1960).

On the relationship between a unilineal descent group and a bifurcate merging kin terminology, see Robert H. Lowie, *Social Organization* (New York: Rinehart, 1949), especially pp. 60–67.

For the first discussion of Arctic bilateralism, consult Waldemar Bogoras, *The Chuckchee—Part III: Social Organization* (Memoirs of the American Museum of Natural History, 1904–1909). For two theoretical discussions on Arctic bilateralism in Lapp society, see Robert A. Pehrson, "Bilateral Kin Groupings as a Structural Type: A Preliminary Statement," *The University of Manila Journal of East Asiatic Studies*, 3:199–202 (January 1954)—also reprinted in Bobbs-Merrill, Series A-181, and *The Bilateral Network of Social Relations in Könkämä Lapp District* (Bloomington: Indiana University Publication, 1957). For bilateralism in an Eskimo society, refer to David Damas, "Igluligmiut Kinship Terminology and Behaviour: Consanguines," pp. 85–105 in V. F. Valentine and F. G. Vallee (eds.), *Eskimo of the Canadian Arctic* (Toronto: Carleton Library, 1968). The thesis concerning the relationship between residence groupings and kinship has been explored in detail in Nelson Graburn, *Taqagmiut Eskimo Kinship Terminology* (Ottawa: Northern Coordination and Research Centre, 64-1, 1964). For a review of the literature on Arctic bilateralism, see Joel S. Savishinsky, "Kinship and the Expression of Values in an Athabascan Bush Community," *Western Canadian Journal of Anthropology*, 1:1:31–59 (1970) (Special Issue: Athabascan Studies).

For an analysis of influence of marriage on the formation of a bifurcate collateral terminology, see George Peter Murdock, *Social Structure* (New York: Macmillan, 1949), especially pp. 145–146, 151. On the concept of "ambilateral lineages," refer to Leslie A. White, *The Evolution of Culture* (New York: McGraw-Hill, 1959), especially pp. 176–182. For a general discussion of nonunilineal descent, see William Davenport, "Nonunilinear Descent and Descent Groups," *American Anthropologist*, 61:557–572 (1959). For purposes of comparison, reference can be made to the more extreme ranking, the ambilineal lineages and kinship of the Northwest Coast Indians and of Polynesia. See Philip Drucker, "Rank, Wealth and Kinship in Northwest Coast Society," *American Anthropologist*, 41:55–65 (1939)—also reprinted in Bobbs-Merrill, Series A-55—and his *Indians of the Northwest Coast* (New York: Natural History Press, 1963). Perhaps the best overall view of Polynesia is Marshall D. Sahlins, *Social Stratification in Polynesia* (Seattle: University of Washington Press, 1958).

The data on the Yukagirs were taken from Waldemar Jochelson, *The Yukaghir and the Yukaghirized Tungus*, in three parts (Memoirs of the American Museum of Natural History, 1910–1926); and from M. V. Stepanova, I. S. Gurvich, and V. V. Khramova, "The Yukagirs," pp. 788–798 in M. G. Levin and L. P. Potapov (eds.), *The Peoples of Siberia* (Chicago: University of Chicago Press, 1964).

The material on the Tanaina was taken mainly from Cornelius Osgood, *The Ethnography of the Tanaina* (Yale University Publications in Anthropology, No. 16; reprinted by Human Relations Area Files Press, 1966). And from Joan Broom Townsend, *Ethnohistory and Cultural Change of the Iliamna*, Ph.D. dissertation, University of California, Los Angeles, 1965 (University Microfilms, Ann Arbor, Michigan), and see also her discussion "The Tanaina of Southwestern Alaska: A Historical Synopsis," *Western Canadian Journal of Anthropology*, 1:1:2–16 (1970) (Special Issue: Athabascan Studies).

The information on Ingalik social structure was taken from Cornelius Osgood's works, *Ingalik Social Culture* (New Haven: Yale University Publications in Anthropology, No. 53, 1958) and *Ingalik Mental Culture* (New Haven: Yale University Publications in Anthropology, No. 56, 1959).

The material on social structure and ranking of the Kutchin was taken mainly from Asen Balikci, *Vunta Kutchin Social Change: A Study of the People of Old Crow, Yukon Territory* (Ottawa: Northern Co-ordination and Research Centre, 1963); Cornelius Osgood, *Contributions to the Ethnography of the Kutchin* (New Haven: Yale University Publications in Anthropology, No. 14, 1936); Robert A. McKennan, *The Chandalar Kutchin* (Arctic Institute of North America: Technical Paper No. 17, 1965); and Richard Slobodin, *Band Organization of the Peel River Kutchin* (Ottawa: National Museum of Canada, Bulletin No. 179).

NINE

AN ECONOMIC HISTORY OF THE KUTCHIN

During the past century or two the most significant factor in the lives of the northern Athabascan Indians has been the presence of whites and the sicknesses, social systems, and material goods they brought with them. The written history of these Indians begins, of course, only at the time of contact with whites, and any history of the northern Athabascans must also be a history of the whites who had an effect on them and lived near them. A study of the history of the small group of humans who have lived and live in the northwestern part of North America is of concern even to those who have little interest in them for the changes in this Indian society brought about by contact with the West reveal the nature of the larger society.

ABORIGINAL TIMES

The Kutchin originally included nine bands, which together formed a larger cultural and linguistic—but not political—grouping. Several of these bands, through epidemics and other causes, have almost disappeared, with perhaps a few individual band members remaining. A number of fair ethnographic studies on the Chandalar, Crow River, and Peel River bands have been done over the past four decades, and a group of community studies on the Mackenzie Flats Kutchin was done in the mid-1960s. Our examination of the lives of the Kutchin in aboriginal times relies primarily on the ethnographic reconstructions of McKennan (for the Chandalar) and Osgood (for the Crow River and Peel River).

In Chapter 7 we examined the patterns of subsistence of the Chandalar and Crow River bands; the Peel River band resembled the Crow River group but with more emphasis on hunting. The Yukon Flats group depended more on salmon and fish than did the more northern mountain groups, and they also had a larger population. Aboriginal population estimates on the Kutchin bands are often contradictory; however, an estimate of around two hundred individuals for each band with some

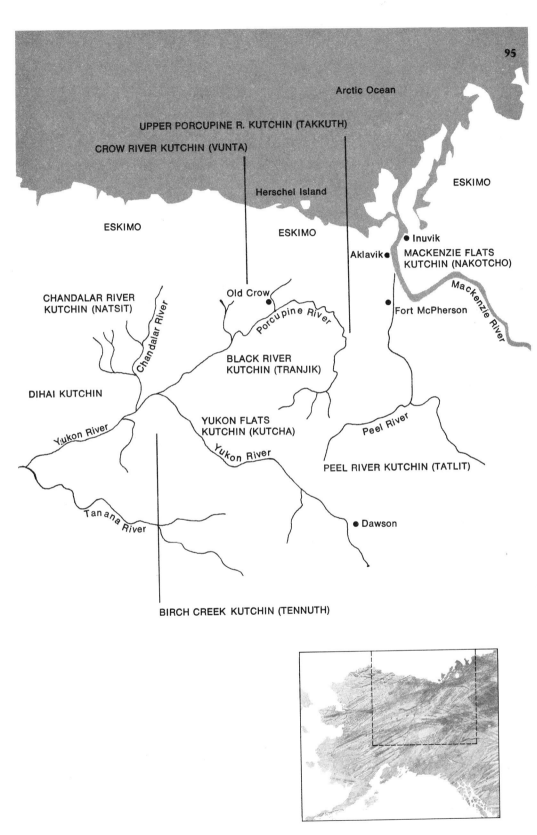

Figure 9.1 Distribution of the Kutchin bands (after Osgood and McKennan).

variations would be safe—the Yukon Flats band may have had a population of around five hundred individuals. Thus the total population of the Kutchin may have been around two thousand.

The Kutchin patterns of subsistence depended upon fishing, hunting, and gathering, according to the prevailing seasonal resources in the area. The most important technology for food production included large surrounds and fences (often used in conjunction with big-game snares), fish weirs (used in conjunction with fish traps), fish nets, fish spears, and a variety of snares. In winter the Kutchin lived in dome-shaped skin tents or in semisubterranean houses. Birch-bark canoes, skin boats, and snowshoes provided means of transportation. The Kutchin wore a distinctive variety of the tailored skin clothing found throughout the Arctic.

These Kutchin bands were divided by three exogamous matriclans, which were not localized and were found in all Kutchin bands. These clans were ranked relative to each other, and chiefs came from the two most prestigious clans. Kutchin society was further differentiated, with chiefs, shamans, wealthy men, and members of prestigious multilineal descent groups at the top of the ranking order and war captives at the bottom. The power of the chief was weak, but the chief and his close kinsmen and supporters commonly made up the prestigious descent group in Kutchin social organization (Slobodin describes a prestigious kin group still functioning as a group in 1947). The position of the chief was based on wealth, membership in a prestigious group, personal ability in the hunt, and a number of personal qualities connected with the particular Kutchin mode of leadership. Shamans also had a position of high prestige in the social order and a marked influence upon it; they received payment for their services and so had a means of amassing wealth and thus raising their ranking. A mark of prestige for chiefs and shamans was that they often had several wives, which implies that they had the means to support them. Division of labor was by age and sex. Most ethnographers on the Kutchin point to the relatively high position of women; they could hold property, manage the household economy, and influence the course of human events in many ways.

A common feature of northern Athabascan social organization shared by the Kutchin was the partnership; two men formed a close working relationship and depended on each other for economic support. One partner, on killing a large game animal, would give it to the other for final distribution to the group.

The Kutchin often shared property, especially food, and the sharing followed various patterns of distribution and redistribution. For instance, a person would give game to a man of a different clan who in turn would provide a feast for the entire group. People with sites for fish weirs had the right of occupancy as long as they were used, and caribou surrounds were "owned" by the person who organized their building, with the builders also having a right to animals killed. Groups

Figure 9.2 Kutchin woman and children. (From Sir John Richardson, **Arctic** *Searching* Expedition, *London: Longman, 1851, Vol. 1, p. 384.)*

were never denied access to strategic resources. Little property was accumulated in aboriginal times, and at death a man's possessions were buried with him; any remainder was divided among his kinsmen. A special category of property, the dentalium shell and a kind of red paint, represented a highly valued form of "primitive money." It was directly connected with the ranking system—a rich man wore large amounts on his clothing as a badge of prestige—and it was individually owned and not included in the pattern of sharing. The Kutchin obtained the dentalium shell through aboriginal trade routes from the Northwest Coast, with intermediate groups of Indians acting as middlemen. Native copper, which the Kutchin made into distinctive knives, also moved through these native trade routes. The Kutchin followed an alternating pattern of raiding and of peaceful trade with the Eskimo to the north.

A potlatch, a feast at which some skins, shells, and other material goods were distributed, was sometimes given in honor of the dead—with some honor going to the living, namely the giver of the potlatch. The receivers of these goods would make a partial repayment to the giver of the potlatch at a later date. In aboriginal times the amount of goods involved was probably rather small. The potlatch for the dead can best be seen as a social device in maintaining and emphasizing the ranking prestige systems—usually wealthy men aided by their kinsmen gave potlatches—and as a means of redistribution of wealth. For these northern Athabascans a man was rich because he had much to give away; a man would be considered very odd if he hoarded his wealth.

Thus, in summary, the aboriginal economy of the Kutchin can be seen as one in which the sharing of food ensured the survival of all if any member had food. Embedded in the economy was the emphasis on prestigious descent groups and ranking, with high rank being based in part on wealth in dentalium shells and in part on the ability to organize kinsmen to present the feast and gifts of the potlatch of the dead.

PERIOD OF WHITE CONTACT AND THE EARLY FUR TRADE

Long before white men arrived in the Kutchin area their influence was felt as goods manufactured by the Russians and English reached the Kutchin through native Indian trade routes and through the Eskimo. The first white contact with the Kutchin occurred in 1789 when Alexander Mackenzie sailed down the river that bears his name. Mackenzie comments briefly on the Kutchin pattern of raiding the Eskimo but says little else about them. The best source on the Kutchin in the days of the early fur trade is the journal of Alexander Murray, the Hudson's Bay Company trader who built Fort Yukon in 1847.

An important aspect of the early fur trade, the introduction of firearms and ammunition, altered native patterns of subsistence. Hunting became more individualized as large numbers of people were no longer needed to drive large game into surrounds. Firearms simplified the hunting of large, nongregarious animals such as bear and moose, and perhaps made possible a shift to greater dependence on large game. However, since ammunition was costly and often in short supply, caribou surrounds continued to be used in some areas until the turn of the century.

Murray emphasizes the demand for firearms and beads by the Kutchin; along with dentalium shells imported by the Hudson's Bay Company, they played an important part in early Kutchin trade. This demand characterizes the early fur trade: very small amounts of provisions, perhaps a little flour and sugar, were traded. Trade goods bought by the Kutchin fell into two categories, the first category being material goods connected with exploitation of the environment, such as firearms, gunpowder, lead bullets, twine for fishing nets, snare wire, steel traps, axes, knives, needles, metal cooking gear, and so on; the second category comprised "luxury" items such as tea, tobacco, and beads. Transportation of trading goods to isolated northern posts such as Fort Yukon required a three-year journey one way from England. Since transportation by canoe and York boat was costly, precluding the importation of large stocks of provisions, the trader had to depend for his trading stock on goods that were necessary, light, and portable. Except for small amounts of imported food, which was regarded as a luxury, Hudson's Bay traders depended on food from the land—large game, fish, and hare. Often the fur traders depended on the Kutchin for a portion of their food supply; for example, Fort McPherson, established in 1840, was primarily a meat post, where game was collected from the Kutchin and distributed to other Hudson's Bay posts. The traders followed special rules; for example, they traded ammunition at certain times only for provisions or, in time of need, they gave it "free" to the Indians. They traded firearms only for special types of fine furs such as marten or fox. High transportation costs restricted trade in cheaper furs such as muskrats. The trading standard was the "made beaver" token, against which all furs were measured. Trade took the form of barter in which no money was used.

In the early days of the trade the Hudson's Bay traders set about creating new demands. They gave stick tobacco to the Kutchin—some of whom, not knowing the uses of tobacco, wore it around their necks. In a short time tobacco and tea became almost a necessity among the Kutchin, as elsewhere in the Arctic. Murray complained that the Kutchin would not trade for the clothing in his stock, arguing that their skin clothing was superior, and Murray wrote in his journal that he had to agree. In a few decades, however, the Kutchin came to depend on European-manufactured clothing and blankets. With the fur trade came the introduction of the toboggan and the dog team, which gave rise to another shift in subsistence pattern as dog teams required large amounts of food. Fishing nets made of cording bought from traders replaced fish traps and spears. Other kinds of change resulted from the fur trade: aboriginal band groupings split as different bands aligned themselves with the various trading posts, and the raiding wars with other Kutchin bands and with the Eskimo stopped after the first decades of trade, the traders having imposed a Company peace upon the area.

The life of the men working for the Hudson's Bay factory was often harsh—at Fort Yukon, for example, their diet consisted mainly of food from the land. Dall and Whymper mention a number of harsh practices of the Company, such as charging its men high prices for the natural products of the region—leather for footwear and clothing, for example—the men being forbidden to trade independently. The Company also maintained a harsh discipline over its workers, and paid

Figure 9.3 Fort Yukon, Hudson Bay Company's post. (From Whymper, op. cit., p. 250.)

the Kutchin only a small fraction of the value of their furs. Many historians of the fur trade, who are not apologists for the Hudson's Bay Company, have pointed out the high transportation costs and overhead of the Company, but nevertheless shareholders in the Hudson's Bay Company at this time did not grow poor.

It is an irony in history that the lives of these northern tribesmen were changed because of the demands of the West for luxury furs. Dall and Whymper, who visited Fort Yukon in the 1860s, mention the rich collection of fur gathered there by the Hudson's Bay Company; thousands of marten and beaver pelts were traded there, and these, together with fox and otter, formed the staple fur in the trade. Shortly after the purchase of Alaska by the United States, an Army captain sent to locate Fort Yukon found it within the United States territory, and he ordered the Hudson's Bay Company to leave. There followed a new era in the Kutchin country. American traders traveling on steamboats collected fur throughout the American section of the Yukon River, and, with the monopoly of the Hudson's Bay Company broken and a number of traders in competition, the Indians often got better prices for their fur. Also, the use of steamboats on the Yukon reduced transportation costs. In the last decades of the nineteenth century, however, the Alaska Commercial Company bought out its competition and made special arrangements with independent traders, thus creating a new monopoly and again lowering fur prices paid to the Indians. The Indians' income from furs was determined by the world fur market and by the nature of the organization of trading companies, factors over which the Indians, of course, had no control.

By the turn of the century the Kutchin had become largely dependent on the fur trade for the technology necessary to exploit the environment to the degree required by their altered pattern of subsistence, and the fur trade also brought them the small luxuries of life. Nevertheless, at this time most of their food came from the land; they were still primarily hunters and fishers who also trapped furbearers, in contrast to their later status of trappers who depended largely on food bought at stores.

Europeans had a more profound effect on the lives of the Kutchin than even the preceding pages would indicate. The whites introduced a number of diseases: smallpox, diphtheria, measles, scarlet fever, influenza, pneumonia, gonorrhea, and tuberculosis. The scarlet-fever epidemic of the 1860s reduced the population of many Kutchin bands. Through this epidemic the Birch Creek band became extinct and the Yukon Flats band was reduced to one family; and the Dihai and Upper Porcupine bands—at least partly through epidemic—no longer exist as independent groupings.

FROM THE GOLD RUSH TO WORLD WAR I

Slobodin, who provides perhaps the best account of the effects of the Yukon gold rush on the lives of the Kutchin, points out that between 1858 and 1898 the purchasing power of the price paid to the Kutchin for their fur increased four times, and between 1898 and 1917 it increased three times. In the period between 1900 and 1914 the prices of fine fur rose throughout the world. Factors other than the world market, however, explain this rise in the price paid to the Indians. Hudson's Bay men found small amounts of gold in the Yukon in the mid-nineteenth century, and in the last two decades of that century a number of white prospectors searched in or near the Kutchin area. In 1896 two Indians and a white man together discovered gold on the Klondike River, and in the following years many white men came to the country of the Kutchin. After the rush to the Klondike men stampeded for a number of years to many other places throughout the North. The heart of the gold area was in the land of the Han—Athabascan neighbors of the Kutchin—and they perhaps suffered most as a nation the ill effects of this period of contact with whites. An effect of the gold rush was the increase in transportation throughout the North; in 1899 there were at least thirty steamboats on the Yukon River, and in 1908 the first Hudson's Bay steamer traveled on the Mackenzie River. Indians were employed by the whites in large numbers for the first time, selling game to the mining camps, cutting wood for steamboats and acting as pilots, working as laborers, and selling native manufactures to the miners.

In roughly the same period, from 1890 to 1907, the whalers wintering at Herschel Island traded with the Kutchin and, together with those miners who acted as free traders, provided competition for the Hudson's Bay Company. By the turn of the century, the money introduced by the gold rush replaced the Hudson's Bay Company made beaver tokens as currency. In his ethnography of the Peel River Kutchin, Slobodin describes an entire generation of men sophisticated in the ways of the whites through experience in the gold-rush mining camps. With the introduction of larger amounts of European-manufactured goods came a revival of the potlatch for the dead—it is recorded that in one potlatch one thousand marten skins were given away. Although some Kutchin groups near mining camps may have come to depend heavily on food bought from stores, the majority of the Kutchin still depended on food from the land throughout this period.

SECOND ERA OF THE FUR TRADE:
WORLD WAR I TO WORLD WAR II

The world fur market fell in 1914, at the beginning of World War I, with prices becoming high again in 1917. In the fur market 1922 was a year of recession, as were several years during the Great Depression of the 1930s. Fur prices rose at other times until the boom in fur during World War II, an era which, taken as a whole, was one of relatively high fur prices in the world market. Because of improved transportation in the North and the increased market for furs, such furs as mink and muskrat assumed a new importance in the economy of the Kutchin. Throughout much of this whole period fine furs such as fox, marten, and lynx brought high prices and became a staple in the fur trade. Otter, ermine, and squirrel were also of some importance.

Muskrats, especially numerous in the Mackenzie Delta, became important in the economy of the Kutchin there. Minks were found in marshes and lakes and marten in the hill country. The fine furbearers found in higher ground were often sought in the early winter and muskrats and beaver in the lowlands in the spring. Snares, often made of wire, continued to be used, but deadfalls gave way to the increasing use of steel traps. The increased exploitation of fur led to changes in the settlement pattern, families or small groups of families scattering throughout the area surrounding their trap lines. It led also to the increased use of dog teams as a means of transportation for visiting trap lines during the winter. The overall effect throughout the North was that more people were spending more time trapping furbearers. The population of white trappers also increased during this period.

The mode of operation of local fur traders was to advance "debt" to the Indians to cover in advance the cost of the supplies necessary for a winter on the trap line, with the trapper later selling his furs to the trader who advanced debt. The better the trapper the more "debt" advanced and carrying a large debt was often a matter of high prestige. The white fur trader thus exercised control over the Indian community through giving or withholding credit.

The improved network of transportation and the higher prices received by the Kutchin for fur led to the establishment of a supply of staple foods. It is difficult to judge from the literature what proportion of food in the diet was purchased, although it is certain that it greatly increased over previous times. Of course, this proportion would vary according to place and season. Osgood says of the Kutchin in 1932 that the land was still the main food source. Slobodin describes a Kutchin group trapping marten in the mountains in 1947 who depended almost entirely on food from the land, mainly caribou, during their winter trip. By the end of World War II, however, these people had come to depend more and more on purchased food and other supplies to the point where they had become primarily trappers who also hunted and fished.

During World War II construction was started on the Alaska Highway, which brought about a new mode of land transportation and introduced air travel in the North. In 1921 the Canadian Kutchin signed a treaty with the Canadian government ceding title to their land, but retaining aboriginal use rights, for the magnificent sum of $5 paid annually to each individual with slightly higher sums for chiefs. In 1946 trap lines were registered in the Mackenzie area by the government; in 1950 they were so registered in the Yukon.

The people's pattern of life in this whole period was increasingly altered by improved modes of transportation, by the growth of the white population, by greater involvement with government and other white institutions (the church, schools, police, game wardens, and so on), and by increased dependence upon the fur trade. Osgood stresses, however, that in the early 1930s the Kutchin still maintained their particular world view to a large degree. Although many aspects of the Kutchin culture had faded (for example, the clan system), other aspects persisted in an altered form; this is evidenced by the revival of the potlatch, the functioning of prestigious kin groups, the use of the Athabascan language after many had learned English, and the continued pattern of sharing large game animals within the group. Furthermore, in spite of the scattering of families over large areas at certain times of the year because of the new emphasis on trapping, the people still lived and worked together in hunting, fishing, and trapping parties larger than family groups, and they gathered for trade, for visits, and for band assemblies.

All these factors would provide an objective basis for the continuation of the ancient Kutchin world view. Little explicit data on this world view appear in the anthropological literature. While we may feel the lack in this respect, we should remember that this important aspect of a people's lives is probably the most difficult for an outsider to grasp and communicate. Nevertheless, it should be stressed that the world had changed greatly for the Kutchin, and their outlook had to change somewhat to meet the new demands imposed upon them. For example, prices of fur and of trade goods became a constant concern and a major topic of conversation.

MODERN ERA: THE 1950S AND 1960S
In 1947 the world fur market fell, with the result that trapping is no longer important in the economy of the Kutchin and, where people do continue to trap, their incomes from this occupation are very low.

Subsistence hunting and fishing continue, and such large game animals as caribou and moose, together with salmon and white fish, make up an important part of the Kutchin diet. The historical trend toward increased exploitation of natural resources by individuals rather than by large groups continues. The harvesting of fish and game by individuals tends away from the communal sharing of food from the land, although sharing does exist. Dependence on subsistence hunting and fishing varies not only from area to area but also within each regional population. Smith, working in the Mackenzie Delta, defines three groups: people who depend mainly on the land for their food; people who do some wage work but who also exploit the natural resources for food; and people who depend mainly on income from wage work to buy food. This classification of degree of dependence on subsistence hunting and fishing, as Smith points out, could probably be extended to many areas throughout the North. For the Kutchin the emphasis is toward the latter two categories, and, in spite of some continued subsistence activity, in the modern period the Kutchin as a group have come to depend more on purchased food.

The cost of food and other supplies is high in the villages in the Kutchin area; prices often run 50–100 per cent above those for the same items in Seattle or Vancouver. Even the relatively small group of people who depend heavily on food from the land must buy, in addition to some supplemental food, a large range of supplies for making a living on the land under modern conditions: rifles, ammunition, outboard motors, steel traps, canvas for tents, and so on. With the fall in fur prices, credit advanced by traders was reduced, making it increasingly difficult for trappers to obtain the supplies necessary for a life on the land.

Permanent jobs—government and other—are generally held by whites, and wage employment for the Kutchin is largely seasonal. It includes various construction jobs, service work in schools and military bases, guiding, cutting fire wood, and the like. Old-age pensions, family allowances, various systems of relief, and wage work account for most of the money income. Under present conditions employment opportunities in the North are limited, and this in turn limits the people's access to the basic needs of life. In some areas the Kutchin have "tea days," days in which only tea and sugar are consumed, a commentary on their place in this century in two of the richest nations in the world. Moving to the South may be a solution to the economic problems of some individuals, but the Kutchin as a nation will remain in the North. Ethnographers of the Kutchin are almost unanimous in describing the desire of the people for permanent work within their own territory.

Today the Kutchin live in a number of settlements with populations ranging from about one hundred to perhaps six hundred and in larger settlements, some of which have total populations of more than two thousand including the whites, Metis, and Eskimo. In this era there has been a pattern of movement away from the lonely bush trap lines to the settlements, and more people, a large proportion of them young, spend more time in these villages. Patterns of transportation have changed. Planes are no longer a novelty in the North and bush pilots fly regularly scheduled flights between settlements. The Alaska Highway brings a network of roads closer to the Kutchin area and provides staging points for flights. Recently snowmobiles have replaced dog teams in the North, obviating the necessity to get the large amounts of food formerly consumed by dogs, with the probable result of another shift in subsistence patterns. In some areas heavy freight is transported on the rivers in motorboats and barges.

In a number of places throughout the Kutchin country various native political organizations have been formed with the view of placing in the hands of the native peoples some control over their lives. In Alaska these organizations are involved in the struggle over the native land claims, and in Canada "native halls" and Indian Brotherhoods have been formed. Village co-op stores have also been started to give the people some control over their economy. Chiefs and counselors continue to be elected by the band.

It is striking that maps of Kutchin settlements by ethnographers working in the modern period show the villages sharply divided into two sections: one occupied by whites, the other by the native people. Many whites working full time in these settlements—fur traders, school teachers, missionaries, policemen—enjoy a social position superior to the Indians. Such jobs are occasionally held by Indians but most are taken by transient whites, who typically spend several years in a village and then move on, often to the South. The villagers who remain in the northern settlements all their lives are denied these permanent, better-paying jobs because of the difficulty they have in obtaining the necessary training and for other reasons. Generally the Kutchin villages have an elementary school run by one or two teachers who spend the winter there. Most young people must travel to other areas to high school, and thus for these years the child is separated from his parents and older kinsmen and from his village, and in some areas Kutchin children learn little of the Athabascan language. The modern era has brought an increase in medical services; people in remote villages who need medical help can radio an airplane to take them to settlements with hospitals. Tuberculosis was once almost endemic in the North, and as a result the lives of many people were divided between their villages and the tuberculosis sanitariums. A campaign against tuberculosis, however, has resulted in a sharp decrease in the Kutchin death rates, and today the Kutchin are a growing nation.

CONCLUSION

We have defined the main outlines of the historic economic movement of the Kutchin. The concept of Marx and Engels of the "four active movements of history" can be used to understand the processes of this economic and social change. It is a basic fact of all societies that men have to make new men—that they must reproduce themselves physically. From the 1860s until almost the present day, the Kutchin were threatened as a nation by various epidemics and in the latter part of that period by endemic tuberculosis; this threat to their physical existence has been largely overcome.

In the aboriginal period the Kutchin met their needs for food, clothing, and shelter through exploitation of the natural production of the land, using an indigenous technology. The fur trade with Europeans introduced a new technology for such exploitation—firearms, ammunition, cording for nets, wire for snares, and so on. New demands were created and the people had to work not only to meet their basic needs but also to harvest furs to trade for the technology now necessary for food production. "Luxuries" introduced by the fur traders—tea, tobacco, sugar, blankets, clothing, beads, and the like—soon became necessities, thus new needs were created.

Men not only reproduce themselves physically but they reproduce their social relations. Sons become fathers, old chiefs die and younger men take their place. We have reviewed the aboriginal economic relationships in Kutchin society, the ancient communal sharing with a degree of ranking based on a chief's or shaman's ability to organize his kinsmen for production. The effect of the fur trade, the gold rush, the period of intensified trapping, and the events of the modern period was that some aboriginal social relations—the clan system, for example—ceased to be reproduced. Other social relationships took their place. The Indian became subordinate to the fur trader, the policeman, the missionary, and to other agents of the white world. The people came to depend more and more on the fur trade not only for the technology necessary for production to meet basic needs but also for these basic needs themselves—for food and clothing.

As history moves on, men continue to work together, to produce to meet their basic needs. As we have seen, however, these specific relationships in production change. The Kutchin in the past decades have changed from independent family trappers to part-time wage laborers, with residence based in the settlements. New needs are in the process of being formed—for example, the need felt by many of the younger people for increased training and a university education. Some aspects of Kutchin social relationships are no longer reproduced and new social relationships are formed. The new Kutchin political and economic movements—the formation of the Kutchin political organizations and co-ops, for example—perhaps hint at the social relationships to come.

ANNOTATED BIBLIOGRAPHY
Perhaps the best overview of the fur trade is Harold Innis' *The Fur Trade in Canada* (New Haven: Yale University Press, 1962). Also, for

a detailed history of the fur trade, see E. E. Rich, *Hudson's Bay Company 1670–1870*, in three volumes (Toronto: McClelland and Stewart, 1960).

For information on distribution of the Kutchin bands, these articles are useful: Cornelius Osgood, "Kutchin Tribal Distribution and Synonymy," *American Anthropologist*, 36:168–179 (1934); Robert A. McKennan, "Anent the Kutchin Tribes," *American Anthropologist*, 37:369 (1935); and Frederick Hadleigh-West, "On the Distribution and Territories of the Western Kutchin Tribes," *Anthropological Papers of the University of Alaska*, 7:2:113–116 (1959).

In their scientific studies of a number of northern Athabascan societies in the late 1920s and 1930s, Osgood and McKennan have both provided reconstructions of the aboriginal life of the Kutchin that give a base line for further study, as well as information on conditions at the time of their field work. The following works of these authors form the basis of any historical study on the Kutchin: Cornelius Osgood, *Contributions to the Ethnography of the Kutchin* (New Haven: Yale University Publications in Anthropology, No. 14, 1936); Robert A. McKennan, *The Chandalar Kutchin* (Arctic Institute of North America, Technical Paper No. 17, 1965). Another monograph useful for the understanding of the Kutchin in aboriginal times is Frederick Hadleigh-West, *The Netsi Kutchin: An Essay in Human Ecology* (unpublished Ph.D. dissertation, Louisiana State University, 1963; available from University Microfilms, Ann Arbor, Michigan).

For early days of the fur trade, see Alexander Hunter Murray's *Journal of the Yukon 1847–48* (Ottawa: Government Printing Bureau, Publications of the Canadian Archives, No. 4, 1910). The accounts of the fur traders Hardisty and Jones also provide some additional bits of information: William L. Hardisty, "The Loucheux Indians," and Strachen Jones, "The Kutchin Tribes," in *Smithsonian Institution Annual Report, 1866* (Washington: U.S. Government Printing Office), pp. 311–327. An account on the Kutchin, based mainly on Murray, is Sir John Richardson, *Arctic Searching Expedition*, in two volumes (London: Longman, Brown, Green, and Longman, 1851; a modern reprinted edition is also available).

Slobodin gives a good account of the Peel River Kutchin in the 1940s and also a historical sketch with useful information on the gold-rush days: Richard Slobodin, *Band Organization of the Peel River Kutchin* (Ottawa: National Museum of Canada, Bulletin No. 179, Anthropological Series, No. 55, 1962), and "Leadership and Participation in a Kutchin Trapping Party," in D. Damas (ed.), *Contribution to Anthropology: Band Societies* (Ottawa: National Museum of Canada, Bulletin No. 228, Anthropological Series, No. 84, 1969). An additional source of information on Kutchin life in the 1940s is Douglas Leechman's *Vanta Kutchin* (Ottawa: National Museum of Canada, Bulletin No. 130, Anthropological Series, No. 33, 1954).

For modern life of Crow River Kutchin together with an account of their historical movement, see Asen Balikci, *Vunta Kutchin Social Change* (Ottawa: Northern Co-ordination and Research Centre, 1963). A number of studies based on field work in the mid-1960s in the Mackenzie Delta give an account of modern conditions there—not only for the Kutchin but also for Eskimo, Metis, and whites: A. M. Ervin, *New Northern Townsmen in Inuvik* (Ottawa. Department of Indian Affairs and Northern Development, Mackenzie Delta Research Project 5, 1968); Jose Maihot, *Inuvik Community Structure—Summer 1965* (Ottawa: Department of Indian Affairs and Northern Development, Mackenzie Delta Research Project 4, 1968); Derek G. Smith, *The Mackenzie Delta—Domestic Economy of the Native Peoples* (Ottawa: Department of Indian Affairs and Northern Development, Mackenzie Delta Research Project 3, n.d.); and John R. Walforth, *The Mackenzie Delta—Its Economic Base and Development* (Ottawa: Department of Indian Affairs and Northern Development, Mackenzie Delta Research Project 1, n.d.); Donald H. J. Clairmont, *Deviance among Indians and Eskimo in Aklavik, NWT* (Ottawa: Northern Co-ordination and Research Centre, Department of Northern Affairs and National Resources, 1963-1969); and John J. and Irma Honigmann, *Arctic Townsmen* (Ottawa: Canadian Research Centre for Anthropology, Saint Paul University, 1970).

For an overview of the role of natural resources in the Yukon in the lives of the native peoples, including the Kutchin, see Adrian Tanner, *Trappers, Hunters and Fishermen: Wildlife Utilization in the Yukon Territory* (Ottawa: Department of Northern Affairs and National Resources, Yukon Research Project Series No. 5, 1966). For historical overviews based on change of settlement pattern, see June Helm and David Damas, "The Contact-Traditional All-Native Community of the Canadian North," *Anthropologica*, n.s., 5:9–21, and Ann Welsh, "Community Pattern and Settlement Pattern in the Development of Old Crow Village, Yukon Territory," *Western Canadian Journal of Anthropology*, 1:1:17–30 (1970), Special Issue: Athabascan Studies. For a brief overview of Canadian Athabascans including the Kutchin, see the pamphlet, *Indians of the Yukon and Northwest Territories* (Ottawa: Department of Indian Affairs and Northern Development, n.d.). For some additional information on the Kutchin in Alaska, see *Alaska Natives and the Land* (Washington: U.S. Government Printing Office, 1968).

The theoretical basis of the concluding paragraphs was taken from the "four active movements of history" of Karl Marx and Frederick Engels, *The German Ideology: Parts I and III* (New York: International Publishers, 1969 [1845–1846]), pp. 16–19.

The main body of data used in this section on the Kutchin comes from the references cited above. For additional sources consult George Peter Murdock, *Ethnographic Bibliography of North America* (New Haven: Human Relations Area Files, 1960), pp. 43–44, and the relevant sections of both R. J. Lotz, *Yukon Bibliography* (Ottawa: Department of Northern Affairs and National Resources, 1964) and Mary Jane Jones, *Mackenzie Delta Bibliography* (Ottawa: Department of Indian Affairs and Northern Development, 1969).

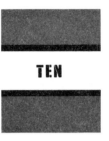

TEN

THE NORTHERN NASKAPI

The Naskapi Indians[1] of what is now northern Quebec are the north-easternmost of the great Cree nation, whose territories stretch more than two thousand miles from the Atlantic coast of Labrador to the Great Plains of Saskatchewan. The Cree group is part of the extensive Algonquian language family, which also includes the Micmac, Malecite, and Passamaquoddy of the east, the Blackfoot and Gros Ventre of the Canadian Great Plains, and the Cheyenne, Ojibwa, and other groups of midwestern North America.

The Indians of this huge area never had political organizations or unity at the tribal level, hence the use of dialects as our criteria for division. They roamed in scattered nomadic bands throughout the taiga and even onto the tundra, with a population density of less than one per forty square miles. In this chapter we are concerned with two major topics in the culture of the northernmost bands who lived around the tree line: (a) the social organization of these bilateral bands, particularly the presence of preferential cross-cousin marriage in this area; and (b) the frequent and hostile relationships with the Eskimos.

The lands of the Naskapi cover more than one hundred thousand square miles of the interior plateau of northern Quebec. Fewer than two thousand people were divided into thirty or forty small bands, each of which followed an annual nomadic cycle, roaming the vast

[1] The designation "Naskapi" is supposedly the name given by the Algonquian Montagnais of the Gulf of St. Lawrence to those Indians who live far to the north of them; there is disagreement as to the meaning of the word itself but it is supposed to have negative connotations. All the eastern Cree call themselves by a word meaning "the people" with dialectical differences: *inuuts* (Naskapi), *iluuts* (Montagnais), and *iyuuts* (James Bay "Cree"). Different authorities have designated the Indian groups quite differently within this area, some calling all of the Montagnais "Naskapi," others referring to the Hudson Bay bands as Cree or Naskapi-Cree, etc. The Indians themselves are quite aware of the dialect differences but label the groups according to their geographical location, such as, e.g., *Washawinuuts* = the people of the bay (Seven Islands), *Waupmauk-stuiiyuuts* = the people of the river of the white whale (Great Whale River).

Figure 10.1 Indians and Eskimos of northern Quebec and Hudson Bay area.

taiga in search of their major source of support, the caribou. The plateau is dissected by a number of very large rivers that run from its center west to Hudson Bay and James Bay, north to Ungava Bay, east to the Atlantic, and south to the Gulf of St. Lawrence. This wooded plateau contains a number of huge lakes, some more than sixty-five miles long. The climate of this area is continental, with short and hot summers accompanied by swarms of mosquitoes and black flies, and long winters with considerable snowfall and temperatures down to –60° F. Because of the forests the snow never hardens, as it does in Eskimo country, in spite of the frequent high winds. The cold climate causes the birch, spruce, and pine of these forests to grow very slowly, and in the northern part, near the tree line, they form little more than a scrub, except in protected areas of the valleys. In summary we may say that the natural environment of the northeastern Algonquians resembles very closely that of the interior northern Athabascans (see Chapters 7 and 9).

MODES OF LIVELIHOOD

Traditionally, Naskapi life was governed by the movements of the vast herds of caribou that inhabited both the forests and the tundra of northern Quebec. These caribou followed a cycle of movement, generally going north or toward the sea in the summer and returning along the main river valleys to the thicker forests in the winter. The Naskapi would try to meet the caribou at the places of their greater concentration, such as at river and lake crossings, at the narrower river valleys, and at the fall rutting places. The Naskapi were extremely skillful in the use of bows and arrows, but they also hunted the caribou with spears in their birch-bark canoes, called *ud*. Whenever possible, they tried to travel by canoe and portage, which was much easier than walking overland in the swampy muskeg—and they thereby also avoided the worst of the insects. During the winter the Naskapi used very wide, closely woven snowshoes made of curved wooden frames laced with *babiche* (dehaired strips of caribou skin which were woven when wet and then dried into a tight matrix). In their annual migrations the Naskapi moved hundreds of miles, so they valued stamina above all.

In the more southerly area, traditionally assigned to the Montagnais, moose were more prevalent than caribou and were less nomadic, more solitary animals, demanding different forms of social organization and of strategic hunting. In the Naskapi area, smaller animals such as beaver, otter, and especially porcupine also provided essential food. These animals became even more important, as did the fox, wolverine, and wolf, during the period of trading and trapping of the last hundred to hundred and fifty years. Fishing, both in the open water and through the ice, was important to the Naskapi and was another reason they tended to stay near the lakes and rivers. Most birds were migratory and in the spring and summer formed a valuable additional food resource, though the majority of the huge flights of ducks and geese passed over Naskapi land to nest farther north in Eskimo land. Luckily for the Naskapi the ptarmigan stayed in their land the year round and formed an emergency winter food resource. In spite of these diverse resources, starvation was very common in this area, especially when a band failed to find the caribou along its usual migration routes.

The Naskapi, emphatically a wood-oriented people, were extremely skillful at working the soft woods abundant in their area. In addition, they burned wood for the fires essential for warmth in the winter and for smoking their meat and skins throughout the year. For winter travel they used two major forms of hand-pulled sleds: the most important, made of planks of wood upturned at the front, were called *utabagan* (from which we get our word "toboggan"); the other, called *utadiaban-askwits*, had two rounded side runners with an open platform on top and was used for carrying wood and heavy objects short distances. These toboggans were pulled by a rawhide line attached around a man's shoulders or forehead, and the same form of tumpline was used for carrying heavy objects on the back.

The Naskapi had two forms of shelter. The usual living accommodation was the large tent, *mijuap*, formed by leaning together several light, straight poles and covering them with caribou skins sewn together (in the more southerly areas the Naskapi sometimes covered them with birch bark, as did some of the Cree and Ojibwa). The interior of the tent contained the central fireplace (the smoke drifted through a hole at the top) on top of fir branches used for flooring, with bedding and belongings arranged around the edge for sitting and sleeping, the senior people being located farthest from the door flap. Another form of structure, the *mɘtɘžan*, was made by sticking a circle of fresh boughs in the ground and bending them inward to meet at the top. This structure served primarily for the ritual sweat bath; stones were heated in the fire and then water was poured over them to produce the steamy cleansing atmosphere. The Naskapi also used the *mɘtɘžan* as an emergency shelter. Fire, essential to these people for warmth, cooking, and the ritual sweat bath, was made by striking flints together over wood shavings or by using a bow-drill. In contrast to the Eskimos, the Naskapi smoked or broiled nearly everything they ate. Occasionally a temporary shelter was made by piling snow on spruce boughs or digging a hole in a drift, but of course fire was not used in this makeshift abode.

Dress was not as warm as one might think necessary for such a climate—perhaps because Naskapi always had wood fires burning in their homes and were strenuously on the move when outside. Both men and women wore knee-length, tubular "dresses" with sleeves and sometimes with hoods, usually made of hairless caribou skin or with the hair turned in. The skins were soaked until the hair could be pulled out, then cured with rotted brains, dried, smoked, and hand-worked until they became as soft as chamois. Ankle-length moccasins were made of caribou or moose hide trimmed with fur and, more recently, decorated with beads. The Naskapi wore no form of trousers, but in the cold season they used leggings, often of rabbit skin, which were attached to the moccasins at the bottom and hung by leather strips from a band around the waist. Sometimes a fur hat and mittens were worn, and the mittens were sometimes decorated with beads and buttons. The standard frock coat had bright-colored geometrical designs around the hem, seams, and sleeves. Except for the moccasins, these forms of clothing have been replaced by cloth and ready-made garments in the last hundred years.

Traditionally, these people had no metals, but this was one of the first things they obtained in trade—via the Montagnais along the St. Lawrence River, or at the Hudson's Bay posts on James Bay and Ungava Bay. They used stone knives and arrowheads and also made great use of bone and antler for blades, points, scrapers, needles, and the like. They did not use stone cooking utensils, as did the Eskimos, but hung their meat and fish above the fire to be smoked or threw small animals and birds into the fire to be roasted.

RELIGION

In common with the other circumpolar peoples, the Naskapi practiced animism and shamanism. Although their huge land may have appeared thinly populated, in a sense it was as full of beings as a metropolitan area. Not only did all animals have souls, but also the woods, streams, lakes, and waterfalls were inhabited by many different kinds of local and nomadic spirit-beings, some of whom were potentially benevolent and all of whom had to be placated by small gifts, singing, or magic (*mitawawin*). Most important among these beings were the *atsan* (probably identical with the *windigo* of the more southerly Algonquians). The *atsan*, in the form of a huge and frightening humanlike monster, would steal people or eat them; indeed, *atsan* were believed to be the reincarnated souls of Indians who had been cannibals. Unlike the Eskimos, the Naskapi had an extreme fear of cannibalism, and even though starvation was frequent, they often chose to die rather than eat the bodies of those around them. Less awesome were the numerous *kačimeiǰasu*—"the one who hides behind (trees)"—also called *bod, upiwaš*, or *ostipwew* in other areas. These humanoid beings sometimes stole children, seduced wives, or threw stones at people, but they were not particularly feared in the daylight. The rivers and waterfalls were inhabited by male and female spirits who were believed to seduce humans into living in the watery underworld and who were blamed for "stealing" those who drowned.

The Naskapi believed in generalized spirit power, *mento* (*manitou* in more southerly Algonquian dialects), that motivated many of the events of the universe. *Məčimento*, evil power, was localized at many dangerous places and had to be warded off by *kwačinokwat*, "magic to keep evil away." The manipulation of this general power, which we might translate as magic, was *mentogasčxo*, a word also used as a synonym for shaman. Through singing, interpreting dreams, or playing the drum (*tawaigən*), every man could influence the spirit powers, but the shaman had the most power to cure, divine, and communicate with the spirit world. The shaman's usual method employed the small "shaking tent" (*kušabičigən*). The shaman entered the tent and summoned the spirit(s) by chanting and drumming; when the spirit(s) arrived, the tent began to shake and the shaman could then ask the spirits important questions.

Each human had a soul (*hečokw*) which made itself known in dreams, and soul loss was a major cause of sickness. The active part of a person's soul (*mistapiu* or *məstabaw*–"great man") was aroused by special magic (*pawmiȷ̵imaw*) for success in hunting. The concept of *məstabaw* seems to have been related to the vaguely known "master of the caribou," a great spirit who was supposed to live far up in the Torngat Mountains of Labrador, and who was responsible for the coming and going of the most important food animal. The spirit entering the *kušabičigən* was said to be the active soul as a representative of this important spirit. *Məstabaw* was also said to be the first man, who was brought to life in a fight with *čikabish*, the trickster.

Relations with the animals depended on magic and the placation of their soul spirit. In general the Naskapi observed taboos and took care that the bones were not eaten by dogs. They cast a small amount of fat into the fire so that the smoke from this sacred grease (*məstahamɨno*) would return to tell the others of the proper treatment. After the kill the Naskapi dragged the animals back to camp with a sacred carrying strap (*ɨnɨntucigən* or *nimaban*) appropriate for each species so that the soul spirits would not be offended. Above all they treated the black bear (*ɨməskw*) most circumspectly and usually referred to it by various circumlocutions; they observed sexual abstinence after a hunt, did not eat various parts of the bear, and disposed of the remains with the greatest care. These customs greatly resemble the treatment of the bear across all the circumpolar regions.

SOCIAL ORGANIZATION

The bilaterally organized bands of Naskapi roamed within a rather ill-specified hunting territory, each containing a mix of the various resources; there was also some trade with adjacent bands for necessities not obtainable within any one zone. Bands consisted of a number of related but relatively independent families who followed the advice of a senior hunting leader (*kawmicɨma*), but the members did not stay together throughout the year. On occasion the men were also organized under a war leader (*dowhendóho*)—see the next section of this chapter. These bands might have ranged in size from as many as sixty people (say, ten families) down to thirty people, and many times during the year single households or individuals existed alone while hunting or fishing. Long arguments have been pursued in the anthropological literature about whether there was individual or family possession of northern Algonquian hunting territories; these rights probably were made explicit only after the rise of commercial trapping. At certain times of the year members of two or three bands would get together at key hunting places where the caribou were massed, and great kills would allow this larger aggregate to form a big camp for as long as a month. At these joyous times news was exchanged and marriages were sometimes arranged. The feasting (*mukušan*) and social intercourse provided a welcome respite from the hard life of most of the year.

Each household consisted of a nuclear or small extended family, with postmarital residence generally matrilocal, at least at first. Sometimes marriages were arranged by the parents; otherwise, if a young couple wished to marry, the girl would first get informal permission from her parents and then the man could move into her house if he brought a gift of reasonably large game for his in-laws. The story is told that some desperate young men would "borrow" game from their friends rather than wait till they had killed their own. The young man would then hunt with and for his in-laws, but he was not usually considered a full man (*napaw*) until after some years of marriage and fatherhood.

Groups of consanguineally related households formed the basis of bands. These people, who called each other *nic'anc'* (*nihanisits*), included those consanguineals within which the incest taboo was enforced—that is, siblings, parallel cousins, and their descendants. The *nic'anc'* cooperated economically and were considered the most trustworthy people outside of one's own household; they were a subgroup within all recognized relatives who were *jinuamituan* or *atahumenánuts* (dialect variations). Few people who could not be reckoned as some kind of relative were trusted at all and nonrelatives were rarely encountered. Members of other bands were usually related through marriage because the small size and consanguineal nature of the groups led to preferential exogamy. Friends or partners who were not related but could be trusted were *nimaiaban*, and even strangers were often cast into the role of "potentially hostile in-law" (*nuija'agɔn*).

The kinship terminology of the Naskapi (see Figures 10.2 and 10.3) differentiated between parallel cousins, classed as siblings, and cross-cousins, classed as siblings-in-law. The Montagnais, however, classed all cousins as siblings, and this may have been one of the major social organizational differences between the two groups. The Naskapi also classified the spouses of uncles and aunts on the mother's side with the uncles and aunts on the father's side, and called both by the same terms as father- and mother-in-law. These features, and scattered ethnographic reports, have long led a number of anthropologists to propose that the Naskapi and other northeastern Algonquians must have practiced preferential bilateral cross-cousin marriage. I have suggested elsewhere that this was not necessarily so (Graburn, 1971). The small size

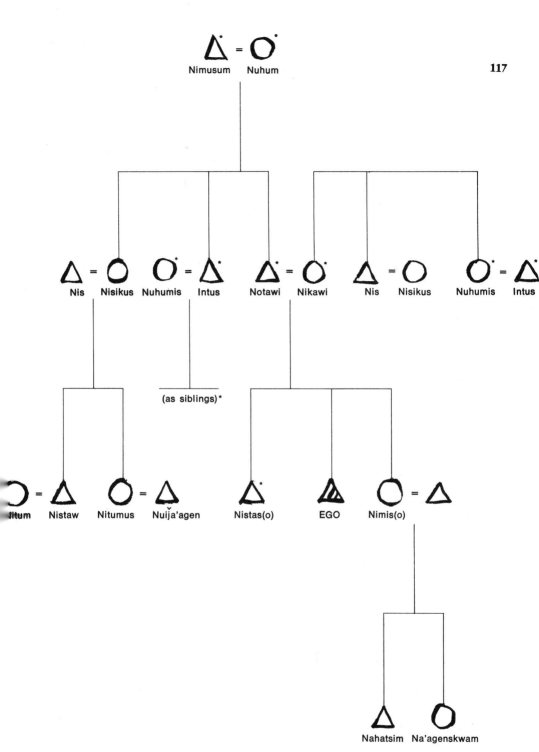

Figure 10.2   Selected consanguineal terminology (male speaking). The asterisk indicates that they are nihanisits.

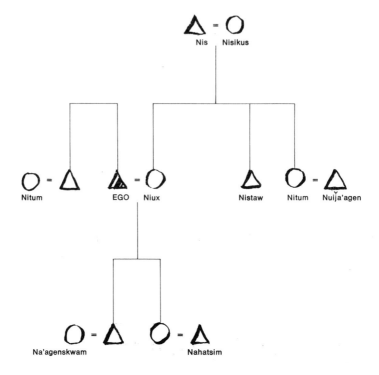

Figure 10.3 Affinal terminology (male speaking).

of the bands and the scattered nature of the populations usually necessitated band exogamy. One could not marry a *nic'anc'* but, as I have mentioned, most people ever encountered were some kind of relative; one had to marry a non-*nic'anc'*—that is, some kind of *jinuamituan* (which included all cross-relatives and affines).

An even more significant feature of the terminology and social system was that an opposite-sexed cross-cousin (*nitumus*) was classed with wife's sister or husband's brother (*nitum*; the *-us* ending is a diminutive of endearment), and sororate and levirate marriages were the rule among these people. Because of the very high death rate, it was the responsibility of a man to marry his wife's younger sister (or a woman, her husband's younger brother), so these people were potential spouses even before widowhood, and sexual joking and relationships often occurred between these pairs. Furthermore, one's wife's sister's husband was *nitum* to one's own wife and one was *nitum* to that man's wife; the two men called each other *nuija'agɔn* and were potentially hostile sexual rivals. Very often sister exchange was the mode of contracting marriage. Thus, if a young man wished to marry a woman, her brother (or his father on his behalf) might say, "Only if you can find a woman for me," that is, only if your sister (or parallel cousin) will marry me. If a cross-cousin marriage did take place, a man's

son (or daughter) married his "sister's" daughter (or son) and terminologically "sister's" children were classified as son-(or daughter-)in-law,
this being the reciprocal of classifying parents-in-law with "cross"-uncle
or -aunt.[2]

INDIAN-ESKIMO
INTERRELATIONSHIPS

As can be seen in Figure 10.1, the Indians were surrounded by Eskimos
on three sides during traditional times: the Cree shared a border with
the Eskimos on James Bay and Hudson Bay; the Naskapi along the
tree line, at the Seal Lakes, near Ungava Bay and the Labrador coast;
and the Montagnais along the eastern part of the St. Lawrence River.
In all these places the relationships between the Indians and Eskimos
were consistently hostile. Though attempts have been made (see the
bibliography) to show that the Eskimos and Indians shared many material and other cultural features, and hence must have "traded," only
one account (Kohlmeister and Kmoch, 1814) mentions friendly intercourse whereas hundreds of others talk of warfare.

Traditionally the Naskapi-Cree territories ran close to the sea in
southeastern Hudson Bay, at Ungava Bay, and along the Labrador coast.
All these places were also visited by Eskimos at times in the spring
and summer. In the barren grounds beyond the tree line the Eskimos
went inland to fish and hunt caribou, and the Indians went north
following these same herds. The Indians never went too far north because they depended on wood for fires, and the Eskimos never went
too far into the taiga area because they feared the Indians and were
ill-adapted to life there. Each group was well aware of the other's presence through the smoke from fires, abandoned campsites, and aspects
of material culture.

The interethnic behavior is described differently from the two sides
(as one would expect), but both agree that when they met they fought
and killed each other. The Eskimos were always afraid of the Indians,
although the Indians have stated that the former often attacked first!
Both agree that the Eskimos lost the skirmishes and usually fled if they
saw the Indians or came across their camps. The Indians would detect
the Eskimos from a distance and then attack by stealth, using bows,
arrows, and knives, hoping to catch the Eskimos unarmed or asleep.
They killed everyone who did not get away, except in rare instances
when they spared an Eskimo girl or woman to take for a wife. Only

---

[2] "Cross"-uncles and -aunts are those of the opposite sex to the linking parent—that
is, FaSi and MoBr. Quotes are used here and above for "sister" to indicate that these
terms include the classificatory extension of the primary meanings; that is, "sister" includes female parallel cousin and uncle or aunt includes the appropriate parallel cousin
of one's parents. It should also be noted that although the past tense is used for consistency
in the above section, this terminological system was still operating until very recently,
as recorded by W. D. Strong (1928) and N. Graburn (1971).

once did the Eskimos win and that was when they were camped on a peninsula jutting into a lake and knew the Indians were going to attack. They fortified the neck of the peninsula with upturned broken caribou shin bones and then pretended to be asleep. When the Indians came in the dark, they tripped over the bones and were cut by them and the Eskimos rose to attack and kill them all.

Although both groups were excellent shots with bow and arrow and were good canoemen, the Eskimos acknowledged the Indians' superiority in inland areas. Each side used their shamans to make them strong in these battles, and the Indians claimed that they won with superior magic. In addition, the Indian parties of men were organized by a "war chief" (*dowhendóho*), and the Eskimos were never organized in such a manner.

The Indians and Eskimos thought of each other in the most hostile and derogatory manner. The Indians referred to the Eskimos as *aijis-timau* (*aijatsimijuu, iičimau*), which means "eaters of raw meat," that is, animal-like, anathema to the Indians. The Eskimos referred to the Indians as *adlat* ("Indians, hostile strangers") or *irqidlit* which means "those with *irqit* (louse eggs) showing in their hair"! The Indians, on the one hand, thought the Eskimos were lazy for using dogs to pull their sleds and smelly from the seal fat and raw meat. One Indian claimed that though the Eskimos in fact had human souls (*hočekw*), they did not know it and acted like animals. Some even said that *atsan*, the cannibal spirit, looked like an Eskimo. The Eskimos, on the other hand, claimed that very long ago the Indians did not wear any clothes, that they were hairy and slept in the snow like dogs. They did not like the smell of the Indians' smoked clothes or food, and, though they knew the Indians used the *mǝtǝzan* as a sweat bath, they thought that the Indians only took off their clothes and washed once a year. Neither group figured prominently in the other's mythology, although the Eskimos associated the *arngnasiutik*, woman-chaser spirit, with the Indians and the tree line where Indians lived.

After the traders established themselves in the northern area in the nineteenth century, they curbed active warfare as they did not want to see their trappers using their time and supplies to shoot each other. The Indians probably had access to guns first, which made them even more feared by the Eskimos. During the first half-century or more of trading at the same settlements, the Indians and Eskimos remained fearful of each other, setting their temporary camps apart. Some intercourse occurred through the traders' efforts, and as familiarity developed the Indians and Eskimos got to know more about each other, especially after both were converted to Christianity around the turn of the twentieth century.

These contacts engendered new stereotypes and modified some old ones. In general the Indians were seen as the more aggressive and hostile, and still superior in such matters as wrestling, carrying weights, canoeing, and shooting. The Eskimos, on the one hand, considered the Indians noisy for singing so much and ridiculed their extreme modesty in urinating. They also thought that the Indians were stricter with their children and that when alcohol became available the Indians drank more. (In fact, in one settlement it was the Indians who eventually taught the Eskimos how to make home brew, long after the former had learned from the white man.) The Indians, on the other hand, had the stereotype of the Eskimos as rather "primitive," and their women as "looser" and uglier than the more modest Indian women. In spite of these hostile expressions, both groups grew to appreciate certain items of the other's material culture and some barter took place. The Eskimos liked the Indians' way of preparing very soft caribou skins and traded for them and for snowshoes, which they themselves never made traditionally. The Indians overcame their olfactory disgust and traded for the waterproof Eskimo summer boots, which were much superior to their moccasins in the swampy flatlands. More recently other cultural interchanges have taken place in such technical matters as inland trapping, skin preparation, and sea hunting. Intermarriage has been rare and sex and mating behavior until recently has always involved Indian men and Eskimo women, never the other way around. The Eskimos have sometimes accused the Indians of using shamanistic magic to seduce away their women!

To what shall we attribute this traditional fear and hate? The two groups competed only slightly for such game as caribou, white whale, and seals, and never fought among themselves for these resources. The Eskimo claim that sheer ignorance and unfamiliarity led to fear and hostility, as they do in other matters too. The Indians, however, believe that such warfare was natural and needs no excuse or explanation.

Eskimo-Indian warfare was common along mutual borders all across North America. Hearne's famous expedition up the Coppermine River (1771) ended with his Athabascan Indian guides massacring the unarmed Eskimos. Farther west, in Alaska, the warfare was more equal as the Eskimos were more numerous and better organized, and they commonly beat some of the interior Subarctic Indians such as the Dihai Kutchin and the Tanaina. In these raids, too, it appears that all the vanquished were killed save for a few young women, but the accounts suggest that material gain and territorial expansion were motives in addition to prestige and plain hatred. In fact in the west there were also fairly frequent peaceful relations involving trade of material items and occasionally women and slaves. Even these relations, however, involved suspicion and hostility except in one area, where the Ingalik learned much from the Eskimos and sided with them against other Athabascans. In general we may state that these interethnic relationships are problem areas for which we have, as yet, no good explanations.

ANNOTATED BIBLIOGRAPHY

In selecting the literature on the Indian peoples of this area we have the problem of the labels used for the groupings, particularly because different authors call the same peoples by different names and because cultural distinctions between the groups are more like gradations than sharp boundaries. In general we have tried to reduce the length of this section by eliminating those references to "Cree" or "Montagnais" when we know that the people described are not normally identified as Naskapi. Luckily for the authors and readers much of the literature on this area is summarized and evaluated in the excellent volume by J. Malaurie and J. Rousseau (eds.), *Le Nouveau-Québec* (Paris: Mouton, 1964), partly in French.

There is very little literature on the physical anthropology of the Indians of this area and even archeological research has been minimal. (See W. E. Taylor, Jr., "The Prehistory of the Quebec-Labrador Peninsula," pp. 181–210 in Malaurie and Rousseau, *op. cit.*). As far as we know the Naskapi (and Cree and Montagnais) have inhabited this area for thousands of years and have long been adapted to the forest and taiga environment. Although there have been sporadic contacts with the littoral Eskimos, it is no longer believed that the two groups once shared the same culture as some ethnologists used to claim—see, for example, K. Birket-Smith, "A Geographic Study of the Early History of the Algonquian Indians," *Internationales Archiv fuer Ethnographie*, 24:174–222 (1918). Even though the two groups share some cultural features, it has been pointed out (E. S. Rogers, "The Eskimo and Indian in the Quebec-Labrador Peninsula," pp. 211–250 in Malaurie and Rousseau, *op. cit.*) that most of these features, such as bear ceremonialism and items of material culture, are shared throughout much of circumpolar Eurasia and North America by peoples of many different physical and linguistic stocks.

Linguistic work on north and central Algonquian has been more extensive. See L. Bloomfield, "Algonquian," pp. 85–129 in H. Hoijer (ed.), *Linguistic Structures of North America* (New York: Viking Fund Publication No. 6, 1946); and C. F. Hockett, "The Proto-Central Algonquian Kinship System," pp. 239–258 in W. H. Goodenough (ed.), *Explorations in Cultural Anthropology* (New York: McGraw-Hill, 1964). The major authority on dialect classification is Truman Michelson, whose "Linguistic Classification of the Cree and Montagnais-Naskapi Dialects," *Bureau of American Ethnology Bulletin*, 123:67–96 (1939), we have followed in this chapter.

The bulk of the ethnographic literature on this area has actually described the more southerly groups, which we have called Montagnais and Cree, even though the authors sometimes called them Naskapi. The extensive writings from the seventeenth and eighteenth centuries, known as the "Jesuit Relations"—R. G. Thwaites (ed.), *The Jesuit Relations and Allied Documents*, 73 volumes (Cleveland, 1896–1901)—provide the earliest descriptions of these groups. Employees of the Hudson's Bay Company of the early nineteenth century have provided valuable documentation of initial cultural contacts and Eskimo-Indian hostilities, especially J. McLean, *Notes of a Twenty-Five Years' Service in* the Hudson's Bay Territory (London, 1849; Publications of the Champlain Society, Vol. 19, 1932); Finlayson and Erlandson in K. G. Davies (ed.), *Northern Quebec and Labrador Journals and Correspondence 1819–35* (London: Hudson's Bay Record Society, Vol. 24, 1963); and the many novels of R. M. Ballantyne. Later in the nineteenth century a number of adventurers, such as Hind, Wallace, and Mrs. Hubbard, wrote rather amateur accounts (see A. Cooke, "The Exploration of New Quebec," pp. 137–180 in Malaurie and Rousseau, *op. cit.*), but it was not until the publication of the major works of Lucien M. Turner that there appeared anything like a professional account of the Indians (and Eskimos) of the northern area—"Indians and Eskimos of the Ungava District, Labrador," *Proceedings and Transactions of the Royal Society of Canada*, Vol. 15 (1888); "Ethnology of the Ungava District, Hudson's Bay Territory," *11th Annual Report of the U.S. Bureau of Ethnology* (1894), pp. 159–350. Though these two reports dwell extensively on material culture, they also give fair accounts of social organization, acculturation, and interethnic relationships.

During the twentieth century there has been considerably more ethnographic work but emphasizing, again, the southern part of the peninsula. Frank G. Speck, who worked in the area from 1906 to 1932, has written the most extensive accounts. His major work, *Naskapi* (Norman: University of Oklahoma Press, 1935), deals mainly with the spiritual life and cosmology of the central Montagnais-Naskapi. Julius E. Lips has also published excellent accounts of aspects of Naskapi life: "Public Opinion and Mutual Assistance among the Montagnais-Naskapi," *American Anthropologist*, 39:222–228 (1937); "Naskapi Trade," *Journal de la Société des Americanistes*, 31:129–195 (1939); "Naskapi Law," *Transactions of the American Philosophical Society*, 37:379–492 (1947); and "Notes on Montagnais-Naskapi Economy," *Ethnos*, 12:1–78 (1947).

These writers and others engaged in two major controversies. The first concerned the aboriginality or recency of the ownership of hunting territories, which generated an extensive literature. See particularly F. G. Speck, "The Family Hunting Band as the Basis of Algonkian Social Organization," *American Anthropologist*, 17:289–305 (1915); "Kinship Terms and the Family Band among the Northeastern Algonkian," *American Anthropologist*, 20:143–161; "Montagnais-Naskapi Bands and Early Eskimo Distribution in the Labrador Peninsula," *American Anthropologist*, 33:557–600 (1931); and, with L. Eiseley, "Montagnais-Naskapi Bands and Family Hunting of the Central and Southeastern Labrador Peninsula," *Proceedings of the American Philosophical Society*, 85:215–242 (1942); Rev. J. M. Cooper, "Is the Algonkian Family Hunting Ground System Pre-Columbian?" *American Anthropologist*, 41:66–90 (1939); A. I. Hallowell, "The Size of Algonkian Hunting Territories: A Function of Ecological Adjustments," *American Anthropologist*, 51:35–45 (1949); and Eleanor Leacock, "The Montagnais 'Hunting Territory' and the Fur Trade," *American Anthropological*

Association Memoir, No. 78 (1954), and her "Matrilocality in a Simple Hunting Economy," *Southwestern Journal of Anthropology,* 11:31–47.

The second controversy had to do with cross-cousin marriage. It had long been noted that the northern Algonquians had a kinship-terminology system suggesting this practice but the relevant ethnographic data were unavailable until this century, and even then the argument has revolved around historical reconstructions as much as functional analyses. Basing his hypotheses mainly on terminology distributions, A. I. Hallowell suggested a widespread former prevalence of this institution: "Was Cross-Cousin Marriage Practised by the North-Central Algonkian?" *Proceedings of the XXIII International Congress of Americanists* (1928), 519–544; "Kinship Terms and Cross-Cousin Marriage of the Montagnais-Naskapi and Cree," *American Anthropologist,* 34:171–199 (1932). W. D. Strong supplied data on the frequency of such marriages for the northeasternmost bands near the tree line in "Cross-Cousin Marriage and the Culture of the Northeastern Algonkians," *American Anthropologist,* 31:277–288 (1929); and R. Flannery for the westernmost groups in "Cross-Cousin Marriage among the Cree and Montagnais of James Bay," *Primitive Man,* 11:29–34 (1938). The problem has been reviewed more recently by Fred Eggan in his *Social Anthropology of the North American Tribes,* 2nd ed. (Chicago: University of Chicago Press, 1955), pp. 519–548; and Nelson Graburn, "Naskapi Family and Kinship," in F. Eggan and A. Spoehr (eds.), *Anthropological Studies in Comparison, Social Structure and Change* (manuscript in preparation, 1971).

Other works concerned with Indian religion, in addition to the work of Speck, are by the Rev. Cooper, "The Northern Algonkian Supreme Being," *Primitive Man,* 6:41–111 (1933), and by his colleague, Regina Flannery, "The Shaking Tent Rite among the Montagnais of James Bay," *Primitive Man,* 11:11–16 (1939). Many cultural features of this area have been discussed in the review works of Cooper, "The Culture of the Northeastern Indian Hunters," pp. 272–305 in F. Johnson (ed.), *Man in Northeastern North America* (Andover, Mass.: Peabody Publications, 1946); J. Fried (ed.), *A Survey of the Aboriginal Populations of Quebec and Labrador* (Montreal: Eastern Canadian Anthropological Publications, No. 1, 1955); P. Garigue, "Social Organization of the Montagnais-Naskapi," *Anthropologica,* 4:107–136 (1957); and, especially, J. J. Honigmann, "Indians of Nouveau Quebec," pp. 315–373 in Malaurie and Rousseau, *op. cit.*

Most recent published works have concerned the Indians around Lake Mistassini and Great Whale River, concentrating on aspects of acculturation and interethnic (including Indian-Eskimo) relationships. See, for example, J. J. Honigmann, *Social Networks at Great Whale River, P.Q.* (Ottawa: National Museum of Canada, Bulletin 178, 1962); E. S. Rogers, "The Individual in Mistassini Society" (Ottawa: National Museum of Canada, Bulletin 190:2:14–36, 1963); and Norman Chance (ed.), *Culture in Conflict: Problems of Developmental Change among the Cree* (Ottawa: Canadian Research Centre for Anthropology, 1968). These authorities, their collaborators and students, and others have done considerably more research work in these areas, as well as at Schefferville, P.Q., and Davis Inlet, Labrador, but their results unfortunately are still unpublished.

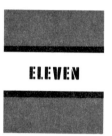

ELEVEN

THE ALEUTS: SUBARCTIC
ISLANDERS

The Aleutian Island chain—with fourteen large islands and more than eighty small ones—runs in an arc nine hundred miles WSW from the Alaska Peninsula (see Figure 1.1). The Japanese Current (Kuro Siwo) keeps the climate from extremes, but the constant meeting of warm and cold air masses results in frequent snow, rain, fog, high winds, and little sunshine. No trees are native to the islands and in many parts the vegetation is swampy or absent altogether. Yet at the time of discovery, more than two hundred years ago, the Aleuts—estimated at 12,000 to 25,000 in number—were the most densely populated peoples in native North America.

The Aleutian peoples,[1] who diverged from the proto-Eskimo-Aleut stock some four thousand or more years ago, spread west along the island chain and adapted their littoral culture to the harsh climate and abundant resources of the area. Though land animals are few, birds, fish, shellfish, and sea mammals abound, and berries and grasses can also be utilized. Living in compact littoral settlements, though with no overall political unity, the Aleuts subsisted on the diverse resources and developed excellent hunting techniques and an ingenious material culture.

The sparse literature on Aleut ethnography, as opposed to physical anthropology and prehistory, reports the unusually early, intense, and disastrous history of their contact first with the Russians and later with the Americans. The initial slaughter of Aleuts and their later virtual enslavement to fur-trading organizations led to the decimation of the population and the disruption of much of the aboriginal Aleut culture. For information about the Aleut traditional culture we have to rely mainly on the early Russian accounts, some of which are summarized

---

[1] The name Aleut was first applied to the islands and their inhabitants by the Russians as early as 1747, but its origin is unknown. The Aleut people referred to themselves as *unangan* (the people) but we have retained the use of the term Aleut in this book, because most of the Aleuts speak English and use the term now.

and translated in Waldemar Jochelson's *History, Ethnology and Anthropology of the Aleut* (1933). In this chapter we emphasize the adaptation of the Aleuts to their unique environment, and their different relationships with the Russians and, after 1867, the Americans.

TRADITIONAL ALEUT SOCIETY: ECOLOGY AND ADAPTATION

Aleut villages crowded the coasts of some of the better-endowed islands, situated on spits or points wherever there was fresh water, a beach for landing boats, and a suitable lookout point for guarding against surprise attacks in the frequent internecine wars. Each village consisted of one or a number of large communal houses called *barabaras*, which were partially underground with sod roofs supported by driftwood or whalebone (see Figure 11.1). The houses had no windows but there were communal exits through the roof. Inside these houses each family had its own "apartment" for sleeping, on benches cut into the soil and covered with straw mats. There were communal urine troughs, used for washing hands and tanning skins. Some houses extended to as much as two hundred forty feet long by fifty feet wide and housed as many as one hundred fifty people.

The climate was damp and cold and there was not enough driftwood for fires. Each family had a stone lamp that burned animal oils and was used for cooking, lighting, and partially warming the house; to get warm, however, individuals usually had to stand over the lamp, letting the air rise inside their parkas. Fire was made either by a bow-drill or by striking stones together and using the spark to ignite down and dry grass and sulfur (gathered from the many volcanic outlets on the islands).

Figure 11.1   Inside a barabara. (From Capt. James Cook and Capt. James King, A Voyage to the Pacific Ocean, London; 1874, p. 110.)

From these settlements the Aleuts foraged and hunted along the coast and out to sea and made short trips inland to gather grasses and other vegetable matter. These settlements consisted of permanent houses, but people might also move from place to place for hunting or for protection from enemies. Unlike the central Eskimos, the Aleuts cannot be considered a nomadic people; they did not have dogs or sleds and they traveled little in the winter. During the summer excursions they might use their upturned boats as shelter or dig a temporary pit house and cover it with mats.

By some standards Aleut social organization was fairly simple. There was probably no overall sociopolitical organization higher than the village or island level, but intervillage mobility, marriage, and trade flourished, often interspersed with inter-Aleut and Aleut-Eskimo warfare. Village members were usually kinsmen, and production and consumption were largely communal. Leaders were skilled older men and family heads, who constituted an informal council that oversaw productive strategies and social controls. The aboriginal "class system," though not clearly recorded or explained, probably consisted of (a) nobles, from whom chiefs were drawn, (b) commoners, and (c) slaves captured in warfare. Kinship was mainly bilateral, but nuclear families traditionally relinquished control of adolescents, the boys being "tutored" in Aleut ways and techniques by older men, often their mother's brothers, and the girls going into semi-isolation, directed by older women in their puberty rites. Thus in social complexity Aleut society fell between the relatively simple Eskimos to their north and east and the more highly stratified Northwest Coast Indians to their south and east.

Aleut religious traditions were modified or eradicated during the period of early contacts. As with other Eskimoid peoples, shamans held important positions and practiced curing, prediction, and witchcraft. In what is recorded of the mythology,[2] both the vision quest and apprenticeship could lead to shamanism, and animal-human transformations and communications were common. The Aleuts used amulets and observed strict taboos, such as avoidance of menstruating women, to guard against failure in the all-important hunting activities.

Strategic hunting and gathering forays made use of the widest diversity of resources, and a very high population was maintained; although hunger was common, population fluctuation through starvation was kept to a minimum. Within their area the Aleut population probably reached and maintained the maximum number supportable with the given technology. Not all the islands were suitable for habitation, however, and the fairly large Commander Islands to the west and the rich Pribilof Islands to the north were not inhabited and may not have been discovered until the coming of the Europeans, after which they were populated by Aleuts transported there by the Russians for commercial (hunting) purposes.

---

[2] See especially Knut Bergsland, "Aleut Dialects of Atka and Attu," *Transactions of the American Philosophical Society*, 49:3 (1959).

The sea-mammal population, though lacking the many walrus of the Bering Straits, included abundant sea lions, various seals, and migrant whales. In addition, the sea otter was originally very abundant, though it nearly passed out of existence before it became internationally protected in 1912. Large cod and halibut were caught offshore, and salmon, herring, and smelt were taken in large quantities during their seasonal runs.

Birds and birds' eggs formed an important part of the summer diet, and included murres, ducks, geese, loons, gulls, ptarmigans, and cormorants—though the one species of the latter has become extinct.

Perhaps the mainstay of the Aleut diet were the very abundant shellfish gathered along the shore; without these to fall back on when hunting failed or storms came, the villages would have been wiped out by starvation. Old Aleut village sites are huge shellfish middens (mounds), many meters thick, consisting of the external remains of mussels, spiny sea urchins, and other creatures gathered at low tide. In addition, various forms of seaweed were gathered and eaten, especially in times of hunger. At certain times, berries, bulbs, and roots of land flora were gathered for food, and other plants contributed much to the diet and the material culture. There was little land fauna, save the caribou and the bears that hunted on the large Unimak Island in the east.

Aboriginally the Aleuts had two types of skin boats: the smaller, which the Russians and the early literature called a *bidarka*, was a form of kayak (see Figure 11.2); the larger, an open boat called by the Russians a *baydar*, resembled the typical Eskimo *umiak* and went out of existence more than a hundred years ago. Both these boats were covered with seal or sea-lion skins, stitched over a driftwood frame bound together with leather thongs. The kayak was about twelve feet long by two feet in beam and was so light it could easily be carried

Figure 11.2   Canoes of Unalaska. (From Cook and King, op. cit., p. 112.)

across land. A peculiarity of the Aleutian kayak was that it was made in both one- and two-hole forms, the latter being used for transporting people and later for hunting with a rifle. After the advent of the Russians the Aleuts made kayaks with as many as three holes, the center hatch being reserved for transporting traders, missionaries, and the like. These kayaks could make over six knots and were very versatile in all kinds of weather. The umiaks, up to thirty feet long and open on top, were used only for transporting families and their goods to and from camps and islands.

When using the kayaks the Aleut hunters wore waterproof seal-gut "parkas" or shirts (*kamleikas*), which were tied around the hatch hole, allowing no water to enter even if the craft were swamped. They also wore large hats, made of flat pieces of wood bent round the back of the head and joined at a point some inches out from the brow, which were painted and decorated with feathers. The kayakmen used a dou-ble-bladed paddle for propulsion, and the craft contained stones for ballast and usually an inflated bladder on deck for extra buoyancy. Each man's kayak was always equipped also with many darts (like small harpoons) and a dart-throwing board for hunting.

Hunting methods varied with the quarry. Sea-otter hunting, in May and June, was a cooperative effort. From five to twenty kayaks would set out together in search of the sea-loving mammal. When one was seen the hunter would point to it and the craft would quickly make a circle up to half a mile in diameter around the spot where the animal dived. When it surfaced for more breath, they would shout at it to make it dive quickly, and close the circle. When close enough, one or more of the men would throw their darts at the animal; the small bone head of the dart was attached to a bladder or float by a line, thus impeding the animal which was dispatched by more darts when it next surfaced. The westernmost Aleuts were also said to net sea otters near the coast with nets made of sinew, and occasionally they clubbed them when they came on shore during bad storms.

Whale hunting was more dangerous, and Aleut methods differed considerably from the techniques of other Eskimoid peoples. Two kayaks set out together and approached a whale from the rear. When quite close the men threw a heavy, stone-pointed spear into the animal's back, and retreated quickly to avoid being capsized. The spear tip was smeared with a powerful alkaloid poison (aconite) from the monkshood plant, which is common on the Aleutians. The whale swam off but after a day or two usually died of the poison, and then drifted to the shore of one of the many islands. The hunter meanwhile went into isolation for three days and prayed for the whale to return to shore. It is estimated that only one in twenty whales was actually retrieved for consumption, but when a whale was retrieved it provided food and oil for many Aleuts for a long time. Each hunter's spear point was specially marked so that the credit and prestige of the kill could be attributed to the successful man when and wherever the whale might land.

The kayaks were also used for fishing, especially for the large cod and halibut, which may weigh hundreds of pounds. These large fish were caught by bone hooks with lines of braided strips of giant kelp, and it often required two kayakmen working together to get them out of the water. The Aleuts used kelp or sinew nets for salmon and trout in the small rivers and near the shore and also sometimes for the large shoals of herring that run near the coast. In addition to nets, they used spears for salmon, mackerel, octopūs, and other sea creatures. Huge shoals of tiny smelt were gathered in dip nets or picked up off the beach. The Aleuts made weirs or dams in the rivers that the salmon ascend in the summer and fall; the trapped salmon were caught in dip nets and shared by all the villagers.

Women did most of the gathering of edible land plants and of the mussels, clams, and sea urchins so abundant along the coast. Only the gonads of the sea urchins were eaten, but they were gathered in huge quantities, especially at low tide during the many storms which made hunting and fishing impossible.

Aleut cooking was rudimentary and consisted of placing the fish or meat on a hot slab of stone over a grass fire or oil-burning lamp. Most fresh foods were eaten raw, but fish, which were often obtained in large quantities at one time, were split and dried outside on wooden racks.

Because of the relatively temperate climate, the Aleutians are inhabited by more birds the whole year round than is the true Arctic; these all-year birds include the ptarmigan, many species of ducks, waders, gulls, murres, and cormorants. Other birds migrate there in large numbers for the summer, including many geese, swans, other species of ducks, and even swallows. Birds and their eggs formed a substantial part of the Aleut diet during the spring and summer. Small birds were caught in nets and snares and larger flying birds were knocked down by bolas (three or four stones tied together with cords). A light bird dart was used with a throwing board for killing birds in flight and on the water. Perhaps because of the prevalence of birds and the absence of extreme cold and of caribou, most Aleut clothing was made of bird skins, tanned in urine and sewn together. Such clothes would be used, for instance, by a hunter under his intestine *kamleika* during wet weather or on the water.

Aleut dress consisted of birdskin parkas without hoods and usually birdskin pants. Sometimes the wives of important men had sea-otter clothing, and men might have trousers of seal or sea lion. All these skins were tanned in the urine collected in the large houses, and were dried and sewn by the women, using bone needles and sinew thread. Early accounts differ as to whether the Aleuts normally wore footgear at all, especially along the western islands. In those accounts that do describe footgear, it is said to consist of waterproof leather boots with sealskin soles and leggings of sea-mammal esophagus.

As was common with Arctic and Subarctic peoples, the Aleuts tatooed the faces of women. Both men and women wore stone or ivory labrets (plugs fastened into the upper or lower lip) and many wore ornaments stuck into holes pierced in the nasal septum or the ears. Both men and women cut their hair, the men on top and the women in front, tying the rest in a knot on top.

Aleut women were known particularly for their skillful weaving of grass, and their mats and baskets exhibit as fine a technique as that of any peoples in North America. They gathered the grasses in summer and left them to dry in caves until needed. They then split the grasses with their fingernails into fine threads, dyed them, and wove them into a tight matrix with intricate geometrical patterns. Traditionally the Aleuts slept on such grass mats in both their temporary and permanent shelters, and used the baskets for carrying gathered foods and for storage.

ALEUT HISTORY AND ACCULTURATION

In the sixteenth and seventeenth centuries Russian adventurers and fur traders pushed across Siberia to Kamchatka. They were interested mainly in the fur trade of such land animals as sable, squirrel, fox, marten, ermine, and bear. Peter the Great supported these activities and early in the eighteenth century he financed two expeditions to travel east from Kamchatka to the American mainland and to explore the ocean in between.

On Bering's second voyage in 1741, he and Chirikov commanded two ships, but they soon became separated. Each sighted and named parts of the Alaskan mainland and the Aleutian Islands, making little contact with the Aleuts. Both halves of the expedition ended in storms and suffered scurvy and other sickness, and many sailors, including Bering himself, died before regaining Kamchatka. Bering's ship was wrecked on the then uninhabited Commander Islands near the Russian coast, where the crew spent the winter living off seals, sea lions, and Stellar's sea cow (or manatee) while they recuperated. They also killed and accumulated the skins of many sea otters, foxes, and fur seals, which they took back with them to Kamchatka the next spring.

The discovery of such abundant sources of skins and hence wealth set off a stampede of Cossack and native Siberian traders and hunters (promyshlenniki), which lasted with little restraint for more than forty years. All who could raise money to outfit expeditions sailed their little boats along the Aleutian chain to the mainland, and later down the Pacific Coast. From the first, through misunderstanding or malice, relations with the Aleuts were hostile and disastrous. More than sixty trading companies were formed, using the Aleut men to hunt the valuable sea otter for them. They employed hundreds of kayakmen at a time to hunt along hundreds of miles of coast, and sometimes they used them as militiamen to make war on recalcitrant tribes or even on the hunters for competing fur companies. Friction was inevitable, and the Russians killed hundreds and sometimes even thousands of

Aleuts at a time. Although the Aleuts ceased their own internecine warfare, they were seldom successful in killing Russians, and they were severely repaid for it when they did.

We do not have very good accounts of the initial changes in Aleut society, but we know that metal for needles, hatchets, and spears was introduced along with beads, baubles, and other ornaments, that disease took the lives of countless thousands of Aleuts, and that some islands soon were depopulated. The animals fared little better. Early traders used the Commander Islands as a provisioning base, and within forty years the slow-moving northern sea cow had become extinct; the spectacled cormorant also disappeared later, and the sea otter rapidly diminished in numbers. Aleut society was broken up by the deaths, the long absences of the men, and the new rapacious political control. The communal houses gave way to small semisubterranean family dwellings; chiefs became the lackeys of tyrant traders; and population movements were often enforced by the Russians.

This state of chaos lasted for only two generations, for the returns from sea-otter hunting diminished to a few thousand pelts a year. By around 1800 Aleut population is said to have fallen to about 2,500. Luckily for the traders, one Pribilof in 1786 discovered the two islands named after him, which were and are the main breeding grounds for the fur seal and the sea lion. These islands, far north of the Aleutians, were probably unknown to the natives, and the animals, untouched by human plundering, numbered in the many millions. The fur seals, which were already being slaughtered on the Commander Islands, overtook the sea otter as a source of revenue, but indiscriminate slaughtering at first threatened their population too. On both these island groups, the Russians soon instituted a more controlled killing, taking only the bachelor males between two and five years old. Aleuts were employed to do the killing, and on the Commander Islands other native peoples as well.

In the 1790s some order was introduced when the richer of the trading companies banded together and, under the name of the Russian-American Company, leased from the czarist government a monopoly on the fur trade in this huge area. In 1791, Alexander Baranov, a shrewd businessman and strong ruler, was appointed governor of the Company, making his headquarters on Kodiak Island and, later, down the coast at Sitka. The Company attempted to expand Russian influence and land claims down the coast, frequently using Aleut kayakmen as warriors, but the latter were too easily slaughtered by the resistant Tlingit.

Under the Russian-American Company, the first organized attempts were made to convert the Aleuts and other native peoples to Christianity. This, together with the cessation of warring between rival companies, led to a relatively peaceful period of six decades for the few remaining Aleuts. Bishop Veniaminov, who lived on Unalaska at times between 1823 and 1842 and visited all of the inhabited islands, recorded much of what we know about Aleut culture and helped introduce literacy through Church Old Slavonic. The majority of the Aleuts have followed the Orthodox Church from then until this day. The Russian-American Company's twenty-year lease was renewed with some misgivings in 1840 but ran out again in 1860. Some San Francisco merchants tried to purchase the third lease for five million dollars, but in 1867 Secretary of State Seward bought the whole of Russian America (Alaska) for the United States for seven million dollars. By then the area had become less profitable, and both the Russian czar and the Company needed the cash to pay off their many creditors.

By this time the Aleuts had become more thoroughly acculturated to the Russian model, not only in their religion but also in many other ways. Literacy in the cyrillic script had been introduced, both in Russian and Aleut, and the Church controlled what education was not left to the Aleut elders themselves. Many Aleuts spoke Russian, intermarried with them, and wore Russian-style clothes. A few adopted Russian-style houses and many more used imported iron stoves in place of their oil lamps. In kinship and marriage they moved somewhat toward Russian patterns, and tea samovars, quilts, tobacco, and a few firearms were also introduced. Berreman, in his analysis of recent Aleut history and acculturation,[3] makes the point that the second half of the Russian occupation represented relative stability and social reintegration compared with the American period especially after the turn of the century.

In 1867 the United States took over all Aleut territory, save the Commander Islands which remained Russian. The Alaska Commercial Company, and later the North American Commercial Company (1890–1911), took the richest gem by leasing a monopoly on the fur seals of the Pribilof Islands, where they continued to employ Aleut slaughterers using relatively conservationist methods, as did the Russians on the Commander Islands. Nevertheless, the annual harvest decreased, probably because these same seals were being increasingly hunted at sea outside the breeding season, until the U. S. government itself took over the Pribilofs in 1911. The rest of the Aleutians were thrown open to competitive capitalist traders, who encouraged sea-otter hunting to near extinction and the trapping of foxes on many of the islands. On a few islands they introduced foxes where there had been none and also experimented with agriculture and livestock breeding, but with little commercial success.

The United States government introduced schools in English in the early 1900s, but at first made little progress with the Aleuts who were already literate in their own language and Russian, and who kept strictly to the Orthodox churches which they continued to support. By 1900 the Aleut population, still racked by diseases and with its social structure broken, had fallen to approximately two thousand in spite of efforts to introduce wooden housing and some rudimentary health

[3] G. D. Berreman, "Inquiry into Community Integration in an Aleut Village," *American Anthropologist*, 57:49–59 (1955).

care. Berreman notes a number of factors that resulted in sociocultural
disintegration in Nikolski on Umnak Island (one of fewer than ten
Aleut villages still existing in 1952). These factors include the introduction of compulsory English education, the monetization of the economy, the great fluctuation in the price of fox skins, the establishment
of a purposeless village council, and the sending of children to the
Alaska mainland for secondary education. One further important factor
was the removal of all Aleuts to the mainland during World War II
after the Japanese had attacked and captured the western islands of
Attu and Kiska in 1942, which were deserted by the Japanese and
retaken by the United States in 1944. After three years spent in a camp
in Southeast Alaska during the war, those who wanted to go were
returned to the islands, but by then the total number of known Aleuts
had dropped to around one thousand.

ANNOTATED BIBLIOGRAPHY

The extensive literature on the Aleutian area is unsatisfactory from
an anthropological point of view because much of its ethnography is
an afterthought written by nonanthropologists engaged in other types
of studies. The bulk of it is in obscure publications or written in Russian
and not translated. The Russian anthropologist Waldemar Jochelson,
who did archeological work on the islands in 1910–1912, haphazardly
summarized much of the ethnography from his own observations and
from earlier Russian sources in his *History, Ethnology and Anthropology of the Aleut* (Washington, D. C.: Carnegie Institution Publications, 1933); a better and more critical ethnohistorical synthesis is Margaret Lantis's excellent "The Aleut Social System, 1750 to 1810, from
Early Historical Sources," pp. 139–301 in M. Lantis (ed.), *Ethnohistory
in Southwestern Alaska and the Southern Yukon* (Lexington: University of Kentucky Press, 1970). The reader should refer to these sources
for early bibliographic references.

The best single account of Aleut ethnography is probably Bishop
Ivan Veniaminov's *Notes on the Islands of the Unalaska Division* (St.
Petersburg: Russian-American Company, 1840, in Russian). In the nineteenth century, explorer-naturalists, such as Dall, performed archeologi-
cal-ethnographic observations that were published as parts of larger volumes on the Alaskan and Pacific area, with many inaccuracies and
ethnocentric biases (e.g., W. H. Dall, *Alaska and Its Resources*, Boston,
1870). Rather more extensive observations, particularly on the natural
history of the area but also including considerable (though "pro-
American") ethnography, were recorded by H. W. Elliot in *Our Arctic
Province: Alaska and the Seal Islands* (New York: Scribner, 1886).

More recent observations, conducted along with archeological work,
appear in the works of Jochelson (see above) and in Ales Hrdlicka's
The Aleutian and Commander Islands and Their Inhabitants (Philadelphia: Wistar Institute, 1945). Reasonably adequate summaries of Aleutian ethnography and prehistory, based mainly on secondary sources,

have been published by George I. Quimby, *The Aleutian Islanders* (Chicago Natural History Museum, Anthropological Leaflet No. 35); by Henry B. Collins, *The Aleutian Islands: Their People and Natural History* (Washington, D. C.: Smithsonian Institution, War Background Studies, No. 21, 1945); and, based partly on observation, by the naturalist Ted Banks II, "The Aleuts," *Scientific American*, 199:5:112–124 (November 1958).

Since World War II there has been renewed work in the area, including the ethnographic works of Gerald Berreman, based on fieldwork in 1952 and 1962: "Effects of a Technological Change on an Aleutian Village," *Arctic*, 7:2:102–107 (1954); "Enquiry into Community Integration in an Aleutian Village," *American Anthropologist*, 57:49–59 (1955); "Aleut Reference Group Alienation, Mobility and Acculturation," *American Anthropologist*, 66:231–250 (1964). However, the bulk of the work has been in prehistory and in physical anthropology, led by William S. Laughlin, "The Aleut-Eskimo Community," *Anthropological Papers of the University of Alaska*, 1:1:25–46. This has been followed by a series of publications based on continuing fieldwork by Laughlin and his associates, much of which has been outlined in their "Aleut-Konyag Prehistory and Ecology," *Arctic Anthropology*, 1:1:104–116 (1961).

TWELVE

THE ESKIMOS

The Eskimos are the best known of all the native peoples of the North, partly because of their unique and exotic way of life, and partly because their traditional lands extend over five thousand miles across the circumpolar region, embracing political domains of four nations—USSR, Alaska (USA), Canada, and Greenland (Denmark). Although the lands of the Eskimos are very extensive, the total population of less than 100,000 is very thinly distributed, generally concentrated at ecologically favored places along the complex coastline. Without the bounty of the seas, the Eskimos who could survive on the resources of the land would be less than one-tenth of the past and present population.

The literature on the Eskimos and their land is more extensive than that of any other "primitive" peoples in the world, in both professional and lay publications. For this reason we not only know more about past and present Eskimo life than about other peoples, but we hold more stereotypes about them which have to be modified. These stereotypes derive from the more romantic desires of the Western world to dramatize the exotic, the different, and the remote. This chapter, in some ways, can provide only a very limited guide to this enormous body of literature, but it can point the way for further serious research.

We wish to stress both the cultural homogeneity of so far-flung a group of peoples and the great variety of adaptations to local circumstances that often go unrealized in the lay mind. The cultural homogeneity of the recent and present Eskimos derives from their having spread from their "homeland" around the Bering Strait in waves of migration during the past two to three thousand years and their frequent interarea travel and intercultural exchange ever since the last major migration of seven hundred to a thousand years ago. The reader should not forget that the Aleut peoples too are part of the Eskimo stock and only diverged from the Alaskan homeland some three thousand years ago, according to archeological and linguistic evidence (see Chapter 11). Basically the Eskimos have the same kind of culture and react in the same kind of ways to social and technical pressures from Siberia in the west to Ammassalik in the east (see Figure 1.1).

The differentiation of Eskimo cultures has involved technological and demographic adaptation to vastly differing ecological niches within the Arctic area, and these have led to superficially different social and physical structures. In Barth's[1] terms, we may say that the same basic cultural patterns and economic strategies have generated different social forms under different pressures and circumstances. In this chapter we hope to show how these different features derive from the basic imperatives of life in the Arctic, but we have space only for illustrative examples.

The Eskimos have endured the penetration and acculturative forces of agents of many nationalities, starting at different times in different geographical areas. As a result the Eskimos have at times been more different after contact than before, as some groups have changed fast while others have been left untouched. With the rapid growth of all forms of communication in the twentieth century, however, nearly all Eskimo groups have "caught up" in their knowledge of the outside world and their demands for a significant place within it (see also Chapter 13).

ESKIMO ENVIRONMENT: LIMITATIONS AND OPPORTUNITIES

The two features that distinguish the environment of the Eskimos and hence their lifeways from that of all other native peoples of North America are residence in the Arctic and dependence on the sea. The majority of the Eskimos live in the typically Arctic environment where the rocky land is underlaid by permafrost which limits the growth of trees and the drainage of water from flat areas in the summer. Long and severe winters contrast with short and only mildly warm summers. The Eskimos therefore represent the people most typical of and best adapted to the Arctic environment as described in Chapter 1.

This does not mean that all Eskimos live in a characteristically Arctic environment or that Eskimos cannot live outside it. The maritime Eskimos of southern Greenland live in a Subarctic environment somewhat similar to that of the Aleuts. As the climate has fluctuated somewhat in the last one or two thousand years, the boundary between the Arctic and the Subarctic in this area—as measured by the presence of permanent offshore winter ice (*tuvak*)—has moved north and south along the coast of Greenland. Similarly, at the other end of their range of habitation, the Eskimos of southwestern Alaska, the Chugach Eskimos, and those around Cook Inlet and Bristol Bay may be said to be Subarctic. Their lands never get as cold and their seas never as clogged by ice as in other areas, and the land surrounding the coast

[1] See Frederick Barth, "Models of Social Organization," *Royal Anthropological Institute Occasional Paper*, No. 33 (1966).

and for many hundreds of miles up the long river valleys is covered
by typically Subarctic forests. It should be noted that the population
density in these two exceptional Subarctic areas is probably as high
or higher than that of the Eskimos in any of the more Arctic areas.
Thus Eskimo culture is basically positively adapted to Subarctic maritime as well as Arctic environments.

The second major characteristic of the majority of Eskimo lifeways
is their orientation toward the sea. Their whole life rests on a land-sea
dichotomy. Much of their land orientation resembles that of other
North American peoples, but most Eskimo groups have an extreme
dependence upon the sea, and in this they resemble in part the Aleuts
(who are prehistorically a kind of "Eskimo" who have become the most
sea-oriented), the maritime Chukchi, and perhaps the Haida of the
islands off the Northwest Coast.

Once again the important exceptions must be noted. In large areas
of west and southwest Alaska, many of the Eskimo groups have a riverine rather than a maritime emphasis and depend more on migratory
fish than on sea mammals as they inhabit the wooded valleys of the
large rivers such as the Noatak, Kobuk, Koyukuk, Yukon, Kuskokwim,
etc. Technologically and ecologically these Eskimo groups resemble
more the Alaskan Athabascans (as described in Chapter 7).

The other important group of exceptions include those Eskimos
known as the Nunamiut (the people of the land) or Caribou Eskimos.
The Nunamiut of the Brooks range of interior northern Alaska are
well adapted to inland hunting but aboriginally they probably always
depended upon economic exchange with the people of the coast to
the north of them. Similarly a few groups of peoples lived in the interior
of the Ungava Peninsula of northern Quebec, but these people too
depended upon exchanges with the coastal peoples or themselves visited
the heads of bays or the tidal portions of rivers where they could find
some maritime resources. The most extreme Nunamiut were the Caribou Eskimos of the Barren Grounds, some half million square miles
north of the tree line west of the Hudson Bay. These scattered populations depended mainly on the vast herds of migratory caribou and the
fish resources of the Thelon, Kazan, Back, and other rivers and lakes.
It has often been noted that these latter peoples, though culturally
typical Eskimos, were economically and technologically the poorest of
all groups. With their limited resources, they had to be more constantly
on the move, made poorer igloos and smaller tents, and were subject
to drastic periods of starvation even in recent times. They did not enjoy
the advantages of the Subarctic Indians round them such as the northern Athabascans and the northern Algonquians who depended upon
the same caribou herds but lived in wooded areas. We may therefore
summarize by saying that Eskimo culture and technology was successfully adaptive for Arctic and Subarctic maritime and riverine environments but less so (in terms of population maintenance) to land-locked
Arctic environments. It should of course be noted that no other peoples

in the world have had to live completely in Arctic tundra areas without complementary access to other environmental niches.

Technology and Production Strategies

No Eskimo groups depend totally upon the natural production of exactly those areas that they inhabit. The Arctic and Subarctic environments are not closed ecosystems, and few if any Eskimos would live in any part of their inhabited range if the Arctic were a closed system. For example, the maritime Eskimos depend partly on sea mammals which spend part of their annual cycle in warmer waters or whose food sources migrate from other areas. Nearly all the Eskimos depend partially or wholly on migratory fish which spend large proportions of the growing period of their lives in warmer areas and richer waters. All groups of Eskimos, especially at certain times of year, rely on migratory birds such as geese, ducks, and swans, which spend winters in temperate climates. Even the Nunamiut and other Eskimos most dependent upon caribou hunt these animals during the summer seasons when they come north to have their fawns, having spent their winters in the more productive wooded areas of the south. There are of course exceptions such as the caribou of Baffin Island, Greenland, and the other islands in the high Arctic; and there are important exceptions in that certain species of fish and a few bird species live all year in the true Arctic. Though not major food sources, many wolves, foxes, and owls are confined to the Arctic. Some minor sources of food, such as crustaceans and mollusks, certain plants and seaweeds, are virtually sessile and therefore part of the local natural production.

We may conveniently classify and discuss most aspects of Eskimo culture in terms of the important dichotomy between the land and the sea. This division is not only technologically and ecologically apparent, but it is fundamental to Eskimo symbolism and world view; at a deeper level of analysis the same dualistic world view could be mapped onto aspects of life such as esthetics, mythology, spatial arrangements, household and household organization, the annual cycle, and religious beliefs and operations. Although it has often been stated that dualism and the opposition of complementary halves is fundamental to all human culture because of such universal features as the symmetry of men and many other creatures, the opposition between the two sexes, etc., this dualism is made most overt in Eskimo society and will be touched upon again and again in later sections of this chapter. To summarize we might say that the Eskimos are an "edge" people who look to the land and the sea, the winter and the summer, the appropriate hunting and domestic technologies for both the seasonal and geographical cycles, and who arrange their living and ideological categories in a series of more or less overt oppositions.

In this section we shall see that the diversity of resources available to the Eskimos is probably greater than that for any other peoples described in this book. The poverty of the Eskimo environment does not lie in the paucity of species or phyla represented but in their uneven and irregular distribution and in the geographical and climatic features which make access to the natural production most difficult. Technologically the Eskimos have invented very sophisticated tools and strategies and make the utmost use of the diversified natural production whenever opportunities present themselves. We shall emphasize the sea and its resources because the majority of the Eskimos excel in this area in comparison to all other groups save their distant cousins the Aleuts and, perhaps, the Maritime Chukchi who may have been influenced by long contact with the Siberian Eskimos.

For the Eskimos living in the true Arctic the sea is not a unified concept, as it is perhaps for us. They find the sea in two forms—wet, windy, and relatively full of diverse resources in the summer, and covered or nearly covered with an immensely thick layer of floating ice especially near the coast and inhabited by relatively few and almost inaccessible resources in the winter. For our purposes we may say that the Subarctic Eskimos see the sea around them in a "permanent state of summer" compared with the majority.

Winter comes early to the Arctic Eskimos and from September on is often stormy or begins to freeze; the smoother fresh water of lakes and large rivers freezes and melts earlier. The sea, especially near the land, gradually freezes over, but the early winter storms keep breaking up the ice so that practically no hunting can be done until weeks or months have passed. Once the surface was fairly solidly frozen, the Eskimos traditionally made use of the few resources under the ice with a special technology. Keeping holes in the ice open with ice chisels and fishing with hooks was common but this was not the most significant contribution or source of food. The near-shore ice mass (*tuvak*) may grow to ten or twenty feet deep, but two species of seals, the ringed or common seal (*natsiq*) and the bearded or square flipper seal (*ujjuk* or *ugrook*), inhabit the underice water and keep open breathing holes to the surface by coming up for air every few minutes and disturbing the newly formed ice that tends to close them. Eskimos used keen-sniffing dogs or thin probes to find these holes in the ice and developed a complex technology for which they are justly famous in order to catch this single most important winter resource.

As has been well described, and filmed, the hunter poked a light indicator through the thin crust of snow above the breathing hole and waited with his harpoon until the indicator moved or the sound of the escaping air was heard. Then he thrust the harpoon down into what he considered to be the center of the breathing hole, hoping to hit the seal in the head or neck. The harpoon head remained attached to the sealskin line but the handle was discarded. The Eskimo quickly made the line fast round his body and arms and braced himself across the hole as the powerful seal tried to swim away. Sooner or later the seal tired and the Eskimo cut away the snow around the hole and tried to pull it out onto the ice surface. For a powerful seal such as

the *ujjuk*, which may weigh six to seven hundred pounds, a man called
upon other hunters for assistance or even used his dog team to get
the animal on the surface of the ice. Though the *tuvak* may stretch
many miles from land, in most areas there is an edge or long wide
leads of open water. At these points the Eskimo tried to harpoon the
seal from the ice or used the traditional summer technology of boats,
harpoons, and floats to hunt seals and walrus. Finally we may say that
even at this point there was an "edge" that symbolically and technologically divided winter and summer. As the winter progressed the sea
ice became thicker and fishing through it impossible. Thus late winter
was the time of great privation except when other land resources or
birds were available.

As the days lengthen and solar radiation becomes warmer in April,
May, or June, both these species of seals like to climb through their
holes and bask on the ice—their skin may in fact become "sunburned"
at this time and of lower quality as they are losing their winter hair.
Hunting became easier at this time and another technology was employed. The seals were visible as little black spots from miles away
on the flat ice. Restraining his dog team, the Eskimo would crawl toward
the seal and shoot or harpoon it before it had a chance to dive down
its nearby hole. The hunter often used a small white blind to remain
unseen, peering over it every now and then to keep an eye on the
seal. Or, dressed in sealskin clothing, he crawled toward the animal
imitating another member of the same species by movement and sound
until he got close enough. The hunter used a harpoon, a bow and arrow
(or more recently a rifle), or in some areas a long, heavy sliding harpoon
made like one runner of a sled, but he had to get within a few feet
of the animal to ensure the kill, at least in traditional times.

Freshwater ice breaks up early in summer or becomes too dangerous
to walk on, but saltwater ice is very resistant and, though large masses
may break up, the individual floes remain floating around in the Arctic
seas for most of the summer. Gradually the massive *tuvak* breaks up
and the open sea approaches the shore, favoring the Eskimo's choice
of summer hunting techniques. Between ice cracks or from floe edges,
small fish were caught by hook and lure and occasionally by leister
(fish spear). The major maritime emphasis turned to seal, walrus, and
whale hunting mainly by kayak.

All Eskimo groups, save the most northerly Polar Eskimos, used
some form of kayak, as did the Aleuts. This vessel varied considerably
in length, breadth, detail, design, and even skin covering, but it was
basically a one-man, closed-deck hunting canoe. The light frame was
made of small pieces of wood and occasionally other materials lashed
together with bones or sinew and covered with a skin—seal or caribou
skin—sewn together with waterproof seams. The man sat on the bottom
slightly aft of the middle in a fairly tight hole, or he may have been
"integrated" with the vessel by wearing a waterproof garment lashed
to the frame of the opening to make the whole unit impermeable.

Kayaks were usually propelled by double-bladed paddles and had no form of rudder; though very fast in smooth water and seaworthy in choppy seas, they could easily be blown off course by side winds and were inherently unstable, requiring constant efforts to remain upright and keep on a straight line. Though superbly adapted to hunting, they were very tiring craft and one can understand why the Eskimos of all areas have quickly taken to other forms of boats for both hunting and long-distance travel.

Hunting from the kayak could be an individual affair for small sea mammals but was often carried out in small or large groups both for companionship as well as safety and effectiveness. Eskimos concentrated on the sea mammals (puiji = those that show their noses, come up to breathe) and until recently neglected large fish such as shark because the hunting techniques did not work on them. The main feature of kayak hunting was to approach the sea mammal at the point where it surfaced to breathe until one got close enough to throw the three-part harpoon and embed the detachable head securely in its flesh. The hunter therefore approached the last-sighted surfacing place of the sea mammal as fast as possible and calculated how far and in what direction it might swim until the next breath. If there were more than one hunter the process was considerably easier and the game could be taken sooner. Having secured the animal the hunter let out the long harpoon line so that the kayak was not swamped and the vessel broken by the powerful sea mammal. With a walrus or whale, a number of hunters often tried to fix their harpoons in the animal, and a float made of an inflated sealskin was attached to the line to impede the animal and mark its progress and direction. For the larger sea mammals a drag—a large circular hoop covered with a skin like a drum—was attached to the line such that it was pulled through the water at right angles to the motion and slowed down even the most powerful animals. Sooner or later the animal tired and the hunter approached closer, drawing his line and further securing it if necessary. Most of the sea mammals were too large to haul on board the kayak or to stuff inside it, so the hunter made for the nearest land or large block of floating ice where the animal could be beached and butchered on the spot.

Though these techniques of kayak hunting were adequate in the open sea, Eskimo hunting strategy used as many methods as possible to increase the efficiency and size of the take. Eskimos knew which areas within their local environment were likely to be crowded with sea mammals and they knew the migration routes and times of appearance of the larger ones such as white whales, baleen whales, walruses, and harp seals. They may have tried to drive such animals into shallow bays where they would be stranded and whole herds could be dispatched like "shooting fish in a barrel." Such large hauls were cached for months and were supposed to supply the needs of the group during difficult times such as late fall and late winter. Occasionally other opportunities arose for catching large quantities of such huge sea mammals as white whales and walrus. For example, white whales sometimes became trapped by the gradually freezing sea and, unlike seals, could not form breathing holes throughout the winter. They therefore became confined to a smaller and smaller patch of open water and by late fall or early winter were found thrashing around gasping for air or even dead from crowding and overexertion.

Walrus, unlike all the other sea mammals, like to haul up on land and were sometimes found in huge herds at favored places. This applied to both the Pacific walrus, the mainstay of some of the Eskimo groups in the Bering Strait, and the slightly different Atlantic walrus, found off the Labrador coast and around the Fox Basin of southern Baffin Island. As the walrus was such a dangerous and aggressive animal, a group of Eskimo hunters preferred to approach a herd on land where they got as close as possible, unseen, and then rushed the herd and harpooned the slower animals. This of course was a very dangerous method because the powerful walrus, if even halfway into the water, could drag a number of men on the other end of the line into the water. This hunting technique often turned into a tug of war in which the Eskimo lost his life or his harpoon or the walrus was killed. Hunting walrus from a kayak was perhaps even more dangerous because in trying to defend the herd the aggressive males attacked the vessel and pierced it with their tusks or sank it by charging.

The large open Eskimo boat, the *umiak*, was found in most maritime Eskimo groups and in some riverine groups too. Like similar vessels among the Aleut and the Chukchi, it was twenty to thirty feet long and was made of a sturdy wooden frame covered with heavy animal skins. Although it had an open deck, it could be quite heavily loaded and was fairly seaworthy. In some places these vessels were occasionally propelled with the aid of small sails but usually they were rowed or paddled by the women of the group, while an old man gave directions and held the steering oar. It might be noted that the oval shape of the *umiak*, commonly known as the woman's boat, closely resembled that of the oil-burning soapstone lamp which was the prototypic possession of all women; whereas the sleek, pointed kayak used exclusively by men resembled the sharp hunting weapons which were prototypically male possessions. Thus we see here again on two levels a dualistic symbolic mapping of two important spheres of Eskimo life. Psychoanalytically minded readers might note (and be supported by the Eskimo) that these two fundamental and opposite forms also find material expression in the shapes of male and female genitalia.

In northwest Alaska the *umiak* was the supreme hunting vessel for the hazardous but exciting chase of the huge baleen whales—though even in this area the boat and its crew were led to the sea by a ritually selected woman who danced and gave gifts to the men. A number of umiaks and their crews, each led by an experienced *umialik* (boat owner, captain), went to the floe edge in April to June to await the migration of the great baleen whales. The key person was the harpoon thrower who, from the prow of the umiak, was supposed to get as close to or even on top of the whale's back and thrust the extra-heavy harpoon deep into its flesh, releasing a long line with at least three floats and drags attached. The whale would then dive, taking the floats with it, and when it surfaced again the other eight or ten umiaks would be in position, hoping to be close to the wounded animal. Again and again they would thrust in their harpoons with floats, slowing down the animal until it was so winded it could hardly struggle, at which point the men dispatched it by thrusting killing spears into vital places in its back. The assembled umiaks then towed the huge animal back to shore where it was cut up and distributed among a large number of families.

Umiaks were generally used for transportation rather than hunting, for carrying whole families or even numbers of households along the coast, to islands, or even far inland up the huge rivers so that they might camp near the best summer hunting places. Most Eskimo groups, except the Subarctic and the most northerly ones, had umiaks although their use dropped off with the advent of wooden boats in most areas. An umiak could be loaded with twenty to thirty or even more people and all their possessions, tents, dogs, and sometimes sleds. It could be dragged over the ice and snow on a sled in the winter but was usually kept for summer use.

Though kayaks were faster, they were much smaller than umiaks and only occasionally used for transportation. Materials and humans might be stowed in the empty fore and aft sections and occasionally on the deck. Kayaks might also be used for hunting other than sea mammals. In many areas water birds were very common and the hunter would use a light, three-pronged bird spear, propelling it with a throwing board, to catch the birds in flight or on the surface of the water. The lightweight kayaks could be carried over the land to lakes and rivers where they might be used for fishing and in some favorite locations for killing caribou as the herds had to cross the waters on their migration routes. The hunters quickly killed as many members of the swimming herd as possible with their killing spears.

Large migratory bird populations formed an important resource for the Eskimos in the spring and summer. They killed these birds with bird spears, bolas, and bows and arrows. Eskimos climbed cliffs to raid the nests of the multitudinous *akpa* (guillemot) and they gladly raided the nests of water birds such as ducks, geese, swans, gulls, and the many waders. In many areas ptarmigan (Arctic grouse) were valuable to fall back on in times of poverty for they did not leave the Eskimo area entirely and were found even in areas of deep snow. Since they are relatively stupid birds they could be killed by throwing stones at them. Of the birds that were widely spread in the Eskimo area and tended to stay around most or all of the year, only the owl and the ptarmigan seemed to be "proper food." The ubiquitous seagulls, though eaten as eggs and embryos, were seen as fit only for a starvation diet and were mythologically thought to be descendants of Eskimo women who had turned to cannibals and eaten their own children. The raven, which stays in the Arctic the whole year round and figures importantly in Eskimo mythology, often with a human personality, is eaten only under dire circumstances.

Before we consider the land animals, we should mention the polar bear, which thrives throughout the circumpolar regions but with special concentrations in certain areas of northern Alaska, the central Canadian Arctic, and northern Greenland. Though they hibernate in dens deep in the snow on land, polar bears, which are excellent swimmers, were most often encountered near the shore or out to sea on floating sea ice where they could scoop their major food source, seals and fish, from the water. Although known by all Eskimo groups, polar bears were not particularly sought as a source of food because they are rarely present in large numbers and perhaps more importantly because they are an awe-inspiring and dangerous animal. In areas of their major concentration, such as in the lands of the Thule or Polar Eskimos, polar bears were and are hunted for clothing since parts of their skin make excellent garments and form a good substitute when caribou are not abundant. Before the advent of rifles, hunting polar bears in water or on land was a dangerous experience. Trying to harpoon the animal from a boat could result in a fatal counterattack. A fast runner and powerful fighter on land, the polar bear could be killed only if the hunter got close enough to hit vital areas with the hand-propelled bow and arrow or spear. The Eskimo's dogs represented his greatest defense; they relentlessly attacked the bear and distracted it while the hunter made his kill. Throughout the Arctic a role reversal commonly took place and hungry polar bears raided igloos or houses in search of food such as stored meat. Though they sometimes broke into the igloo and terrified the inhabitants, people were only incidental quarry for polar bears searching for food just as the polar bear was only an incidental quarry of sea-mammal-hunting Eskimos. Along with the walrus, the polar bear was regarded by the Eskimos as the most awe-inspiring and respected member of the animal world. Their humanoid characteristics and their worthiness as opponents are well reflected in Eskimo mythology and tales where human/polar-bear transformations are common.

Of the land animals, the caribou (*Rangifer arcticus*) was by far the most important and was found in nearly all areas inhabited by Eskimos. In the mainland areas the Eskimos usually encountered large numbers of caribou in spring, summer, and early fall, as the animals came north to drop their fawns and to feed on the young tundra grasses and mosses. In the late summer in most areas the Eskimos made a concerted effort to hunt caribou herds in order to supply themselves with the best skins with which to make new sets of clothing for the coming winter. In some areas caribou were also found in smaller or larger numbers in the winter. Although the hair is thick on their skins at this time, it was deemed lower quality because the long hair broke off or fell out; it was commonly used only for bedding. Although most Eskimos considered caribou meat and back fat to be one of the most tasty foods, they depended for the bulk of their diet on sea mammals or fish. The Eskimos stated that caribou meat "strengthens one" but it was not as good for feeding humans or for the all-important dog teams as sea-mammal meat which contained a higher proportion of fat. In caribou hunting, usually a communal affair, the object was to meet the herds where they were most concentrated as at important crossing places (mentioned earlier) or in narrow valleys and defiles along the migration routes. Here the caribou would mass or be frightened by "beaters" and stone "imitation men" (*inukshuks*) into places where other hunters were lying in wait with their bows and arrows or with their kayaks and spears. At other times of the year caribou furnished an appreciated bonus when found in small numbers or as stragglers from the main herd.

Other land animals were of minor importance until the fads and fashions of the white world created a great demand for white and other fox pelts during this century. Although occasionally caught, trapped, or shot in the past, foxes provided very little meat. Muskoxen, though they might have been distributed widely prehistorically, have been found in historic times only in the northernmost regions of the Canadian mainland and on the high Arctic islands. In these places they may have been an important source of food because, rather than running away when confronted, the herds drew together and stood their ground as though opposing wolves. They were therefore "sitting ducks" for Eskimos with bows and arrows. The most numerous land animals in the Arctic, the ubiquitous lemmings, live on the seeds and other vegetable materials of the tundra. These tiny animals burrow along the surface of the ground and under the snow in the winter. In their enormous numbers they form the basis of the land-based carnivorous food chain supplying the bulk of the diet for foxes, owls, other birds of prey, and probably wolves. Thus they are the prime movers of the natural production which turns the weak solar energy into vegetable foodstuffs and then into the predatory chain. The Eskimos rarely ate lemmings except in times of starvation, but young boys practicing their male roles often "hunted" them with stones or bows and arrows.

Fishing has always been of importance to nearly all Eskimo groups and could be practiced by various methods in lakes, rivers, and sea at most times of year. Few purely marine fish were of great importance, though cod and sculpin were abundant and the huge Greenland shark has become of major commercial importance in the eastern seas. The major fish resources were the anadromous migratory fish such as the Atlantic salmon in the easternmost part of the range and the Pacific salmon all up the western part of Alaska, and the purely freshwater fish of the larger lakes of the whole area. Traditionally Eskimo fishing occurred in three major forms. Hooks with or without lures were used for jigging both at sea and in fresh water, often through cracks or holes in the ice. Even the oldest and weakest people could usually undertake this activity. The three-pronged fish spear was almost universal among Eskimos and could be used for medium-sized fish such as whitefish, lake trout, and salmon at all times of the year. In the winter they might be used through holes kept open in the ice, where a lure was jigged below the entrance of the hole while the hunter watched with his spear in the other hand. The barbs easily caught fish of varying sizes which were hauled up onto the land or ice surface. At other times of the year the leister could also be used at the constructed fishing weirs, which were dams of large boulders made across the shallow streams where the fish migrated. The men, and sometimes women, would wade in and spear the thrashing fish by the hundreds in favored locations. The leister was also used from the banks of streams and rivers and sometime from kayaks. In the west of Alaska those Eskimo groups that specialized in fishing for the major source of their diet developed more sophisticated techniques, resembling those of their neighbors, the Athabascan Indians. The main device was the fish trap, of varying form, which would direct and catch the large shoals of migrating fish near the shores of the huge rivers.

There has been some controversy in the literature about the recency and distribution of nets for both fishing and hunting in the Arctic. As far as we know these devices were confined solely to the far western and to the (eastern) Greenland areas. Sealing nets, made of strips of sealskin or braided baleen ("whalebone"), could be used in the open water for those seals that migrated in large herds, but more often they were placed at restricted areas such as the entrance to bays and rivers. The distribution of sealing by net occurred conversely to the distribution of *maupuk* or hunting through breathing holes in the ice; in the more Subarctic conditions the latter technique was rarely usable and the use of nets much more feasible. Net fishing, using the same materials or finer ones such as vegetable matter, also occurred in these two more temperate marginal areas. The nets could be used in streams, along river edges, along the seashore, or even strung under the ice. All these net forms have given way to more efficient nets of imported materials which are now widespread throughout the whole Arctic. Only in the far southwest of the Eskimo range did deep-sea fishing occur aboriginally. The huge halibut and cod of the warmer waters of the Northwest Coast were caught at great depths by lines that held a number of hooks. More recently deep-sea fishing has become the economic mainstay of the Greenlanders (see Chapter 13).

Technology and Materials

Although traditional Eskimos have often been said to be "stone age" people, this gives a very distorted picture of the important materials in Eskimo life. Following Balikci[2] we may say that the raw materials

---

[2] A. Balikci, "The Netsilik Eskimos: Adaptive Processes," in R. B. Lee and I. DeVore (eds.), *Man the Hunter* (Chicago: Aldine, 1968), p. 78.

fall into a number of complexes: snow and ice (snowhouses, icehouses, ice caches, etc.); skin (clothing, kayaks, *umiaks*, tents, etc.); bone, antler, and ivory (the important parts of weapons, tools, needles, etc); stone (hard stone for cutting edges, points, scrapers, and soft stone for oil lamps and cooking pots); and we may add wood, the most variable resource throughout the Eskimo range (tool and weapon handles, tent poles, boat frames, and, where abundant, house-building materials). Other materials included iron, occasionally worked in northern Green-land, copper used by the Copper Eskimos, and even frozen meat and fish were utilized when necessary as structural materials for sleds, etc.

Eskimo housing is popularly thought of in terms of the well-known igloo (snowhouse). This was the major form of winter residence for the central Eskimos and was occasionally used by the western and Greenland Eskimos as a temporary shelter. The igloo and the skin tent used in the summer in the same areas had the same basic plan. The back half, away from the door, was raised considerably above the floor level and may be called the sleeping platform; the people sat and slept, facing the door, on this platform and many of the women's materials were stored there. It was usually covered with skins and clothes over a mat of willow twigs which insulated the people from the earth and snow beneath. Just in front of the edge of the bed next to one (or both) of the walls was the oil-burning *qullik*, made of soapstone, above which might be the cooking pots or a netlike rack used for drying clothes. On the floor, on either side of the doorway to the porch, or the outside in the case of a tent, lay meat supplies, spare skins, tools, and sometimes even dogs. A permanent winter family igloo may have been as much as ten or fifteen feet across and would allow six to ten people to lie side by side on the sleeping platform with the women on or near the outside wall next to the lamp which they tended continu-ously.

It should be pointed out that the remarkable building of the igloo depended not so much on the spiral arch of blocks and the structure or the architecture as on the properties of the hard snow cut from deep drifts: each block was cut into a square or rectangle and placed on top of and next to the lower blocks in the spiral. Then it was given sharp blows down and horizontally against the adjacent block; each blow instantaneously melted the ice crystals at the point of contact through pressure and this momentary creation of water immediately froze again to cement the two blocks together. The points where the blocks did not touch were then filled with loose snow chips which were banged into place. The whole igloo became then a physically integrated structure; as it aged the constant melting of the upper inside walls, due to the heat rising from the lamps and then freezing again at night, formed a layer of ice which further strengthened the structure. The passageway to the outside sloped downward through the snow so that the lowest point of the igloo was the floor at the entrance. This basic feature of Eskimo housebuilding trapped the cold air that might flow in at the lowest level, and the heat rose to warm the upper part,

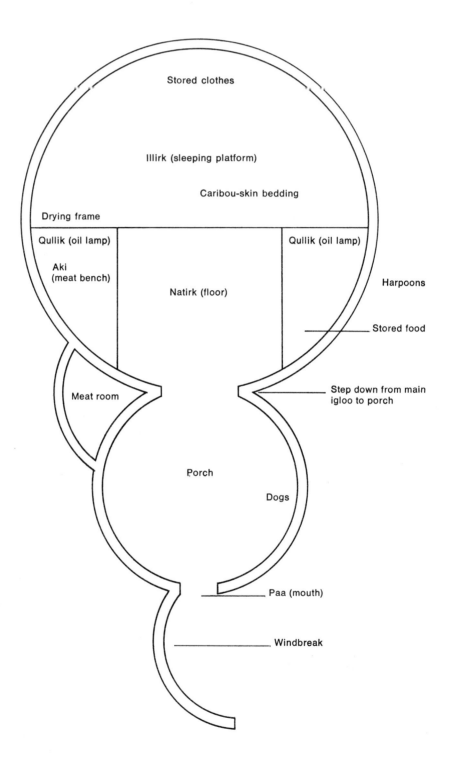

Figure 12.1 Eskimo technology: igloo and contents.

particularly around the bed, while excessive smoke and dirty air escaped through a small "nose" in the top of the dome.

Throughout the west coast of Alaska the more permanently settled Eskimo groups lived in houses with wooden frames and sod-covered roofs. These semisubterranean houses were built on the same thermodynamic principle in that a long, sloping passage was dug down from the surface and under the walls of the house (also called igloo) so that the entrance was at the lowest point in the floor, again trapping the cold air in the passage or at floor level. Across the back of the main structure, or in some cases around the edge, were the sleeping benches, raised considerably above floor level. These houses were of course oblong or square rather than round and were inhabited for up to ten months of the year. Only in the Subarctic southwestern area did the houses have direct entrances through the roof from the outside, for in these areas there was no need for a "cold trap."

At the other end of the Eskimos' range, both the Polar Eskimos of northern Greenland and the majority of Eskimos of south and western Greenland normally built stone houses rather than igloos. The southern Greenlanders built large stone houses, also utilizing whalebone and sod, which somewhat resembled the wooden houses of western Alaska. These more permanently settled populations also lived in a less severe climate, near more constantly abundant resources. In all Eskimo areas buildings larger than domestic households were to be found, built according to the local technologies. These *kashgi, karigi*, or *qaggi* have been called ceremonial houses, men's houses, or meeting houses according to the functions emphasized in each particular locality.

All Eskimo groups used tents in the summer when they were more nomadic. The use of the igloo as the main living quarters was probably a recent innovation, for throughout the central Arctic semisubterranean houses were pre- and protohistorically inhabited; these turf-covered houses were made of whalebone, stone, or occasionally wood. Though the present Eskimos identify these houses as those of the mythical Tunit, they were probably inhabited by the direct ancestors of the present Eskimos, the Thule Eskimos, who depended far more on hunting the large whales than did the historical populations.

In the use of materials and technology, the division of labor was quite sharp. Generally the women were responsible for and used those things to do with the inside of the house such as maintaining the lamp, cooking, making clothes, sewing boots, the final apportionment of animal products, etc. Thus women dealt mainly with the technology of the skin and soft stone complex, with the end products of hunting, and with the gathering of vegetable products such as berries and seaweed for food and dry grass for lamp wicks. The woman's major tools, the ivory needles and their sinew threads, the semicircular woman's knife (*ulu*), and the scrapers, etc., were made from harder materials but their manufacture was usually done by the men.

The men's material world comprised tools and instruments of the outside, those concerned with hunting, production and manufacture, movement, and the ice, snow, bone-horn-antler, stone, and wood complexes. For instance, they build the frames of the kayaks and *umiaks* and the women covered them with skins; they made and erected the tent poles and the women put on the skin cover; they made and used the ubiquitous stone-tipped harpoons, spears, and arrows, and they used the long-bladed forms of knives, while the women handled the final distribution of the products of the hunt. The men built the main structure of the igloos and the women chinked them to make them airtight.

We might pursue our dualistic symbolism by saying that the men were concerned with the hard, pointed, cutting and thrusting materials of the outside mobile world, whereas the women were responsible for the softer, pliable, enclosing materials of the inside world. Even the dwelling spaces themselves were divided half and half into the soft-covered sleeping platform, primarily the domain of women, and the colder floor and storage area. We might extend the simile through other aspects of life—for example, color symbolism—and suggest that even the material of the living spaces can be mapped as a symbolic microcosm of the whole world with its obvious dichotomies to show the Eskimos as an "edge" people.

SOCIOECONOMIC ORGANIZATION

The Annual Cycle

It has long been known that the single major feature of Eskimo social organization was the annual cycle of movement between camps, which involved the splitting up of large groups to smaller ones and even to nuclear family households and reunion again in a fairly regular way throughout the year. This cycle of changing socioeconomic organization was forced upon the Eskimos by the variation in the nature and location of many of the resources at different times of year. The annual cycle therefore varied greatly from area to area depending upon the local ecological circumstances and specializations. The most nomadic groups, found among the more "typical" Eskimos of the central Canadian Arctic, depended on poor, scattered resources, and they moved six or more times a year; the more permanently settled Eskimos of the richer and more temperate areas of southwestern Alaska moved only between two locations and spent at least nine months of the year in the major large village. The great number of variations in annual cycles and resource strategies at different times of year, across the whole Arctic, is well illustrated in the comparative series of charts by E. M. Weyer.[3]

In general we may think of Eskimo social organization in terms of their graded series of units. Eskimos have no "tribes" in the sense of territorially and politically unified and identified groups. Eskimos identify themselves and others according to the locations where they usually live, by suffixing "-*miut*" (the people of) to any geographical

---

[3] E. M. Weyer, *The Eskimos* (New Haven: Yale University Press, 1932), pp. 80–84.

name. The people of an area who felt themselves to be a unity through their kinship connections and their at least annual coresidence may be called a band; such groups of people formed more permanent villages in western Alaska and Greenland or temporary villages in the central Arctic, comprised of sixty to three hundred people who were probably related to each other through bilateral kinship reckoning. There was sometimes a core kin group consisting of a powerful family whose relatives decided to live with them, and other families with less significant economic connections might attach themselves to this group (discussed further later in this chapter). The members of a band lived together in the largest unit of the annual cycle, usually the winter camp or village, for a few or many months of the year depending upon the area. The next level unit we may call camps and these varied most in that the member households of a camp might at one time of year constitute the whole band but at other times of the yearly cycle the group might split up to form smaller and smaller camps, occasionally down to the level of a single household.

The next level of social organization, the household, usually included the nuclear family of parents and their children, but quite often also contained aged grandparents, newly married children and their spouses and children, and sometimes more distant relatives or unfortunates who had no family. Though the household varied from the minimal nuclear family to quite large extended families in some areas, residence of a single individual or even one adult male and his or her children was quite rare and usually temporary because the division of labor required that an economic unit be minimally based upon at least one adult male and one adult female. Within the household the adult men and women made decisions within their own spheres, but the males probably had more important overall decisions about movement and economic strategies.

The camps and villages usually had a *de facto* leader, whose experience and seniority led his advice to be heeded by most of the other members, though this was rarely obligatory. There was little formal differentiation in terms of rich and poor but obviously some people were more successful than others. In the more permanent villages of western Alaska the leader or advisor may have been considered a "chief" in that he had more formal authority in social, ritual, and economic affairs and was more likely to retain his position permanently and perhaps even pass it on to his son. *Umialiks* usually constituted one kind of *de facto* camp or band leader. It should also be stated at this point that religious leaders, shamans (*angakuk*), were present in many villages and bands. They also exercised a certain kind of leadership function in the community in that their superior control over the supernatural put the rest of the community in fear of them or at least in debt to them. Shamans may not have been liked, but they were always important people and exercised considerable control over the lives of all the individuals in their area. Occasionally secular leaders and shamans belonged to the same close family, or even more rarely were the same person, in which case the small family or the powerful individual exercised much greater "political" control over the rest of the people. In these rare cases incipient class differences may have developed within the population, with some people serving others, and social and economic affairs running on a much less flexible basis In any case, both the secular leader and the shaman tended to oversee many of the socioeconomic relationships in the village, such as the apportionment of big game, the organization of cooperative hunts, the arbitration of quarrels, and the relationship between men and animals and the supernatural as represented in the many taboos which all Eskimo groups observed.

Let us examine two divergent examples of Eskimo socioeconomic organization and annual cycle, each of which was typical within its area but neither of which should be taken as prototypical of all Eskimos.

Taking the popularly best-known Eskimos, the igloo-living peoples of the seacoast of the central Canadian Arctic, we may start with the winter phase. At a geographical location near expanses of *tuvak* where many seal breathing holes were found, rather large aggregations (up to a hundred people) lived together in their snowhouses for a few months, with the men constantly migrating to the productive areas and coming back with their sea mammals. As the days grew longer and the weather improved in March and April, the large camp split up and each subcamp, often an extended family unit, built smaller igloo villages at strategic points along the coast. From here they continued to hunt seals through the ice and, as it got warmer, basking seals on the surface of the ice. At the same time sea ice became less extensive and walrus hunting took place by boat at the far edge in the open sea. This cooperative effort required the services of the men of a number of households and continued until the *tuvak* ice broke up in June or July. In the same period of the early spring some of the caribou migrated and approached the area in larger numbers during this season. Some of the more active men may have gone on a cooperative caribou hunt over the inland snows, dragging the caribou back to the coastal camps.

By May or June warm sun and winds often caved in the roofs of the igloos, but these were covered with skins to form a modified kind of dwelling called *qarmat*. By early summer, however, when living in igloos became impossible, sealskin tents were erected on patches of land that were bare of snow. The rivers began to run fast and salmon and char fishing at weirs and by leister became important. The coastal camps may have split further as families wandered to suitable places along the coast or to inland rivers and lakes for fishing, hunting, and gathering birds' eggs. The dog sleds were put on blocks until the next winter and the dogs were fitted with backpacks to help move the family belongings. The "richer" men refurbished their large *umiaks* and transported their whole extended families or camps to inland fishing sites or coastal hunting places. From these latter places the men hunted singly or in small groups from their kayaks, harpooning the relatively abundant seals in the water. By the end of the summer, many families left the coast and moved with their tents and paraphernalia inland to fish and engage in the most important caribou hunting of the year. These were usually large cooperative hunts which caught the massed caribou as they began to migrate south, killing them, caching their meat, but most importantly, getting many skins in the best condition so that new clothes could be made for the coming winter. Caribou hunting continued into the fall as long as the herds were around, and the Eskimos were loath to return to the coast until the stormy fall was over and the new sea ice was strong enough to go *maupuk* hunting again.

Thus in early winter the large winter villages reassembled and reactivated social and ceremonial life, but the Eskimos braced themselves, especially during bad weather, against near and actual starvation. Dog sleds were refurbished, the dogs were better fed on seal meat and fat to strengthen them for their winter tasks, and the women completed the new sets of garments for their families. During the late fall and difficult periods in the winter sociopsychological conflicts and illness most often appeared, probably from unspoken tensions and apprehensions about their very livelihood.

The Eskimos of Subarctic southwestern Alaska, such as the Chugach and the Konyag, illustrate a second type of social organization and annual cycle. The climate was less harsh and the far more abundant resources allowed population densities ten to fifty times greater than those for the central groups just described. Villages, usually larger in terms of the number of houses, were permanent in that the large, rectangular, wooden structures covered with sod remained the same year after year. These villages were found (and this paragraph is more of a reconstruction because the aboriginal patterns had been disturbed far earlier) near the mouths of major rivers and richly endowed coastal points in the area. They were inhabited for at least nine months of the year, for nomadism was not essential for existence most of the time.

Since very little sea ice and no *tuvak* occurred in this area, sea mammals could be hunted from kayaks nearly all year. During the winter and especially in the spring and early summer, the men hunted sea otters, fur seals, and whales from one- and often two-holed kayaks, though only the best men, knowledgeable in the appropriate rituals, dared hunt the largest mammals. During the summer the men commonly went deep-sea fishing for halibut and cod, but some families migrated with tents up the large rivers to net and trap the abundant migratory salmon. Throughout the year, but especially in the fall, plant foods were more available in this area than in others, and berries, tubers, roots, and even some kelp and seaweed were harvested by women. A great variety of shellfish available along the coast could be gathered, especially in the winter when other resources diminished or the stormy weather discouraged sea hunting. The hunting of land animals, though not so important, could be undertaken throughout the year. Bears and mountain goats were hunted and trapped as were small land animals, including many Subarctic species hardly known in other areas, such as the marten and mink.

Rather than a constant splitting up and coming together of groups, we may think of these people as having permanent social organizations as well as dwelling structures. Villages were larger, people were in constant interaction for most of the year, and more formalized social relationships were found. There were generally village chiefs or near-chiefs who might pass the office on hereditarily. Such chiefs might have larger houses with extended families living in them, and their houses might also be used as ceremonial centers for the more frequent and elaborate ritual life of the winters. Most Alaskan Eskimo villages had a ceremonial or "men's house" (*kashgi*) that formed the center of village ritual and social activities and often served as sleeping places for men.

In these areas hierarchical ranks emerged by which people were often hereditarily assigned to positions of power or, at the other end of the scale, servitude. The servants or slaves, often captured in warfare which occurred commonly in the area, performed many of the menial tasks around the village, their lives treated very cheaply by their "owners." Thus we can see that in many ways the annual cycle and social organization of these peoples resembles their not-too-distant cousins, the Aleuts (see Chapter 11).

Kinship and Social Structure

The classical features of the Eskimo type of social organization have often been said to resemble in many ways those of Euro-American kinship structure:

> The Eskimo type includes all societies with Eskimo cousin terminology and no exogamous unilinear kin groups. In addition, as theory leads us to expect, it is characterized by monogamy, independent nuclear families, lineal terms for aunts and nieces, and a bilateral extension of incest taboos, and the frequent presence of such bilateral kin groups as kindreds and demes though these may often be unreported.[4]

Murdock goes on to state that variations in this basic structure may be brought about by rules of postmarital residence other than the normal neolocal one, by polygyny, by extended families, etc. This picture is based on the earlier excellent ethnographies of the central Canadian Eskimos. The heart of the system, represented by the bilateral kinship terminology, "the Eskimo type," differentiates siblings from cousins, and uncles and aunts from parents and from each other (Figure 12.2).

Such a system would lead us to expect equal reckoning of degrees of relationship on either side—bilaterally, that is, through both mother

---

[4] G. P. Murdock, *Social Structure* (New York: Macmillan, 1949), pp. 226–228.

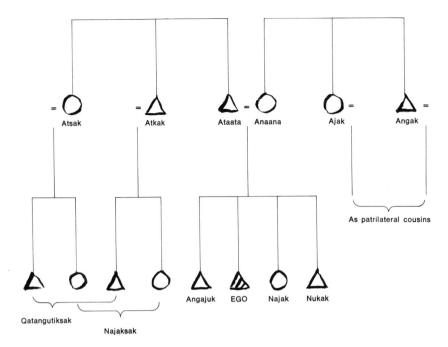

Figure 12.2 Bilateral kinship terminology (the Eskimo type) which differentiates siblings from cousins, and uncles and aunts from parents and from each other.

and father—and perhaps statistically equal choices of residence and alliance with either the mother's group or the father's group. Such bilaterally organized societies are said to be most amenable to flexible social structures, which is necessary for and found throughout most Eskimo groups.

Recent comparative evidence, however, has shown us that such a simple basis by no means accounts for the majority of Eskimo social organizations, and that strict bilateralism, even in the central area, usually occurs to a lesser extent than the tendency toward emphasizing kinship relationships on the father's side. This trend occurs not only in the kinship terminology system but also in a general tendency toward patrilocal residence and kinship groups composed of fathers and their married sons or sibling groups of brothers.

The greatest degree of variation and deviance from the bilateral norm has been found among the more densely populated and permanently settled peoples of western Alaska. A well-documented example is the social organization of the St. Lawrence Island Eskimos as reported by Hughes.[5] These Eskimos do not have the familiar bilateral cousin terminology; although they usually differentiate between siblings and cousins, they lump cross-cousins together and use different sets of terms for maternal and paternal parallel cousins—in fact, paternal cous-

---

[5] C. C. Hughes, "An Eskimo Deviant from the 'Eskimo' Type of Social Organization," *American Anthropologist*, 60:1140–1147 (1958).

ins are often called by the same terms as siblings, emphasizing the closeness of the male/male link through the father (Figure 12.3).

The kinship terminology appears to reflect an "un-Eskimo" social organization, differentiating greatly between the relatives on the father's and the mother's side in actual behavior and residential rules. Patrilateral relatives are more important and the kinship terminology for people on this side is more greatly developed. The underlying bilateral reckoning of relatives by all Eskimo groups leads to a vague aggregation which we often call the "kindred" (i.e., those people to whom one considers oneself related; corresponding to the concept of "relatives" in English). The St. Lawrence Island Eskimos, however, have an overriding organization which Hughes has translated as "patriclan," and from birth all individuals belong to the clan of their fathers. Male members of these clans remain coresidential throughout their lives, but the women leave to join the clans of their husbands. Unlike other areas, these clans are not exogamous. Under conditions of stability all Eskimo groups would probably tend to emphasize patrilineal kinship and to establish patrilocal residences because the cooperative productive group is based on the number of males, and in a kin-based world this generally means groups of brothers. Furthermore, it is more advantageous for men to live permanently in one area during their lives, for a man raised in an area knows its ecological productive possibilities best, whereas a stranger faces great disadvantage when outside his own territory. Even within the northwestern Alaskan area, Heinrich[6] has shown how variations in kinship terminology and in kinship relationships can be correlated with the local ecological imperatives and the consequent need for certain kinds of cooperation. Damas[7] has shown that there is considerable variation in Eskimo kinship terminology within the various subregions of the "typical" central Canadian Eskimos. These variations involve deviations from the "Eskimo type" particularly in overriding the distinction between siblings and cousins and in differentiating matrilateral from parallel cousins, often emphasizing the patrilateral consanguineal kin group. He emphasizes that perhaps one cannot explain all variations on the basis of functional-adaptive correlations, but that some of the variations may result from "historical accident" or "microdiffusion."

Let us now demonstrate, in one case of "typical" central Eskimo social organization, how the kinship terminology and social relationships are functionally adaptive for the kind of existence that requires constant splitting and coming together of groups and dependence upon a flexible set of ties to other bands and camps outside one's own area, whom one may have to visit or depend upon in times of local privation.

[6] A. Heinrich, "The Structural Features of Northwestern Alaskan Eskimo Kinship," *Southwestern Journal of Anthropology*, 16:110–126 (1960).

[7] D. Damas, *Igluligmiut Kinship and Social Groupings: A Structural Approach* (Ottawa: National Museum of Canada, Bulletin No. 196, 1963), especially pp. 189–212.

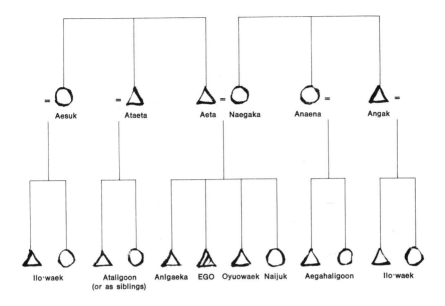

Figure 12.3 A deviation in kinship terminology which distinguishes paternal parallel cousins and emphasizes the male/male link through the father.

At the same time, minor variations from the strictly bilateral system are quite relevant to a patrilateral-patrilocal bias where any degree of stability may hold.

In this social organization, diagrammed in Figure 12.4, postmarital residence is matri-patrilocal, whereby the man goes to live in or near the household of his new bride and hunts with his father-in-law for a year or more, at least until the first baby is born. Thus he will be incorporated into his father-in-law's camp and area for a relatively short period of his life, one in which he is ill-at-ease and is in a subordinate position while proving himself. Ideally and in fact, the young couple move back to the husband's father's territory or camp for the rest of their lives, returning presumably to an area familiar to the man. Since most of the essential tasks of women do not depend upon location, they can be performed equally well in anybody's camp. Given such a residence rule, a man will have in his own camp his father (if alive), his brother and his family and their descendants, and most probably his father's brother and his wife and children. His father's sister will live in another camp, having moved there fairly soon after her marriage; his mother's brother will live in yet another camp with his own brother and father and children; and his mother's sister, if she has been married for more than a few years, will be living in another camp with her husband and his family.

Thus children raised in any given camp are likely to know best (apart from the members of their own household) their father's brother

Generation	Own (Father's) Camp				Other Camps			
	Male		**Female**		**Male**		**Female**	
+2 GrParents	Ataatacia		Aanak*		Ataatacia		Anaanacia	

Generation	Own Household Male	Own Household Female	Other House Male	Other House Female	FaSi Camp Male	FaSi Camp Female	MoSi Camp Male	MoSi Camp Female	MoBr Camp Male	MoBr Camp Female
+1 Parents	Ataata	Anaana	Atkak	Arngnajuk*	Ningauk	Atsak	Ningauk	Ajak	Angak	Ukuak

Generation			Male	Female
+0 Older	Angajuk	Najak	Male	Female
+0 Younger	Nukak		Qatangutiksak	Najaksak

Figure 12.4 Kinship terminology and residential alignments of Ego, an unmarried male (using terms presented in Figure 12.2). Note that the patrilocal, patrilateral bias of the special terms for females aanak *and* arngnajuk *(indicated by asterisks), who are found only in Ego's (father's) camp, is also reflected in the affinal kinship terminology used by married men and women. (After Graburn, Taqagmiut Eskimo Kinship Terminology, 1964, Fig. 6, p. 84.)*

and his wife and children. And perhaps for short periods of time when they are younger, they will know well their father's sister and her husband, and occasionally their mother's sister if she is unmarried or newly married, and their mother's brother and/or father who remain at the camp that their mother originally came from. Siblings living in the household of the growing Eskimos are terminologically distinguished from cousins living in other households, for extended family residence is rarely permanent. Among all the cousins, father's brother's children are most likely to be coresident in the camp, at least for certain times of the year, and in many areas this is reflected by their terminological differentiation from all other cousins who may live in nearby camps and who may visit or be visited by the household in which Ego lives. Thus a person grows up having a series of graduated consanguineal ties within his own camp and with camps in adjacent areas.

As he goes through his life cycle the individual develops further ties. For instance, when a man's sister marries, her new husband will join them for a time before returning with her and their children to his original camp; the man's brother may go to live in another camp

with his new bride and then return later with his young family to
his patrilocal camp; and later, of course, a man's children marry and
form further links to other camps.

The rule of exogamy is not well demarcated in Eskimo culture.
Although Eskimos usually distinguish siblings from cousins terminologically, this perhaps reflects the nature of the residence groups rather
than the allowability of sexual access. Most Eskimo groups permit sexual
access to first cousins, but they discourage it. Marriage preferences,
often arranged by parents during their children's youth, often reflect
the desire to create or cement ties with more distant families through
marriage with distant relatives. Endogamy does occur but the majority
of the population frown upon it. On the other hand, although it might
be advantageous to have alliances through marriage with very distant
groups, the Eskimos' great fear of strangers and the risk involved usually
prevent such arrangements. Thus marriages most often take place between distant relatives or not-too-distant nonrelatives.

Partnerships

A major characteristic of Eskimo social organization, the partnership,
enables Eskimos to extend their ties and to create trustworthy relationships through alliances outside the circle of *ilagiit* (bilaterally reckoned kinsmen). Throughout the range of Eskimo groups various forms
of partnership receive more or less formal or ritual recognition.[8] In the
most well-known form—wife exchange—two friends who are almost
always nonkinsmen agree to swap wives for a period of time, sometimes
to emphasize their friendship but often connected with a practical necessity such as being able to travel with a nonpregnant woman. The
children of both couples involved in an exchange relationship are considered to be full siblings to each other, thus extending the number
of people that these individuals will later be able to count as close
relatives.

A number of other forms of non-kin-based partnerships occur
throughout the Arctic but vary in concept and function from place
to place. Very commonly partnerships are based on friendship and economic cooperation, and the formal social recognition of two men as
partners serves to bind an already existing relationship. Such men become partners often for life, and must help each other, generously share
their goods, and may even practice wife exchange, though this last is
not the main purpose of such relationships. Partners may have to defend
each other and even avenge the other's death in case of murder. Such
economically based partnerships may extend across local and even tribal
boundaries, especially in the western Arctic where long-distance trade
occurs more frequently. Men inherit or create trading partnerships with
other men who have access to different ecological resources. Whenever
the two groups meet, which may be at specified annual times, each

[8] Lee Guemple (ed.), *Alliance in Eskimo Society* (Proceedings of the American Ethnological Society, 1972).

man seeks out his trading partner to exchange, for instance, products of the land for products of the sea, without haggling or hostility, even though each individual may be hostile to or suspicious of other members of the out-group. In some places in western and southwestern Alaska such trading partnerships extend even to non-Eskimos with whom contact is not too hostile.

Partnerships may function in other ways too. For example, very common across the Arctic are forms of "joking relationships," which may or may not be combined with the preceding kinds of partnerships. Such men—who may have formed friendships in their youth or who may actually inherit joking relationships from their fathers, as is obligatory between the children of half-cross-cousins on Nunivak Island— must constantly insult each other. They often compose songs and rhymes to disparage each other and sing them in public without getting angry in return. This latter type has often been called "song (contest) partnership" and in the central Arctic such a pair are known as *illuriik* (see also the following section on "Social Control").

A further means of extending friendly and more or less permanent relationships to nonkinsmen is illustrated by the very common "namesake" system found throughout most of the Arctic. Two people with the same name call each other *saunik* (bone) or *atitsiak* (good name) and have a special relationship based on the fact that the Eskimos believe that one of the souls that governs an individual's personality is attached to his name; thus two people with the same name are in a way spiritually identical. If an Eskimo enters a new and distant village and feels uneasy in the social group, he strikes up a special relationship with a namesake, thus creating an ally. Perhaps more important, he can then put himself in this person's place in the local kinship system and call upon his namesake's relatives for aid and comfort in the same way as the real relative would. This leads to a wide network of often incongruous relationships, for names are not sex-specific. Thus one may hear an old woman calling a much younger man "my mother" because the young man has the same name as the old woman's deceased mother. All kinds of joking and friendship develop where otherwise hostility or awkwardness might exist.

Though the kinship system forms the continuing basis of Eskimo social organization, Eskimo social and ecological imperatives often disrupt the stable group and make the finding of allies a crucial determinant of life or death. The hazards of the environmental supply and the relatively weak social control (see below) often create circumstances wherein the normal social ties and the first line of economic cooperation break down. Those with secondary or tertiary relationships to fall back on are the ones who survive.

Leadership and Social Control
The annual cycle and unforeseen ecological circumstances force the constant splitting up and coming together of small groups of Eskimos.

Even groups that reunite regularly at times of the year are not "territorial"—that is, there are no inherited or permanent rights to the resources of the land and the sea. Thus the Eskimos do not have a territorially based political system, and the groups in which they live have relatively little continuity or rigid organization. As the reader will perceive, these statements apply only partially to the more densely and permanently populated Subarctic areas at the western and eastern extremes of the Eskimo range.

Aside from kinship, very few recognized statuses exist in Eskimo society, and none of these are primarily political or legal in nature. Secular leaders—*umialiks* and *isumataks* (advisors, thinkers)—are leaders primarily because they can bestow economic benefits upon their followers. They may be "rich" or skillful men who can organize hunts, advise on seasonal movements, and oversee the important and equitable distribution of game products. As senior males they usually represent authority in their own nuclear or extended families, but their sway is only voluntary over other adults. Their social-control functions, primarily in the economic sphere, usually take the form of advice which may or may not be heeded by other adults or families. All senior men and women, however, do have authority and command respect among children, regardless of kin ties. More specific Eskimo social controls are exercised by the shaman (*angakuk*), and the many taboos that he oversees. Though these taboos regulate social intercourse to some extent, they mostly concern ecological imperatives and the uncertain, dangerous forces of the supernatural.

Eskimo life at the best of times is peaceful, cooperative, and joyous, embracing much that the Western mind often envisages as the "simple, happy life of the close-to-nature primitive!" As we have seen, however, the best of times are frequently interspersed with the worst of times. Two constantly recurring anxieties pervade Eskimo life: the anxiety about food and material well-being, which are governed by the unpredictable forces of climatic and temporal accident; and, especially for the men, the anxiety about one's performance in the prestige competition for the acquisition of women (spouses) and many children, especially males. These two themes often come together in that the successful hunter can provide the most necessities and hence support the largest number of wives and offspring. Thus the competition between men in one sphere relates to competition in the other.

In every family or camp group, physical skill and factors of personality allow the emergence of *de facto* leaders, as described earlier. Though these men lead, they also instill fear and jealousy. Thus others in the prestige "rat race" try to compete or even overthrow the dominating persons. If they do not succeed, they may acquiesce to their lower status for the sake of economic security or they may leave and join other groups in distant areas where they may be more successful. At the other end of the scale are the relative incompetents who cannot perform successfully in these two spheres. Women also compete against each other for desirable men and for many healthy offspring. Those at the lowest end of the scale are often felt to be burdens on the community; they become the butt of jokes or may even become the servants of others. If they cannot bear their lot, or if they unexpectedly fail in their endeavors, they may abandon the group or commit suicide.

Various forms of what to us would be unacceptable violence are condoned under certain circumstances by nearly all Eskimo groups. This violence includes infanticide—particularly of female children, the killing of the weaker of twins, the killing or assisting in the suicide of aged people who can no longer compete and feel themselves to be a burden, suicide, and cannibalism under starvation conditions. People who perform such acts receive no punishment, but other common forms of violence, seen as a threat to the group or to an individual, may incur preventive measures or revenge. For example, the stealing of provisions and sometimes equipment may be excused in cases of need, but the stealing of wives or even the threat of unsanctioned seduction is a cause for action. Most violence and murder in Eskimo society, and probably most suicide, springs from the competition for women. Men often try to take, physically or otherwise, the wives or women of other men. Some kill to do it, whereas others hope to get away with it nonviolently. Before or after the fact, the offended man may try, with least personal risk, to kill his rival; sometimes a noted philanderer will be killed by the other men in the group, all acting to protect themselves. Killings ("justified" or otherwise) bring on further violence and killing for in many areas the partners, close relatives, or even the children of the dead man may try to avenge the murder at any time later. This leads to long-term feuds which often end the life of the most productive and essential people in the group—the young and able men. In some areas every single adult male has been involved in a killing at some time or another in his life, and this kind of behavior probably represents as much a threat to the continued existence of viable Eskimo social groups as the many hazards of the environment. Thus we can see that the creation of alliances and relationships to as wide a circle of people as possible, as described earlier, becomes a valuable asset.

At the best of times nearly everyone in the group has security, but anxiety over food rarely disappears for long and crisis occurs frequently. This factor, combined with the social instability mentioned earlier, accounts for much of the breaking up of Eskimo social groups and even the hostility and termination of such close relationships as siblinghood or marriage.

There come times, particularly during periods of starvation, when the rule is "every man for himself." The living eat the dead, those with some provisions hide them from their closest kin in order to survive, and the more mobile and fit leave the less well-equipped to fend for themselves or die, and marriages and families break up, never to come together again. The mother-child bond is probably as strong and protective as any, but during the worst times the very young die or are killed and eaten by the most able members of the society, the old people commit suicide or are killed, and in the end even the fit adults wait for each other to die so that the survivors may eat—and sometimes they do not wait. Apparently women generally last longer than men, possibly because of their metabolic nature or because the men must make more strenuous efforts to continue to provide food for the crisis-stricken group. Thus small groups of women occasionally wind up eating their husbands and are later themselves found in the last stages of starvation.

The pervasive, well-known threat of the escalation of violence into killing and murder leads to other mechanisms of conflict resolution or avoidance in many cases of minor social irritations. We have already mentioned how the unsuccessful or unpopular may leave the group to join other groups or even try to live by themselves. The reverse of this is ostracism, whereby the majority of the group avoid or even secretly abandon the offender, though the latter may rejoin the group later if he or she survives and ceases to offend. Constant offense usually leads to killing. Another reaction, however, is to pretend that the problem does not exist—not by ignoring the offender completely, but by protecting one's interest, such as wife, food, or social group, when the social irritant is present.

Quite often the shaman was called in to deal with the offender through supernatural means by finding out if the offender had broken taboos or by trying to perform evil magic to harm the offender or threat. Of course shamans themselves were very often major social irritants or offenders, such as thieves and adulterers, in their own group, but fear of them was such that very little could be done about it apart from leaving the area.

In some areas the partnership labeled earlier as a "joking relationship" developed from its primary function of entertainment into a social-control mechanism. Two people with a disagreement or quarrel would be encouraged to make up insulting songs about each other and perform these in turn in front of the rest of the group; the rest of the community would then choose the winner. Another form of usually nonfatal competition involved boxing contests, in which two men who disliked each other or merely competed for prestige took turns in hitting each other as hard as they could on the side of the head. The last man standing won, and thus gained both the prestige of the social group and implicitly the judgment that his view was justified in the quarrel. Other more common but less drastic forms of social control included the constant scolding of young offenders by elders and leaders in the community, particularly members of their own family, to make them obedient. This often succeeded in minor cases or with relatively unassertive young people, but occasionally it led the young person to leave the group or commit suicide. And constant malicious gossip, in which one heard about the social offenses of all one's neighbors, sometimes brought resolving mechanisms to bear, but much of the gossip merely represented a spicy way of passing the time and expressing commitment to Eskimo moral values.

Thus Eskimo social life was rife with competition and violence, but perhaps somewhat less so in those areas in Subarctic southwest Alaska where the central core of the social organization had more rigidity and continuity. In these latter areas, however, other forms of violence commonly occurred, particularly warfare and feuding with neighboring out-groups. These groups fought other Eskimo groups not only for prestige and sometimes for material gain, but to acquire captives as wives or servants. We have already seen in Chapter 10 the widespread and sometimes organized nature of warfare and hostility between nearly all neighboring Eskimo and Indian groups.

RELIGIOUS IDEOLOGY AND ORGANIZATION

What we would call the "supernatural" played a very large part in the traditional life of all Eskimo groups. The distinction between the natural and supernatural, however, was not nearly so sharply defined and control over both spheres of life was tenuous for the majority of Eskimos. Only the shamans had a positive control over supernatural forces and beings, the majority of Eskimos exercising a negative control by adhering to taboos whose infractions would bring severe supernatural sanction to themselves or even to the whole group. This section will not dwell at length on Eskimo religion because it has been well described elsewhere.[9]

There were many local and regional variations in Eskimo religious practices, beliefs, and personalities, but they revolved around the two major components: shamanism—the presence of a special status for one who has superior control over the supernatural; and animism—the belief that people, animals, inanimate objects, and the world in general are populated by spirits or souls which are important to Eskimo life. The names, appearance, and numbers of these spirits varied from area to area as did some of the conceptions of human souls; similarly the practices, status, and acquisition and degrees of shamanism varied from area to area but their fundamental nature was the same.

Each person was conceived of as a relatively unimportant physical body inhabited by a number of soul spirits. The most important spirit was the *tangnirk* (in eastern Arctic dialect) whose loss became a major cause of diseases or death. This soul spirit did not determine the individual's personality, but his existence; and after his death this soul went to reside in an extraterritorial afterworld, the nature of which usually

[9] See, for example, Margaret Lantis, "The Religion of the Eskimos," pp. 309–340 in Vergilius Ferm (ed.), *Forgotten Religions* (New York: Philosophical Library, 1950); Wendell H. Oswalt, *Alaskan Eskimos* (San Francisco: Chandler, 1967), Chap. 9; E. M. Weyer, *The Eskimos* (New Haven: Yale University Press, 1932), Chaps. 16–26.

depended on the individual's behavior during his lifetime. Thus these afterworlds were conceived of as a hierarchy from good to bad, and were often located in the heavens, near the surface of the earth, deep in the earth, or deep at the bottom of the sea, though the concepts were not exact and varied somewhat regionally. The individual's *atirk* (his name) represented the social aspects of the soul, for the possession of the name to some extent determined the individual's social personality and characteristics. These characteristics went with the name and were reincarnated time and time again. Thus when an individual died his *atirk* was let loose into the atmosphere, at which time it was potentially dangerous; shortly before or at birth, the mother or others present chose an *atirk* for the newborn child who would sometimes grow up in the social likeness of a deceased person. In the past, if someone led an unhappy life, they might change their name in order to acquire a more beneficial social personality. The name-soul belief accounts for the special relationship between two people who are *sauniriik* because they share the same name. A third kind of soul spirit was the breath-soul which left the body at death and disappeared without harm or destination; thus for both animals and humans we might translate this as "life." In addition to these individual soul spirits, parts of the body, particularly the joints, were said to be inhabited by *inua*, which literally means "its person." *Inua* were locationally fixed spirits that inhabited not only humans but animals and significant inanimate objects in the world too. The loss or angering of these could lead to illness and disaster.

All of these phenomena, which we must not look upon as "supernatural" because they were in fact the "nature" of things, existed inside (*ilu*) some thing or person. Their presence was normally accepted and their loss was a statement of abnormality. The whole world, however, was also conceived of as being inhabited by free-roaming spirits of the outside (*sila*), many of which were called *turngak* (or variations in the different dialects). *Turngak* could be large or small, could assume many appearances—natural or unnatural and awesome—and as a class could not be considered necessarily good or bad. The acquisition of personal *turngaks* represented the major avenue to becoming a shaman, for then the spirits would do one's bidding in controlling other elements of the supernatural world. Other *turngaks* were never personally acquired but were harmful when encountered; one might try to avoid them or use magic to keep them away, or wear amulets, not only for good luck but to prevent bad luck. Since *turngaks* very often became visible in animal form, one could not always be sure that one saw a "natural" animal or object or a *turngak* one. Much of the inexplicable was interpreted as being a *turngak*. In a few areas a very powerful *turngak* was elevated almost to the status of a deity and was believed to have control over much of the natural world such as animals and the weather. *Turngaks* occasionally assumed human form and unpopular or outcast people were even said to have married them and had children by them.

Many other classes of beings that we would call supernatural existed. For instance, other "humanoids" were *ijuruk*, the visible manifestations of the souls of dead people. Another class, *inuragulligak*, consisted of perfectly formed but very small Eskimo-like people who could be both benevolent or malevolent and who were endowed with great physical and supernatural powers. Eskimo mythology is full of stories about families or races of giants, misshapen humanoids, the former inhabitants of the area called *tunit* who were exceptionally strong but rather stupid, and man/animal transformations.

Most of the taboos in Eskimo society represented mechanisms to avoid angering the souls of the all-important animals or the spirits and deities that controlled the animals and the weather. Therefore personal and community disasters became expressions of the transgressions of taboos. In nearly all Eskimo areas, the supreme power, particularly over the sea and sea mammals, resided with an old and angry woman who lived somewhere deep in the sea. This woman, who according to myth was outcast as a young Eskimo girl, is often called *Sedna* in the literature, but it is unlikely that the Eskimos actually used this word for her; *Sedna* is probably a corruption of a term meaning "down at the bottom of." The ethnographic record shows that the name for her varies from area to area, but she is commonly called *nuliajuk* ("the one who is a wife/fornicates"), *arngnaluk* ("the big/bad woman"), *niqilik* ("there is food"), and *niqipvilik* ("there is a place for food"); the latter two names refer to the belief that in her igloo are found all the abundant animals of the sea.[10] The belief in the female undersea deity was strongest from north Alaska east through Greenland, and was entirely absent as a major feature in west Alaska and among the caribou Eskimo of the Canadian barren lands. More variable was a belief in another all-powerful spirit, who controlled the weather and sometimes land animals. This was *sila*, the "great outside," the weather. This more impersonal force had less direct concern with individual Eskimo's lives, but where anthropomorphized is seen as male, residing somewhere above.

The personality and individual origin of Eskimo shamans has been subject to some debate, but there is no overriding evidence that these people were "psychopathic" personalities as has often been alleged for Siberian shamans. No doubt shamans possessed powerful personalities, were extremely perceptive, and, though not necessarily likable, were capable of exercising leadership or control over others. Eskimos both feared shamans for their unique powers and welcomed them for their positive contributions. There was no one way by which Eskimos became shamans and both men and women practiced the art. In some areas young people specifically sought to acquire a familiar *turngak* since this was an absolute prerequisite to exercising the powers necessary for a shaman; this kind of spirit quest could be achieved by going off by one's self, hunting or meditating, and waiting for a dream, a vision,

---

[10] See especially Weyer, *op. cit.,* pp. 339–355.

or a sign with some message that one had more than ordinary powers. Equally common was the unintended acquisition of spirit power through personal circumstances such as starvation, isolation, accident, or illness. Shamans were often the children of shamans and thus perhaps were psychologically and socially more disposed to acquire the spirit power.

In any case, in order to become an accepted shaman, one had to learn the many practices at the hand of an established shaman by a relatively long-term apprenticeship. A shaman not only had to have a special relationship to the supernatural, through the ability to use his familiar spirits and to project his soul on flights, but also he had to be able to put on performances in front of the social group which would convince the community of his power and keep them entertained. These "tricks," probably learned from another shaman, were awe-inspiring and convincing. Though entertainment was one function of a shaman, all full-fledged shamans had to be able to benefit individuals or the community as a whole. In times of individual illness or crisis, they were called upon to cure, usually by asking verbally or by signs whether the particular individual or related individuals had broken a series of taboos recently and hence caused the misfortune; sometimes the person or even an object was "lifted" by a strap, and its lightness or heaviness gave a positive or negative answer. Sometimes the shaman cured by "sucking" a foreign body or spirit from the sick person; in other cases he might send his spirit or his soul to look for the errant soul of an ailing person. More critical was the shaman's performance on the behalf of the community as a whole when some general disaster of weather or game supply struck them. He would try to find out if one or more persons had broken some of the more important taboos—for instance, a woman hiding a miscarriage or a man using the same weapons to hunt both land and sea animals at certain times of the year. Even if he could diagnose the cause, very often the shaman had to send his soul on a flight to visit *arngnaluk* at the bottom of the sea and try to soothe and appease her to allow the seas to become calmer or the animals to return and make themselves available for the hunters. This dangerous and not always successful journey required considerable preparation, psychic energy, and cooperation from the local group. In those areas where this personage was not the supreme deity, the shaman, again going into a trance, would have to project his soul to appease the other controlling forces.

Shamans could be used on an individual "consultant" basis. Someone might ask them to perform magic against another person with whom they had quarreled, or to make a woman more willing or to make a wife pregnant or bear sons. They were usually paid for individual and sometimes community services in material goods. Shamans often used their powers for their own advancement; they might use evil magic by sending their familiar spirits to harm someone with whom they had quarreled or whose wife they wished to use. Generally speaking, therefore, ordinary Eskimos had considerable ambivalence toward shamans. Shamans might not be ordinarily successful men, but they sometimes formed alliances with such men, trading power for material goods. Occasionally such an alliance would be fused in that a very successful hunter and leader would also be a shaman, in which case he took an even more elevated status over his family and the other members of the community and could actively command the running of the social organization, rather than just advise. Such "un-Eskimo" organizations often produced very well-run but fear-ridden communities with stable but hierarchical social organizations and considerable economic success. They lasted, however, only as long as the leading individual kept his powers.

The more densely populated, stable communities of western and southwestern Alaska had a more complex social organization of religion. The annual cycle was punctuated by a series of gatherings or feasts wherein whole communities or neighboring communities joined together to perform rituals deemed necessary for the maintenance of ordinary successful life. At many of these the hosts put on performances using masks, each of which represented the *inua* of animals or the natural world, in order to please them and express the proper relationships between them. Considerable economic exchange and trade accompanied these rituals. One such feast in the Bering Sea area was called the "bladder feast" and the bladders of animals were kept throughout the year to be displayed at this ceremony. The bladders were believed to contain the souls of the deceased animals, so they were worshiped and appeased to thank the species for its bountifulness; after the ceremony the remains were put back in the sea. Also in this area there were more elaborate ceremonials involving commemoration of the dead; these elaborate feasts brought together the bereaved and encouraged the soul on its path to the afterworld. It is not surprising that in this western area is found the highest development of the "ceremonial house" complex. These larger house structures called *kashgi* or *karigi* in the west (and *qaggi* in the eastern Arctic) formed the center of village ceremonial and social life; in some areas the men slept in these houses most of the time and they were sometimes called "men's houses." In the central and eastern Arctic the *qaggi* was constructed as a huge igloo on top of dwelling igloos in the middle of the winter and was used for community games and shamans' rituals for a relatively short period of time. During this period the one major annual ceremony, "the midwinter feast" (*qitingirk*), took place; people from the whole area gathered to feast, play competitive games, watch shamans' performances, and exchange wives in the "putting out the lamps" ritual.

Eskimo religion, like that of most other peoples, functioned to restore balance when the outside forces of the world threatened and to provide mechanisms to reduce personal anxiety. Though technologically sophisticated, the ecological pressures on the Eskimos were overpowering and unpredictable. The Eskimos never believed that they had anything like complete control over the world around them or even the animals they depended upon, and the individual Eskimo had relatively little power, save in warding off certain kinds of evil. Supernatural power was channeled through the shaman, a specialist who represented the community in bargaining with the usually malevolent outside forces of the world. Eskimo mythology and creation stories explained the relationships between all things without delving too deeply. A major function of this large body of folklore was to provoke humor and thereby lessen the ever-present tensions about the nature and actions of the inevitable, imponderable forces of the world.

ANNOTATED BIBLIOGRAPHY

The literature on the Eskimos is so vast that we can mention only the most important and accessible works in this brief section. Further important references to Eskimo culture will be found in the bibliography to Chapter 13; other ethnographic information appears in the many films listed in the "Guide to Ethnographic Films" at the end of this book. For a deeper and broader knowledge of the literature one must examine the bibliographies of the following works and, ultimately, the voluminous *Arctic Bibliography*. General books on the Eskimos as well as more specialized works suffer from uneven concentration on specific areas to the neglect of other important ones, as we shall note.

Perhaps the best overall introduction to Eskimo culture, including language history and prehistory, remains *The Eskimos* by the Danish anthropologist Kaj Birket-Smith (Frome: Butler and Tanner; published in Danish and translated into English in 1936; enlarged and revised edition, 1959). Though the author's ideas on prehistory are no longer in favor, the general treatment is excellent save for, perhaps, the understandable emphasis on Greenland culture. Perhaps a better, though more dated, source book limited to traditional Eskimo culture is E. M. Weyer's *The Eskimos* (New Haven: Yale University Press, 1932), which is a massive comparative compilation of all previous sources on Eskimo culture, though it is weak in the areas of social organization and in the paucity of information on the western Alaskan area. Readers might also consult N. Giffen, *The Roles of Men and Women in Eskimo Culture* (Chicago: University of Chicago Press, 1930) for a short but detailed comparative work on aspects of Eskimo social organization. An older but still illuminating secondary source is M. Mauss, "Essai sur les variations saisonnières des sociétés Eskimo," *L'Année Sociologique* (Paris, 1904).

The Eskimo language was first well described and analyzed by the Danish authorities in S. Kleinschmidt, *Den Grønlandske Ordbog* (Copenhagen, 1871), and W. Thalbitzer, "A Phonetical Study of the Eskimo Language," *Meddelelser om Grønland*, 31 (abbreviated to *MoG* from here on) (Copenhagen, 1904), and other works. M. Swadesh has provided a short structural analysis of the Eskimo language in his "South Greenlandic (Eskimo)," Chapter 2 in C. Osgood (ed.), *Linguistic Struc-*

tures of Native America (New York: Viking Fund, 1946). There are a number of grammars, dictionaries, and guides to the Eskimo language for those who wish to learn a little bit; we will pass over the earlier ones such as those of Peck and Thibert to mention the two most useful recent authorities (both restricted to Canadian Eskimo dialect): A. E. Spalding's *Salliq: An Eskimo Grammar* (Ottawa: DIAND, Education Branch, 1969) is a low level but useful introduction to spoken Eskimo for the English speaker; more thorough are the works for French-speaking scholars by L. Schneider, OMI, including his *Dictionnaire Alphabét-ico-Syllabique du Langage Esquimau de l'Ungava* (Travaux et Documents du Centre d'Études Nordiques, 3, Quebec: Les Presses de l'Université Laval, 1966), his dictionary of infixes and his Eskimo grammar.

The focus and brevity of this book prevent us from listing at length the many works on the fascinating prehistory and archeology of the Eskimos, which exhibit the greatest time depth and cultural complexity in western Alaska. Aspects of this area have been covered by such authorities as Ackerman, M. M. Campbell, Chard, H. B. Collins, Giddings, Harp, Larsen, Laughlin, Rainey, and others; the central Canadian Eskimos have been explored in the works of W. E. Taylor, McNeish, Mathiassen, and others; and the prehistory of the Greenland area by Meldgaard, Steensby, Mathiassen, and others. For more exact references or for recent overviews of the field the reader should consult H.-G. Bandi, *Eskimo Prehistory* (College, Alaska: University of Alaska Press, 1969), J. L. Giddings, *Ancient Men of the Arctic* (New York: Knopf, 1967), F. Rainey, "The Ipiutak Culture: Excavations at Point Hope, Alaska," McCaleb Module 8 (Reading, Mass.: Addison-Wesley, 1972) or, for the larger perspective, "The Arctic and Sub-Arctic," Chapter 7 in Gordon R. Willey, *An Introduction to American Archaeology* (Englewood Cliffs, N.J.: Prentice-Hall, 1966).

There are many ethnographies and regional studies of the traditional and near-traditional society and culture of most groups of Eskimos. Here we will mention the most important in terms of geographical groupings (many further references are to be found in the bibliography following Chapter 13, but the dividing line between "modern" and "traditional" is very complex). The historically minded scholar should also consult the many works of explorers and traders which are often interesting but incomplete or biased in their descriptions.

Siberian Eskimo culture is the least well described and we have to resort to the work of W. Bogoras, *The Eskimo of Siberia* (Publications of the Jesup North Pacific Expedition, Vol. 8, 1913), and secondary sources.

Descriptions of Alaskan Eskimo culture are the most numerous, if not the best known, of all major regions. Historical sources from near traditional times include those of explorers such as Lisiansky and Zagoskin, and the rather biased synthetic works of H. H. Bancroft, *The Native Races of the Pacific States of North America*, Vol. 1 (New York: Appleton, 1875), Chap. 2, and H. W. Elliott, *Our Arctic Province* (New

York: Scribner, 1886), Chaps. 12, 13, 14. A better synthesis with an **173**
anthropological perspective is Wendell Oswalt, *Alaskan Eskimos* (San
Francisco: Chandler, 1967). Regional descriptions and ethnographies are
more abundant but more likely to be removed from traditional conditions. Early classic accounts include those of E. W. Nelson, *The Eskimo
about Bering Strait* (Bureau of American Ethnology, 18th Annual Report, Washington, 1899), and J. Murdoch, *Ethnological Results of the
Point Barrow Expedition* (Bureau of American Ethnology, 9th Annual
Report, Washington, 1892). The Northern (Inupik-speaking) Eskimos
have received greater attention, considering their numbers. A short
synthetic account is N. A. Chance, *The Eskimo of North Alaska* (New
York: Holt, Rinehart and Winston, 1966) which uses the more thorough
North Alaskan Eskimo (Bureau of American Ethnology, Bulletin 171,
Washington, 1959) by R. F. Spencer. The inland Nunamiut of the Brooks
range have been subject to almost as many investigations as there are
households there, including the major publication *Nunamiut* (New
York: Norton, 1954) by H. Ingstad, and the better ethnography, *The
Nunamiut Eskimos Hunters of Caribou* (New Haven and London: Yale
University Press, 1965) by N. J. Gubser. The southernmost Chugach
Eskimo culture was reconstructed from the few remaining informants
by K. Birket-Smith in his "The Chugach Eskimo," *Nationalmus.
Skrifter, Etnogr. Raekke.*, Vol. 6, (Copenhagen, 1953) and the "Subarc-
tic" Nunivak Islanders have been the subject of long research and many
publications by M. Lantis, e.g., *The Social Culture of the Nunivak
Eskimo* (Transactions of the American Philosophical Society, n.s., Vol.
53, Part 3, 1946). The Bering Strait Eskimo and their woodland cousins
have been least investigated, but the reader may start by consulting
J. L. Giddings, *Kobuk River People* (University of Alaska Studies of
Northern Peoples, No. 1, 1961) or Oswalt's *Napaskiak, An Alaskan
Eskimo Community* (Tucson: University of Arizona Press, 1963), as
well as the more modern studies listed at the end of the next chapter.

The central or Canadian Eskimos (excluding those of the Mackenzie region) have been subject to the most extensive research and of
the best-known works, partly because they were the most isolated and
therefore were "found" most recently in the traditional state. General
works are few, but include the important early work of F. Boas, *The
Central Eskimo* (Lincoln: University of Nebraska Press, 1964; originally
published as part of the Sixth Annual Report of the Bureau of Ethnology,
Smithsonian Institution, Washington, 1888), and V. F. Valentine and
F. G. Vallee's anthology, *Eskimo of the Canadian Arctic* (Princeton,
N.J.: Van Nostrand, 1968). Among the earlier works one might examine
the many adventures of early explorers including especially those of
Captain Lyon, Hall, Gordon, Low, etc. More strictly ethnographic early
works include the fairly sketchy work of L. M. Turner, "Ethnology
of the Ungava District," *11th Annual Report of the Bureau of Ethnology* (Washington, 1894); E. W. Hawkes, *The Labrador Eskimo* (Ottawa: Geological Survey of Canada, Memo 91, Anthropology Series 14,

1916); and the more narrative accounts of V. Stefanson, e.g., *Hunters of the Great North* (New York: Harcourt and Brace, 1922), and Diamond Jenness, *The People of the Twilight* (Chicago: University of Chicago Press, 1959; originally published in 1928).

The best accounts, probably for any Eskimo groups, are published in the reports of the Fifth Thule Expedition, led by Danish Greenlanders who crossed from Greenland to Alaska by dogsled in 1921–1924. A narrative of this immense expedition appears in K. Rasmussen, *Across Arctic America* (New York: Putnam, 1927), but the major ethnographic results, which have formed a baseline for many later works, include K. Birket-Smith, *The Caribou Eskimos*, Vol. 5 (Copenhagen: Glyndadalske Boghaindeln, 1920); T. Mathiassen, *The Material Culture of the Iglulik Eskimo*, Vol. 6, no. 1 (1928); K. Rassmussen, *The Intellectual Culture of the Iglulik Eskimo*, Vol. 5, no. 2 (1929); *The Intellectual Culture of the Caribou Eskimo*, Vol. 7, No. 2 (1930); *Netsilik Eskimo: Social Life and Spiritual Culture*, Vol. 8, Nos. 1, 2 (1931); and *The Intellectual Culture of the Copper Eskimo*, Vol. 9 (1932).

Other more recent works which include descriptions of near traditional culture or of cultural aspects which have not undergone much change include A. Balikci, *The Netsilik Eskimo* (Garden City, N.Y.: Natural History Press, 1970) (based partly on Rasmussen, 1931), and his regional summary, "The Eskimos of the Quebec-Labrador Peninsula," pp. 375ff. in J. Malaurie (ed.), *Le Nouveau-Quebec* (Paris: Mouton, 1964); the first part of N. H. H. Graburn, *Eskimos without Igloos* (Boston: Little, Brown, 1969); J. Briggs, *Never in Anger* (Cambridge: Harvard University Press, 1970), which is a narrative account of her fieldwork with an analysis of Eskimo emotional life; and D. Damas, *Igluligmiut Kinship and Social Groupings: A Structural Approach* (Ottawa: National Museum of Canada, Bulletin No. 196, 1963), whose title is self-explanatory. Additional references for Nouveau Quebec may be found in J. Fried (ed.), *A Survey of the Aboriginal Populations of Quebec and Labrador* (Montreal: McGill University, 1955).

Greenland, ethnographically and bibliographically, may be divided into three major regions: the Polar/Thule Eskimos, the West Greenlanders (the majority people), and the East Greenland or Ammassalik Eskimos. Danish authorities concentrated on the West Greenlanders, who underwent sociocultural changes earlier than all other Eskimo groups, so our publications in general are earlier than those for other areas—for instance, D. Crantz's monumental *The History of Greenland*, 2 vols. (London: The Brethren's Society for the Furtherance of the Gospel, 1767). In the last century the works of the famous Eskimologist H. Rink, *Danish Greenland, Its People and Its Products* (London, 1877) and "The Eskimo Tribes," *MoG.*, Vol 11 (1891) made the Greenlanders famous outside of Denmark and buttressed his pleas for administrative reform to the Danish government. In this century, K. Birket-Smith's "The Greenlanders of the Present Day," *Greenland*, Vol. II (Copenhagen and London, 1928) provided an introduction to the history and culture of the Greenland natives which has not been surpassed.

The Polar Eskimos, since their discovery as an isolated tribe in 1818, have become the most celebrated single Eskimo group, and are well described in H. P. Steensby's "Contributions to the Ethnology and Anthropogeography of the Polar Eskimos," *MoG.*, 34:255–405 (1910), and E. Holtved's "The Polar Eskimos: Language and Folklore," *MoG.*, 151:1,2 (1951), and, more popularly by P. Freuchen, *Eskimo* (New York: Horace Liveright, 1931), and J. Malaurie, *The Last Kings of Thule: A Year among the Polar Eskimos of Greenland* (New York: Crowell, 1956). Similarly the few but more exotic Ammassalik Eskimos have been well studied, especially at the end of the last century by such authorities as W. Thalbitzer, "The Ammassalik Eskimo; Contributions to the Ethnology of the East Greenland Natives," *MoG.*, 60 (1923); G. Holm, "Ethnological Sketch of the Angmagssalik Eskimo," *MoG.*, 39 (1914); and M. P. Porsild, "Studies on the Material Culture of the Eskimo in West Greenland," *MoG.*, 51:113–250 (1915). The eminent K. Birket-Smith has also provided us with a thorough ethnography, "Ethnography of the Egedesminde District," *MoG.*, 66 (1924), from part of the west Greenland area, but most of the works of this century concern problems of acculturation and administration, which we shall touch upon in the next chapter.

To conclude this compressed bibliography, we would like to mention some more specialized works, relating particularly to outstanding aspects of Eskimo culture that have been stressed in the text. The following, therefore, supplement and often enlarge on the information contained in the more general previous references.

Eskimo ecology, economics, and hunting techniques have been noted as outstanding, for the Eskimos are the foremost hunting (meat-oriented as opposed to gathering) people in the world. The best descriptions and analyses have come from the central Canadian Arctic, probably because it changed last. For an excellent overview and "controlled comparison," see D. Damas, "Environment, History and Central Eskimo Society," pp. 40–65 in D. Damas (ed.), *Contributions to Anthropology: Ecological Essays* (National Museum of Canada, Bulletin 230, 1969), and A. Balikci, "The Netsilik Eskimos: Adaptive Processes," in R. Lee and I. DeVore (eds.), *Man the Hunter* (Chicago: Aldine, 1968). Balikci's *The Netsilik Eskimo* (Garden City, N.Y.: Natural History Press, 1970) gives a more rounded, yet detailed, description from one area, and N. H. H. Graburn, "Traditional Economic Institutions and the Acculturation of the Canadian Eskimos," Chap. 8, pp. 107–121 in G. Dalton (ed.), *Studies in Economic Anthropology* (American Anthropological Association, Anthropological Studies No. 7, 1971) discusses the relationship between the ecological/demographic imperatives and the socioeconomic system. However, for excellence of descriptive detail of hunting techniques and Eskimo ideas of the relevant parts of the natural world, the reader must turn to R. K. Nelson, *Hunters of the Northern Ice* (Chicago: University of Chicago Press, 1969), although it concerns a more modern (Alaskan) Eskimo community.

Eskimo kinship and social structure has generated interest, not only for its own internal variation, but as a proposed "basic type" of system to be compared with others around the world—see G. P. Murdock, *Social Structure* (New York: Macmillan, 1949). More detailed examinations by a number of investigators have questioned its uniformity and added to our understanding of intracultural variation and adaptability. A. Heinrich, "An Outline of the Kinship Systems of the Bering Strait Eskimos" (unpublished M.A. dissertation, Department of Education, University of Alaska, 1955), and "The Structural Features of the Northwestern Alaskan Eskimo Kinship," *Southwestern Journal of Anthropology,* 16:110–126 (1960) have shown and classified the variant systems even within one smallish area, and attempt to provide explanation for such forms. In the central Arctic, D. Damas, "Characteristics of Central Eskimo Band Structure," pp. 116–142 in D. Damas (ed.), *Contributions to Anthropology: Band Societies* (National Museum of Canada, Bulletin 228, 1969) and *Igluligmiut Kinship and Local Groupings: A Structural Approach* (National Museum of Canada, Bulletin 196, 1963) provide us with the detailed workings and explanatory analysis of fairly typical systems, as has N. H. H. Graburn's *Taqagmiut Eskimo Kinship Terminology* (Ottawa: Northern Co-ordination and Research Centre, 1964) for the Hudson Strait area; however, J. L. Giddings in "Observations on the 'Eskimo Type' of Kinship and Social Structure," *Anthropological Papers of the University of Alaska,* 1:5–10 (1952), and C. C. Hughes, "An Eskimo Deviant from the 'Eskimo Type' of Social Organization," *American Anthropologist,* 60:1140–1147 (1958) have questioned the applicability of the "Eskimo type" model to various groups of the Eskimos themselves. B. S. D'Anglure's "Nom et Parenté Chez les Esquimaux Tarramiut du Nouveau-Québec (Canada)," in J. Pouillon and P. Maranda (eds.), *Echanges et Communications* (Paris: Mouton, n.d.) has extended the consideration of the Eskimo kinship system to show how the naming system both modifies and reflects the underlying principles.

Eskimo dyadic relationships and social structural units based on pseudo-kinship partnership relationships have received considerable attention in their various forms. Wife exchange and polygyny have received special note and L. Guemple's *Innuit Spouse Exchange* (Department of Anthropology, University of Chicago, 1962) provides a thorough comparative description and analysis, while A. J. Rubel's "Partnership and Wife Exchange among the Eskimo and Aleut of Northern North America," *Anthropological Papers of the University of Alaska,* 10:59–72 (1961) is shorter but more extensive. Other relationships have been examined in R. F. Spencer, "Eskimo Polyandry and Social Organization," *Proceedings of the Thirty-Second Congress of Americanists,* pp. 539–544 (Copenhagen, 1958); R. Dunning, "An Aspect of Recent Eskimo Polygyny and Wife-lending in the Eastern Arctic," *Human Organization,* 21:17–20 (1962); and L. Guemple, "The Eskimo Ritual Sponsor: A Problem in the Fusion of Semantic Domains," *Ethnology,* 8:4 (1969).

The maintenance, flexibility, and breakdown of Eskimo social organization have been made famous by E. A. Hoebel, "Law-ways of the

Primitive Eskimos," *Journal of Criminal Law and Criminology,* 31:6:663–683 (1941), and *The Law of Primitive Man* (Cambridge, Mass.: Harvard University Press, 1954). More detailed reports of Eskimo law and social control have appeared in L. Pospisil, "Law and Societal Structure among the Nunamiut Eskimo," pp. 395–432 in W. Goodenough (ed.), *Explorations in Cultural Anthropology* (New York: McGraw-Hill, 1964), and G. van Den Steenhoven, "Research Report on Caribou Eskimo Law," (mimeo) (Ottawa: Northern Co-ordination and Research Centre, 1956) and *Legal Concepts among the Netsilik Eskimos of Pelly Bay* (Ottawa: Northern Co-ordination and Research Centre, 1959). A comparative analytic overview with ethnographic illustration is N. H. H. Graburn, "Eskimo Law in Light of Self- and Group-interest," *Law and Society Review,* 4:1:45–60 (1969). Other aspects of internal dysfunction, for which the Eskimos are well known, have been described and analyzed in A. Balikci, "Suicidal Behavior among the Netsilik Eskimos," in B. Blishen (ed.), *Canadian Society: Sociological Perspectives* (New York: Free Press of Glencoe, 1961), and "Female Infanticide on the Arctic Coast," *Man,* 2:615–625 (1967); and F. Van de Velde, "L'infanticide chez les Esquimaux," *Eskimo,* 34:6–8 (1954), for the central Arctic and in C. C. Hughes, "Anomie, the Ammassalik, and the Standardization of Error," *Southwestern Journal of Anthropology,* 14:352–377 (1958) for the easternmost Eskimos.

Our final major topic, Eskimo religion, has generated interest both for its unique features and for its contribution to our comparative understanding of shamanism and animism. The best overview is still in M. Lantis, "The Religion of the Eskimos," pp. 309ff. in V. Ferm (ed.), *Forgotten Religions* (New York: Philosophical Library, 1950), which supplements her masterly *Alaskan Eskimo Ceremonialism* (New York: Augustin, 1947) and G. H. Marsh's "A Comparative Survey of Eskimo-Aleut Religion," *Anthropological Papers of the University of Alaska,* 3:21–36 (1954). Early good descriptions of the richest area of Eskimo ceremonialism appear in E. W. Hawkes, "The 'Inviting-in' Feast of the Alaska Eskimo" (Canada Department of Mines, Anthropological Series No. 3, 1913), and "The Dance Festivals of the Alaskan Eskimo" (University of Pennsylvania, The University Museum, Anthropological Publications, Vol. 6, No. 2, 1914), and a more recent analysis in A. Balikci, "Shamanistic Behavior among the Netsilik Eskimos," *Southwestern Journal of Anthropology,* 19:380–396 (1963). D. J. Ray's *Eskimo Masks: Art and Ceremony* (Seattle: University of Washington Press, 1967) is the most extensive and thorough examination of Eskimo masks, both in connection with religion and in the ethnohistory of the area. Eskimo folklore has been described extensively in many of the above-mentioned works, but the most masterful analytical attempt in modern times is R. Savard, *Mythologie Esquimaude: Analyse de Textes Nord-Groenlandais* (Quebec: Centre d'Études Nordiques, Université Laval, 1966), and much work remains to be done.

THIRTEEN

MODERN CONDITIONS

All the peoples of the circumpolar regions were aboriginally characterized by relatively small populations and low population density, and
a low level of technology or energy harnessing; few of them were politically unified and as a whole, even when they were, they formed scattered populations easily subjected to colonial policies of "divide and
rule." All these populations, at very differing times, have been overrun
by intrusive Western civilizations. The representatives of these larger
national entities came to the northern lands for exploitation, first of
fur and animal resources and later for minerals, lumber, and hydro-
electricity. For a long time these peoples were exploited along with the
animals and other resources of their area (with the possible exception
of Greenland) with little thought given for their welfare beyond maintaining them at the level necessary to produce the labor and consequent
income for the exploiters. Thus they have all become minorities within
the nations that colonized their territories, and many of these peoples
have become overrun by intrusive populations, especially in parts of
Scandinavia and Siberia.

As a result of historical events and social movements, the exploitative national governments at various times have reviewed the relationships of their agents and peopl s with the native groups and have for-
mulated policies to establish g als and regularize the nature of intercultural contacts. Though "hi nane" national legal policies may have
upheld the rights of the native groups, until this century national governments have had relatively little effect on the actual behavior of their
agents in attempting to diminish exploitation and discrimination (again
with the possible exception of Greenland where the church-state monopoly held a tight control supposedly for the good of the natives).
Fundamental to most of the ethnocentric "native policies" of the national governments has been the assumption that, with education and
acculturation and with modern technology and vastly better economic
opportunities, the native peoples would "assimilate," giving up their

traditional life styles and taking on many of the attributes of the national populations. In many ways this has come about though the diminution of a separate identity has not always accompanied the assimilation in life styles.

The great problem with any comparative overview of the recent and present conditions of northern peoples is a differential access of information. For Scandinavia we have the reports of local and national well-meaning intellectuals; for Siberia we have accounts by government administrative officials and government-employed intellectuals; for Greenland we have the accounts of both government reports and independent national anthropologists; for Alaska and northern Canada—where we probably have the best data, at least as far as local conditions and community developments are concerned—we have not only many government reports but also easy access to anthropologists and others whose research reports are rife. On the other hand, the activities of governments have differed greatly too, and some of them are more easily described than others. For Scandinavia we find the problem of three or four national entities attempting to govern and administer policies for the one minority group, the Samek; for the USSR, since the 1920s and 1930s, we have had a well-declared national policy toward Siberian and other minorities in the various republics, and these policies have been pursued with considerable vigor from relatively centralized agencies; for Greenland we have the clearest and most long-standing accounts of national policy, including the inputs, the implementation, and the results of the great changes of the 1950s; for northern Canada and Alaska we have extremely diffuse government policies, if present at all, administered by a variety of often competing public and private agencies. For these North American areas we have the least well-defined goals for the native people set out in public policies and the most quixotic policy changes emerging from relatively laissez-faire national-provincial-territorial political relations, and, perhaps, the most catastrophic effects of huge exploitative developments occurring within areas where no rational framework and guidelines have yet been established.

SIBERIAN NATIVE PEOPLES

English-language accounts of modern conditions of the native peoples of Siberia (the Yakut, Yukagirs, Chukchi, and Evenks) are scattered throughout the literature, but there is no single thorough analysis of the process of cultural changes since the Revolution. Although exact processes of change have not been defined, the outline of cultural change has been established. The czarist government may have had a humane official policy toward the Siberian native peoples, but it carried out an actual policy of general neglect. For all practical purposes the native Siberians were illiterate, since virtually none of the native populations had access to public schools. There was a general lack of

Western medicine and thousands died in epidemics. A host of unscrupulous traders exploited the people and demanded tribute in furs, labor, and service.

With the Russian Revolution, conditions changed for the native Siberians. A number of phases occurred in the development of Soviet policy toward the national question, but we can point to two main periods: (1) the precollective period, from 1917 through the 1930s, in which the native peoples were protected from harmful outside influences, such as the exploiting traders, and prepared for collectivization by the formation of local political organizations; and (2) the period from the 1930s until the end of World War II, in which, with the exact date depending on local variations, the great majority of households were collectivized. One of the first steps in the formation of Siberian socialist political organizations was the creation of "clan"-based soviets, but about 1930 there was a transition from the clan soviet to a wider one based on territory, with the creation of national districts (*Okrug*)—these territorial political divisions, somewhat comparable to the states or provinces of other countries, are integrated politically into the USSR and form a national homeland for the group after which they are named. In 1930 both the Chukchi and the Evenk National Districts were formed. Even earlier, in 1922, the Yakut Autonomous Soviet Socialist (ASSR) Republic was formed as a political and territorial unit, an autonomous republic, a step or two higher than the national district. Generally, the ASSR is formed for larger minority populations, and thus naturally has greater representation in the higher political organizations of the USSR than the national district. The Yukagirs, apparently because of their small population, have no national district.

From the earliest days of the Soviet government, formation of suitable political organizations for the various minority groups was of prime concern. Both Lenin and Stalin (a commissar for nationalities in the early days of the Soviet government and himself a member of a minority group) wrote extensively on the national question and developed a policy, represented by the slogan "national in form, socialist in content," in which political structures were to be developed that would protect the national language and culture of minority peoples while creating conditions favorable for the formation of socialism. Thus the native Siberians and perhaps the Greenlanders represent the only peoples of the circumpolar regions to have advanced politically to the point of having their own states.

Prior to the general introduction of collective farms in 1929, the formation of trading cooperatives ended the old exploitative methods of the individual traders. Approximately a decade after the beginnings of collectivization, three-quarters of the native Siberian households had joined a collective farm, and the process of collectivization was completed during World War II. The following figures indicate the time span involved in this process: in the Yakut ASSR a little over 40 per cent of households were collectivized in 1932; in the Evenk National District

86 per cent of the native population were members of primary production units in 1937, and two years later these units were changed to collective farms; we have no comparable figures for the Chukchi National District, but the Chukchi also were organized into collective farms, as were the Yukagirs, most of them in the Yakut ASSR.

In collectivization, organization for production (that is, the manner in which people work together) is rationalized and individual labor becomes more productive than under the old pattern in which the household constituted the major unit of production. Production increases to the point necessary for the support of a relatively high standard of living (modern education, medical care, and other amenities of modern life) and, with this increase in production and with the nationalization of collective life, leisure also increases. For example, under the shift system of reindeer breeding, half the herdsmen tend the reindeer while the other half live and work in the settlement, whereas under the old conditions herdsmen would be scattered away from settlements most of the time. With rationalization of labor came rationalization of the economic system, of supply, credit, and the distribution of goods. Workers can obtain supplies without the waste of time and effort required by the primitive prerevolutionary conditions of transportation and trade. They can obtain credit from the state, and no longer need to depend on the usurious interest rates of traders. There is a much more equitable distribution of goods under the collective. In addition to the technological innovations introduced in the Soviet north, these purely economic and social innovations brought about through collectivization had great importance for the lives of the native Siberians.

An important aspect of postrevolutionary economic development in the North is that a major part of it is based on traditional occupations to which modern technology and new rational methods have been applied. Important traditional occupations that serve as the base of the native Siberian economy include hunting, trapping, sea-mammal hunting, fishing, and reindeer and livestock breeding (especially cattle); in addition, innovative occupations such as agriculture (in protected valleys), fur farming, mining, lumbering, and manufacturing have assumed new importance. There is not only subsistence hunting for food and skins for clothing, but also commercial hunting and trapping for fur—squirrel, fox, and sable. Animals such as sable, hunted almost to the point of extinction during the time of the czars, have been restored to commercial importance through the introduction of breeding stock to new areas and protective legislation. To conserve and harvest animals like the polar fox, feeding stations have been established and stocked with large quantities of waste meat and fish to support great numbers of fox and provide a prime trapping area for the hunter. The Chukchi, in particular, depend on sea-mammal hunting both for subsistence and commodity production, using modern mechanized technology such as motor-powered whaling boats. Fur farms provide an additional source of income. In the USSR, the world's greatest producer of fur, fur is not used chiefly as a luxury but for everyday clothing throughout the long winters. Reindeer breeding, pursued on a large scale, holds special importance for the Evenks and Chukchi, and reindeer provide an important source of food to support the local population. Veterinary services, insecticides, and the use of aircraft for supply and for spotting lost animals have increased the efficiency of reindeer breeding. To solve the problem often discussed by Soviet ethnographers—that of reconciling the nomadic movement required by reindeer herding with the cultural advantages of life in the settlements—numerous strategies have been worked out to ensure periods of settlement life for each worker—for example, the shift rotation of brigade (team) workers and improved transportation, including aircraft. Fishing, with the use of modern techniques, represents an important occupation, and fish form a staple food for all Siberians. Livestock breeding is also an important occupation in the Yakut ASSR, and modern techniques and improved breeds of cattle have increased production. Vegetables are frequently grown in gardens for local use.

Many minerals, among them large gold deposits in the Chukchi National District and diamonds in the Yakut ASSR, are mined in northern Siberia, and the extensive forests are also exploited. Means of transportation include aircraft, the fleets navigating the large rivers, and winter roads. Many manufacturing plants are located in Siberia, in contrast to the other regions of the North. Academic centers and entirely new cities have been and are being built in Siberia, and there is an increasing movement of people from the southern areas to the North.

Medicine in Siberia has improved from the almost nonexistent health care at the time of the czars to the point where the doctor-patient ratio of the Yakut ASSR and the Chukchi and Evenk national districts compares favorably to that of the most medically advanced states in the United States. Numerous hospitals and health clinics have been established, and special campaigns have been carried out against diseases endemic to Siberia, such as trachoma and tuberculosis.

A particular feature of Soviet national policy has been to establish written scripts for the native languages, to undertake a program of publishing in the native languages, using the scripts, and to conduct the first years of education in the native language before introducing instruction in Russian. The Yakut language had long been recorded and by 1931 the script and grammars for the Chukchi and Evenks had been established and a publication program in those languages launched. Many publications are written in Yakut and seventeen newspapers are printed in the Yakut language. The first phase of education of the Yakut, Evenks, and Chukchi is conducted in the native language, but because the Yukagir constitute an extremely small population (440), either Russian or Yakut is spoken in the schools and apparently there are no publications in Yukagir. Education is widespread in Siberia, illiteracy is practically nonexistent, and students have the opportunity to advance to the highest levels in the university systems. By as early as 1925 a special northern department had been established in Leningrad University by Bogoras and others for the express purpose of meeting the higher educational needs of the native Siberians and thus forming an educated Siberian class. Since that time a number of special problem-oriented branches of higher education have been established, directed toward the particular needs of northern peoples. A native intelligentsia of teachers, writers, political workers, doctors, and other professionals has existed for some time.

In summary, the following developments in Siberia hold particular interest in a comparison of native peoples of the North. (1) Special political organizations have formed to ensure a measure of self-determination. (2) A modern technical economy has been constructed based on traditional occupations. (3) The worst features of exploitation by class have been eliminated. (4) Aspects of native culture have been continued—for example, native languages have been put into written form, publication in native languages has been undertaken, and education in the first years is generally conducted in the native language. The historical movement of the Siberians is not solely toward a wholesale adoption of the culture and ways of the West, but in large measure represents an advancement along Siberian national lines.

ALASKAN NATIVE PEOPLES

This section, based mainly on various United States government reports, emphasizes the native villages and small towns of Alaska (excluding the southeastern panhandle)—in other words, rural Alaska as opposed to the cities. Although it is difficult to speak of Alaska natives (Eskimos, Athabascans, and Aleuts) as a monolithic group—since education, occupation, degree of "acculturation," degree of dependence upon food from the land, and life style vary greatly—basic structural features are common to village Alaska.

Alaska natives constitute a minority in Alaska; projected figures for the State of Alaska for 1970 give a total population of 302,361, of which 50,885 are Alaska natives. Most Alaska natives (about 70 per cent of them) live in the 178 native villages scattered throughout the state.

Three major sectors dominate the economy of Alaska: government expenditures (at the federal and state levels); extractive industries (petroleum, natural gas, minerals, fisheries, and forest products); and the distributive and service sectors. The Alaska economy is growing at a rapid rate both in terms of employment and in value of production: between 1959 and 1969 numbers of individuals employed, employment income, and Alaska gross product more than doubled. This decade of almost unprecedented economic growth, however, had relatively little effect upon the rural Alaska natives.

A brief review of the present economic position of the native peoples of rural Alaska shows that they do not enjoy the economic advantages of white Alaskans. Only approximately 10 per cent of the natives of rural Alaska work full time; for most of the year most of them are unemployed. Seasonal employment, concentrated on fishing, construction, and fighting forest fires, leaves most of the native labor force unemployed during the long winter months. The commodity production that historically has occupied the native peoples—fur trapping, fishing and cannery work, and handicraft—makes up only a minute portion of the gross income of Alaska, and it is difficult to see how it can be expanded to provide a stable economic base. Fishing cannot be greatly expanded because of problems concerning natural production. Fur prices have been low since the 1950s and fur production is now of little financial importance. Most of the people involved in traditional crafts make a very small income from their art. Alaska natives have been underrepresented in government jobs, and most employed in this sector hold lower-level jobs. It seems that better representation in employment in the government sector, development of mineral resources, manufacture, and service industries are the likely directions for economic expansion in the future.

While the annual income for Alaska natives is low, the prices of supplies are high in rural Alaska, with prices almost twice those paid by families in other states. Needless to say, a low income (in 1960 rural Alaska natives had only one-fourth the median personal income of urban white Alaskans) coupled with a high cost of living leads to a poor living standard, and Alaska natives are no exception to the fact that, of all U.S. minority groups, the native Americans have the most unfavorable economic position. As a measure of the level of poverty in rural Alaska, it can be noted that a study by the Bureau of Indian Affairs in the 1960s pointed out that more than 90 per cent of the housing needed to be replaced.

This low standard of living affects many aspects of the people's lives. For example, the death rate of Alaska natives exceeds twice that of whites in Alaska; the infant mortality rate ranges from twice to four times that of Alaska whites. For Alaska natives infliction by tuberculosis is twenty times that of Alaskan whites, and deaths from influenza and pneumonia are ten times the rate for whites in Alaska. Various health campaigns have been successful—for example, the campaign against tuberculosis has resulted in a drastic decline in the death rate from this disease since the 1940s when it infected 80 to 90 per cent of native children in wide regions. The state of health of Alaska natives is directly linked to economic causes: to deficiencies in diet, general malnutrition, and housing conditions.

The low standard of living of Alaska natives is reflected in the educational levels achieved. The average level ranges from six to eight years of school—for the interior and the entire western and northern coast less than six years, and for some large regions two years or less. The average level of education for whites in Alaska exceeds twelve years. Many Alaska native children must live apart from their families in boarding schools during the school year. Education in the native languages is still at an experimental stage.

We may ask why, in the richest country on earth, one sector of the population should occupy such an economically backward position. Part of the explanation for this situation has been pointed out by Jorgensen in his study of the basic contradiction between the city and the countryside as it applies to native Americans. That is, the predominant sources of economic activity, income, education, medical care, cultural activity, and the "good things" of Western life occur in the city, whereas native Americans generally live in the countryside. The Alaska countryside sends basic resources—raw minerals, crude petroleum, fish, fur, timber, and the like—to the city at low prices, whereas the city sends costly manufactured goods to the underdeveloped countrysides of the world. Thus rural native Alaskans, together with a number of other ethnic groups and classes (white small farmers, black sharecroppers, Chicano migrant laborers), share a disadvantaged position inherent in the nature of the larger North American social and economic systems—that of a predominantly capitalist society which emphasizes profit on capital rather than production ultimately directed toward human needs as emphasized in socialistic economies. Even a brief review of histories dealing with the past century of American rule in Alaska reveals the common themes throughout of control of the Alaska economy by monopolies operated mainly for the benefit of capitalists living outside Alaska.

It cannot be expected that these conditions should exist without a response from the people affected. This response came in the 1960s in the form of a statewide political struggle of the native peoples for settlement of aboriginal claims to the land which led to the passage of the Alaska Native Claims Settlement Act in December 1971. Prior to the 1960s the only Alaska native political organization was the Alaska Native Brotherhood formed in 1912. Primarily an organization of Tlingit and Haida of the southeastern panhandle, the Brotherhood had relatively little influence on the rest of Alaska. At the time of settlement of the land claims only two reservations in Alaska had been confirmed by act of Congress—a number of other "reservations" had been created by executive order and by the Department of the Interior, but these did not have the legal status of reservations in other states of the United States.

Around 1960 the native peoples' right to the land and its use reached a crisis. After the Statehood Act of 1958 the State of Alaska, under terms of the Act, began to select some of the most valuable lands for transfer to state ownership. This expropriation of land formed the major stimulus for the aboriginal land-claims issue, which in turn stimulated the rapid formation of native political organizations throughout Alaska. Between 1961 and 1967 twelve regional Alaska native political organizations were formed: seven Eskimo organizations, three Athabascan, one Aleut, and one Northwest Coast Indian. These regional associations together formed a statewide organization, the Alaska Federation of Natives, which guided the filing of aboriginal land claims and represented the Alaska natives as a whole through the regional associations. In the early 1960s the villages and regional associations began filing claims to the land based on aboriginal title and filed protests against state land selection. By the mid-1960s, because of this activity, the federal government put a freeze on selection of all federal lands in Alaska, including state selection. The "land freeze" led to increasing pressure for settlement of the land-claims issue, as varied economic interests were concerned about obtaining clear title to certain land—for example, the oil companies active in the North Slope. Thus enough political pressure was put on the government to ensure passage of the land-claims bill.

Major features of the Alaska Native Claims Settlement Act include:

1. Forty million acres settlement in land, with both surface and subsurface rights granted (in certain cases other formulas may apply).
2. Payment of $462,500,000 from U.S. Treasury over a period of eleven years, and $500,000,000 from royalties on minerals from public land for the total payment of $962,500,000.
3. The twelve Alaska native regional associations are to administer the settlement land and funds, together with the villages in each association. Land is to be divided on the basis of land area of each regional corporation (those with largest land area receive largest share of land) and money is to be shared on the basis of the population of each regional corporation.

Thus in settlement of the land claims, the native peoples gave up claim to 325,481,600 acres of Alaska's land surface.

To the question of what effect the land-claims settlement may have on the economy of the Alaska natives, several points can be made. The economic history of Indian reservations in the lower forty-eight states is largely a very sad history of economic ghettos of a people living at a standard far lower than their neighbors. The reservations historically have had a declining land base. A crucial difference exists, however, between most Indian reservations in the United States and the case of the Alaska natives at the time of settlement of land claims. Many U.S. Indian reservations are characterized by relatively small populations, a small land base, and little in the way of formal Indian organizations connecting the groups in order to pool resources and provide a unified political front. The distinguishing feature of the Alaska case is that of a relatively large population holding a relatively large land base, united under twelve regional corporations, which in turn form a statewide native political organization—the Alaska Federation of Natives. Thus human and economic resources can be pooled and the Alaska natives can present a unified political front in the struggle for their interests. Consequently a new type of political and economic organization, organized on a larger scale and on different lines from other U.S. Indian reservations, has entered the scene, and it can be expected that the results may be different and more favorable to the native Americans than those achieved previously. Large-scale cooperatives currently being organized, however, operate at a great disadvantage because of the backward state of economic development among the Alaska natives, and economic development in Alaska occurs in the context (largely unfavorable to rural and nonwhite ethnic groups) of the U.S. national economy of capitalism, of production for the profit of the small capital-holding class.

Alaska natives form part of one of the fastest-growing populations (native Americans) in North America. While some aspects of the modern conditions of Alaska natives are peculiar to that region and also to northern Canada, many of the most basic problems are shared by a number of ethnic groups and working classes throughout the world. The future for the Alaska natives depends to a large degree on political movements and economic formations developed by themselves, but for better or for worse it also depends on relations with the larger white majority and on the national institutions of the United States.

CANADIAN INDIANS

The Indians of the Canadian Subarctic perhaps have more in common with their brethren in Alaska than with the Canadian Eskimos in respect to history and modern conditions. For the most part both the Algonquians and the Athabascans have been the objects of trade and exploitation longer than the Eskimos, especially in the more southerly and easterly regions. These formerly scattered groups have been "colonialized" longer and their economic and social organization was more totally disrupted at an earlier period (see, for instance, Chapter 9 on the Kutchin of the Mackenzie area). For the majority of the Indian groups, seasonal trapping and wage labor for the white man became the main livelihood in the last century or before. Dependence on the trading posts and imported material goods became complete and irreversible and, particularly with the great declines of caribou and other game animals, trapped animals such as beaver and muskrat became crucial.

Missionaries followed in the wake of the traders, making overt conversions among the bulk of the population who took the new religion, and the accompanying literacy, as seriously as the old. The distinction between spiritually powerful shamans and others is not so strong among the Indians as the Eskimos, and the demise of shamans and ritual performances such as divination and "shaking-tent rites" was slower. Though hymns and prayers were learned and church faithfully attended, a syncretism rather than a substitution has emerged. Many aspects of aboriginal beliefs—mythology, cosmology, and taboos—have been retained alongside the new monotheistic religion.

Provisions were made in the British North America Act of 1867, which granted dominion status to Canada, for the protection and support of the native population and the maintenance of treaties and agreements on their behalf. These statutory rules applied to most of the Indians in southern Canada who had been granted reservations, as their former lands came under territorial pressure from the whites. The Subarctic Indians fell mainly under the hegemony of the Hudson's Bay Company who ceded sovereignty over Rupert's Land to Canada in the 1860s. A few of the Subarctic groups were treated on the southern model and granted reservations, rights, and treaty money. The majority, some of whom were not even in regular contact by the 1860s, fell into the awkward status of being ex-servants of the Hudson's Bay Company and new wards of the government that was very slow to look after their welfare. These Indian peoples were not full citizens—they could not vote, had no internal political organization, received no schooling or medical attention, and for a hundred years were denied the use of alcohol. They were left to the mercies of the same Company that had long exploited them but which was no longer officially responsible for their welfare. Only the paternalism of post managers and the efforts of the churches provided amelioration.

Thus the general picture for northern Canadian Indians resembles that of the Alaskan natives, or has been worse due to lesser government involvement until recently. Until after World War II the only significant changes from the debt-trapping pattern of life took place in the Mackenzie Delta. Here the massive but temporary presence of the whalers, the more favorable climate, and cheaper river transportation brought some aspects of "civilization" before World War II, including a church-organized education, often in hostels, literacy and the use of the English language, social relations and intermarriage with a fairly large white population, and acculturation to a "frontier life style." The high prices for pelts in the 1920s and 1930s brought material wealth to many along with increased expectations and a high turnover of both money and possessions as a result of the prevalent drinking and gambling that characterized North American frontier life. In World War II military activities combined with mineral extraction and transportation ameliorated the aftereffects of the Depression, but, as in the rest of the Canadian North, the massive changes were reserved for the government efforts of the 1950s and '60s.

There emerged in many northern Indian villages and towns processes of ethnic stratification and identity resembling many parts of Alaska but not found in the simpler situations of the Canadian and Greenland Eskimos. The stratified colonial settlements started with the structure of whites, post servants, and "bush" Indians, but the long period of dominance and contact has caused it to grow more complicated in some areas. The families of post servants tried to emulate the life style of the whites and both groups depended on the exploitation of the hunting and trapping "bush" people. In some areas two new groups emerged: the daughters of many post servants married whites and their offspring, known as "metis" or "half-castes," were placed culturally and economically below the whites but above the "pure-bloods"; also in some areas the local Indians were granted reservation status along with rights to education and welfare. This latter group ranked below the post servants but above the more completely "bush" people, who were legally "squatters" as Indians with whom treaties had not been signed, who therefore had no reservation status or rights, and who might be more nomadic or might have come from another distant "treaty status group." Thus the following complex picture became and is still visible in some places:

Ruling whites: Dominate all institutions; "southern" life style and pay; domiciled elsewhere but work in the North temporarily.

Metis: Physically part Indian, part white; usually only English speaking; "citizens" rather than "Indians"; poor-white life style; usually lower echelon employment.

Post servants: May be partially white; unskilled jobs; often bilingual or English speaking; emulate poor-white life style; look down upon Indians and Indian life style except as recreation.

Treaty Indians: "Wards of the government"; territorial and economic rights; sometimes monolingual Indian and "pureblood"; unemployed or seasonally employed; some dependence on trapping and hunting with seasonal "bush" life.

"Squatters" or "bush": Little or no rights to government housing, welfare, education; monolingual or smattering of English; live in shacks with no sanitation; economically marginal with dependence on bush life, occasional employment, and relief.

This complicated model of stratification becomes further confused in some communities and regions, such as the Mackenzie Delta, by the presence of Eskimo groups and in others by the presence of multiple Indian ethnic groups. Furthermore, the sociopolitical structure of the North itself is changing, as community social systems give way to regional or national sociopolitical organizations, with increased mobility for more acculturated Indians and the ever-increasing importance of government policies and actions. In the past few years the federal government has proposed the abrogation of the British North America Act with its Federal-Indian ties, and it is possible that each Indian group may have to renegotiate its statuses and rights as provincial and territorial governments take more control over the populations within their own boundaries. Although this may work to the advantage of the more politically conscious and better organized of the Indian groups, it will probably be disadvantageous for those northern groups whose education and welfare have been neglected until of late and whose understanding of the workings of the world at large makes any matter of renegotiation an unequal affair.

The acculturation stages to which the northern Indians have been subjected resemble those of the Canadian Eskimos (see next section) with: contacts with explorers and occasional trading; trading and dependence on trapping for furs; missionization and some syncretistic movements; government concern and organization—into bands and through treaties; and lastly, massive unemployment, "welfare state" with dependence on government for education, health care, relief, housing, jobs, social control, and the like.

The period of intensive trapping upset the aboriginal hunting patterns for the two are not compatible; furthermore, the lack of aboriginal concepts of exclusive territoriality gave way in many areas to the "ownership" of trap-line areas, some of which have gained legal sanction from the government. Leadership that once was based on hunting prowess and organizational wisdom was replaced by often arbitrary "chieftainship" based on dealing with outside agents and government treaty obligations. Even the new social organizational units, registered as "bands" by the government, have created different population patterns and new allegiances and identities.

The Indian population of the Northwest Territories has grown very little over the past decade, with Indians now in the minority compared with Eskimos in mixed areas and compared with whites in nearly all regions. No wonder that some small bands are reported to be demoralized when their lands and communities are overrun and they become mere appendages of the modern world without having to lift a finger! The North, however, has not yet been inundated by the outside as compared with Indian areas of the United States and southern Canada— nor even compared with many of the "Russianized" lands of Siberian peoples. Many groups retain their integrity in spite of enforced schooling and economic hardships.

The education of northern Indians, apart from earlier church-run efforts, has only recently been implemented with full force. Even here the Indians appear to have fallen behind the Eskimos where they attend the same institutions; these facts are reflected by the unemployment rates for Indians and their per-capita wage earnings of less than 25 per cent of that for Canada as a whole. Apart from government jobs, employment patterns are seasonal and offer little security, yet the possibilities of subsisting on hunting and trapping are minimal.

Indian health also compares unfavorably with that of Canadian whites, with infant mortality over three times that of the rate for whites. Life expectancy, however, about doubles that for Eskimos within the same Northwest Territories, and appears to be improving faster than that for either whites or Eskimos because of increasing medical facilities and changing life styles in the North.

Large-scale exploitative developments have been few and far between in the lands of the Subarctic Indians. Huge iron-ore mines with their infrastructures of communities, roads, and railways have been developed at Schefferville and Wabush, but have provided practically no employment (and no royalties) for the Indians in whose lands they are located. Similarly, the huge grain port at Churchill, and the gold and other mines in the Great Bear Lake region (around the new territorial capital of Yellowknife) have done little for the Indians, except to bring a huge influx of white outsiders. Developments in the Mackenzie Delta have been slower but have taken better account of the native populations, as far as employment is concerned. A huge new hydroelectric power development, involving the flooding of over eight thousand square miles of Indian lands, is planned between Mistassini and James Bay. It provides some employment for local Indians, but they were not forewarned or consulted until "after the fact." The political and ecological consequences of this, the biggest project so far, are unknown or have not yet been made public. Further immense developments in Indian lands are likely to come about—for instance, oil and gas drilling are underway around James Bay and in the Northwest Territories. So far in these and other areas the native inhabitants are neither consulted nor employed at anything above the temporary, unskilled level.

Obviously, political action is necessary to avoid further social disintegration and loss of rights. The leaders are emerging from among the more educated English- or French-speaking Indians, with some white help, and local and national Native Brotherhoods have been formed as the realization of a common identity and similar problems increases. Once again we have a people outside the mainstream of the economic and political life of the larger society; their small numbers and educational neglect have rendered them unable so far to meet the threats to their sociocultural fabric and their lands. Perhaps the model of successful action by the Alaskan natives will soon bring a better life and a measure of control over their lives for the Indians of northern Canada.

CANADIAN ESKIMOS

History and Acculturation

We may describe the history of the changes leading up to the modern conditions of the Canadian Eskimos as a series of stages, each stage marked by the nature of the external material and cultural influences and the resultant changes in Eskimo culture and society. The Canadian Eskimos cover a large land area with different parts subjected to different outside forces at different times; nevertheless, nearly all Canadian Eskimo groups have gone through the same series of stages, though at different times and with different durations.

Traditional Eskimo life as described in Chapter 12 continued in some parts of northern Canada well into the twentieth century, but temporary modifications resulted from the incursion of traders' and explorers' ships into the eastern Arctic nearly four hundred years ago. The first stage of contact, therefore, might be called "modified-traditional," starting in Baffin Island and the Labrador coast nearly four hundred years ago, in the Hudson Bay area nearly three hundred years ago, and in the lands between not much more than fifty years ago. During this period large parties of whites came to the Eskimos' land mainly to explore the area, to find routes to established trading areas, to harvest the sea resources such as whales and walrus, and occasionally to exploit minerals; secondarily to all these, they came to trade with the Eskimos. This early and sporadic trade usually provided metal and metal products for the Eskimos in exchange for skins, sometimes meat and aid, or the company of Eskimo women. It effected little permanent change on the Eskimo traditional life, save that metal knives, needles, and harpoon heads improved the technology of the material culture. The Eskimo did not suffer shortages of skins or animals through the infrequent contacts. Of a local significance was the unwitting introduction of diseases to the contacting Eskimo groups who had little immunity to such epidemics as flu, pneumonia, whooping cough, measles, and the like. This may have caused temporary local population declines in some areas.

The second stage was the fundamental revolution caused by the introduction of extensive fox trapping. Until the present century trading posts were few, found at the south end of Hudson Bay where the main purpose was to trade with Indians, along the Labrador coast in association with the missions, and for some years on the eastern and southern shores of Baffin Island in association with the whalers. In the first three decades of this century, however, the white Arctic fox fur became popular, and the Hudson's Bay and some other companies set up permanent trading posts at over thirty advantageous points throughout the eastern Arctic and in the west. Only a few groups in the central, most landlocked area were not immediately subject to this revolution. The companies would extend credit to Eskimos in the fall, "grubstaking" them with traps, metal objects, guns, ammunition, and sometimes food, to trap along the coast and inland during the winter so that they would bring the valuable white pelts to the trader in the spring and pay off their debts. In order to undertake these extensive journeys inland and run long and lucrative trap lines, the Eskimos had to concentrate more on the provision of dog food to have strong and fast teams. This necessitated more intensive summer hunting with rifles and, more recently, modern boats in order to cache large amounts of food to last their dog teams through the winter and to provide food for their families who often would not accompany them on the trapping trips. The winter hunting techniques changed because of displacement of harpoons by rifles and because of the shorter time that the hunter was able to spend on the coast during the winter. These factors, combined with the problematic decline of the large caribou herds, forced the Eskimos to depend more on imported foods.

Unanticipated and irreversible consequences occurred for the Eskimos at this stage. First, they became trapped in the "credit" system and their livelihood depended on the fluctuations of the outside market. Second, the annual cycle was disrupted by a new emphasis on inland exploitation in the winter and coastal exploitation during the summer. These factors combined with the possibility of handouts and occasional wage labor started the trend for "post living," with important consequences (see below).

In areas far from trading posts there arose the need for long annual or semiannual journeys from the hunting and trapping grounds to the points of exchange, increasing once more the need for dog food and, again, meaning the absence of the more capable men from their families and communities for months at a time.

In this century, soon after the establishment of these many trading posts, other white agencies followed (or occasionally set up independent establishments) with the coming of the Royal Canadian Mounted Police to the North; the police came not only to "keep order" in the land, but also to establish with certainty Canadian claims to the far northern territory that were at times threatened. The RCMP took on additional functions such as handing out relief, taking censuses and demographic records, and establishing respect for the Queen and Canadian sovereignty. In many areas missions soon followed too. In the eastern Arctic the Anglican Church (Church of England in Canada) moved north from their work with the Cree Indians to convert the Eskimos to Christianity and introduce literacy in the form of syllabics. In the area west of Hudson Bay, the Roman Catholic church set up similar missions, though usually with more permanence. In the Mackenzie area, both churches operated from the nineteenth century, setting up schools and hostels.

These latter two agencies combined with the efforts of the Hudson's Bay Company were relatively successful in reducing the rate of violence, both among the Eskimos and between the Eskimos and Indians. It was to the Company's advantage to have their clients trapping and hunting rather than fighting. The Christian gospel and the leadership of the missions went a long way toward relieving the Eskimos of their many fears of the supernatural and of the sometimes malevolent power of the shamans. The appearance of the police and their ability to wield authoritarian power and to take social offenders away from the community also helped repress some kinds of violence.

The price of fox pelts fell drastically during the Depression and until World War II. In most places the Eskimos' livelihood was seriously threatened through diminished credit and irreversible dependence on imported goods. The annual trading ship continued to come, bringing with it communicable diseases, but in some areas where the Eskimos had become materially rich and had bought schooners and other expensive capital goods, they could no longer obtain them. In a few areas the trading posts pulled out altogether, forcing the local Eskimos to become more subsistence-dependent or to visit or move to other areas where posts still operated. The early effects of World War II exacerbated these conditions, meaning less credit, less material goods and ammunition, and more infrequent visits from supply ships.

After the Americans entered World War II an "invasion" took place in certain areas of the eastern and western Arctic where supply bases, airstrips, and meteorological and navigation stations were set up "instantly." In such "favored" areas, tens of ships arrived within weeks, disgorging thousands of tons of supplies, and hundreds of houses were built where few or none had been before. It was like a miracle for the Eskimos in those areas who had been reduced to the most abject state and were even starving. In some localities the mere waste discarded by the huge operations provided food, clothing, and housing for Eskimos and many others who migrated from distant places to partake in this bounty. The generosity of the newcomers was notable compared with the behavior of the previous whites. Medical services, handouts, and luxuries suddenly became available. In these few favored areas, wage employment became the norm for many able-bodied men whereas before it had usually been sporadic for all but a few. Although this human invasion produced further mortal epidemics, the overall effect was better health and population increase due to greater material and medical security.

Although the American and Canadian military withdrew sooner or later from nearly all these bases, they left behind much of the material equipment, the airstrips, and, most importantly, Eskimos with a taste for wage labor, cash rather than debt, and luxuries and post living rather than insecurity and camp life. These values also filtered to some of the areas less touched by the military efforts, and during the 1950s other events of a similar nature spread the new way of life throughout much of the previously isolated parts. All across northern Alaska and Canada near the sixty-eighth parallel, the construction of the DEW line brought a similar invasion of material equipment, ships, housing, waste, white workers, diseases, and access to employment and security. In the southernmost region along the Indian-Eskimo border, the mid-Canada radar line brought similar effects to such Eskimo settlements as Great Whale River and to many Indian communities. Although fox prices rose during World War II and have been fair since that time, the second stage of acculturation, the "trapping," was never reestablished as a major focus of most Canadian Eskimos. Soon after World War II a number of events led to the Canadian government taking more notice of and spending more money on its northernmost inhabitants. The establishment of a family-allowance system of $6–8 per child per month for all Canadians was extended to Eskimos, and the RCMP or HBC handed out or administered these payments, often considerable for fertile Eskimo families.

In the late 1940s came an increasing awareness of the relation between rich governments and minority and Third World peoples within and outside their boundaries. The annual Arctic patrol trip, then equipped as a hospital ship, screened all Eskimos yearly for tuberculosis and other major diseases, which were attended to in hospitals outside the North.

During the 1950s and early 1960s federal day schools were set up throughout all settlements large and small in the Arctic, supplementing or displacing those few in the west run by the churches. Compulsory school attendance meant that the children had to be at the "post" most of the year, and Eskimos, being loath to leave their children during this period in hostels even though they were provided, accelerated their trend to year-round post living. The schools for the most part taught English and elementary subjects in English, but until recently had relatively little success in doing anything but delaying the training of Eskimos for their semitraditional life of trapping and mechanized hunting (see below). During the same decade, nursing stations and a few small hospitals, set up within the larger Eskimo settlements, provided an increased level of constant medical surveillance for those living in the post and eventually led to lowered mortality rates and ever-increasing populations.

With these newly installed government agencies, the government administration itself had to move to the north in the form of Northern Service Officers. Generating plants had to be built, construction had to be supervised, employees had to be chosen and paid, and these government offices were the liaison between Ottawa and all government activities on the local scene. In addition, they assumed the task of administering welfare and pensions, being responsible for the families of those sent out to hospital, and even the purchasing of handicrafts to help the failing economies of some settlements. The opportunities for wage labor grew with the increasing number of white agencies, both for menial jobs and for interpreters, construction men, clerks, etc. After World War II transportation frequency also increased vastly; not only did more government ships visit the settlements every year, but the introduction of general air transportation ensured that few settlements would be without relatively regular air service. This of course meant that the flurry of introduced diseases became more and more frequent, but at the same time the presence of medical personnel in most areas combatted the effects.

Since the 1950s the majority of the Canadian Eskimos have lived in settlements or even "towns" in relatively permanent dwellings and have engaged in a variety of occupations. Only in the more isolated and more abundant areas has sea-mammal hunting continued to be a major source of livelihood. Although the meat is much valued, sealskins have fetched relatively low prices save for exceptional years, and the cost of hunting with manufactured canoes or wooden boats, outboard or inboard motors, and gasoline, to say nothing of rifles and ammunition, precludes the viability of this occupation except where subsidized by other forms of income. Sea mammals no longer come close to human habitation because of the noise and possible pollution, so hunters must go farther and farther for them. Trapping has become a less important occupation too, not only because fox pelts have remained relatively static in price for the last twenty years, but because settlement living means longer journeys to the trap lines and the ancillary costs of trapping make it less profitable. Trapping by dog team has to be supported by successful summer hunting which, as noted earlier, must be subsidized; trapping by snowmobile has become very common but brings a profit only in those areas with an abundance of white fox because the initial price and the costs of use and rapid depreciation of these small and rather fragile vehicles far outweighs the income from pelts for most people. The point has been reached in some settlements where only those Eskimos with reliable wage labor can afford to go hunting and trapping with good equipment.

In addition to the family allowance, many Eskimo families, especially in the eastern and central Arctic, derive other forms of direct federal subsidy from welfare, pensions, rehabilitation allowances, etc., and there have been times when such forms of income have constituted more than half the total income of whole communities and areas. Wage employment obviously represents the most important growing sector of the monetary economy. Only a small proportion of Eskimos, however, have permanent wage employment. These jobs, usually at relatively unskilled levels and low rates of pay, include clerks, interpreters, janitors, assistant store managers, teachers' aides, nurses' aides, vehicle drivers, mechanics, and general manual labor; except in the Mackenzie Delta probably less than one-fifth of the total adult male population enjoys permanent jobs. Most adult men are also employed on temporary jobs, particularly in the construction of transport fields during the summers, and sometimes periods of full employment last for a few months at a time. Most women hold a lesser proportion of jobs—involved for most of their life in running households with many children—but a few occupy the kinds of positions noted above.

The outstanding feature of the economy of the central and eastern Canadian Arctic in the last two decades has been the growth and income from art and handicrafts manufacture. Though such activities brought in occasional income before and during World War II, with sales of souvenirs and clothing to resident traders, ships' crews, and other visitors, it was not until the early 1950s that this source of livelihood was encouraged and became widespread. Canadian government agents and Hudson's Bay Company traders encourage the Eskimos to make soapstone, and some ivory, sculptures for sale rather than as toys and trinkets; the total income from these grew from a few thousand dollars a year in 1950 and 1951 to hundreds of thousands a year by 1960. The majority of unemployed adult Eskimos turn their hand to carving and many make good incomes from this occupation. These small sculptures are sold through the local stores, now including cooperatives, and go through government-subsidized distributorships to dealers and retailers in Canada, the United States, and the rest of the world. In the late 1950s lithographic printmaking was also started, first at Cape Dorset and since then at four other settlements; this also now produces income to the Eskimos of more than half a million dollars a year while the total income from carving has grown to two million dollars net a year. Art and handicrafts are not necessarily a very favored occupation, for the majority of Eskimos would rather be able to hunt in an economical way and the younger members would rather have jobs "like the white man." It has been the savior of the economy, however, for many settlements. When a man wishes to go hunting he may subsidize it from his carving and hence be able to live a more "traditional" life than he would if he had no other income. In many instances when a man asks for relief the government administrator encourages him to carve, and the store managers encourage carvings to put money in the pockets of their customers who will then spend it on other goods in the stores. Sociologically, carving represents a suitable occupation for it does not make unreasonable demands on the majority of adult Eskimos; it allows a man to be his own boss and imposes no time schedule; it fits well with Eskimo concepts of work and manliness in many cases; and the carvers do not pay income tax on the income thus derived. Carving allows people to work for an income rather than depend on welfare, and it allows them to partake in a competitive, skilled, and ethnically distinctive enterprise. Furthermore, it is upon the production of carving and prints that the establishment and existence of the new cooperative institutions has depended. In a time when only a few Eskimos have security of good wage employment, this independent occupation allows others less literate or with fewer opportunities to reduce the potential difference in the standard of living between themselves and more fortunate members of their own community. In fact, it has come to the point where some long-employed people have given up their jobs in order to have the freedom of carving and hunting, and in a few cases they make a larger net income thereby.

Present Conditions

From external appearances Eskimo life now differs almost completely from that of twenty or thirty years ago. Mainly through government efforts, the face of the Arctic has changed almost completely, and the conditions of life, save for early childhood and some aspects of family life, would not be recognizable or even understandable to the grandfathers of the present adults.

Conversion to Christianity has been complete. Most of the church services and affairs are run by Eskimo elders, sometimes in association with resident missionaries in the case of the Anglican Church, which has made strenuous efforts to train and ordain Eskimo ministers; the Catholic Church, however, has fewer adherents in most areas and its affairs are run almost entirely by priests trained in Europe. Only in a few areas, particularly in the Mackenzie Delta, have these churches been responsible for general education of the Eskimos, and even these functions recently have been taken from the churches by the government with its implementation of universal, compulsory, secular education throughout the North.

This universal secular education appears in the form of federal day schools in all settlements and towns, staffed almost entirely by white government employees. The success in getting children to school is illustrated by the fact that throughout the Northwest Territories 1,425 Eskimos were enrolled in 1959–1960 and 4,493 in 1972–1973. As with many other occupations in the North, however, the problem remains that those in charge—with the high salaries, the respect, and the authority—remain white outsiders, for secondary education has not fared so well. The thrust of the educational effort has been to teach almost entirely in the English language following curricula approximately similar to models in southern Canada. Thus children progress through the grades according to their demonstrated abilities as measured by standardized tests, and those who do well may reach the sixth to ninth grades in the day schools in their own settlements. Until very recently there have been no high schools in the North except in the Mackenzie Delta, but they have now been opened or are under construction in at least three other large settlements. The majority pattern has been for Eskimo teenagers to go to special apprenticeship or vocational training programs in such centers as Churchill in Manitoba or more recently to complete high school in cities such as Ottawa or Montreal. Though some hundreds of Eskimos enroll in these various secondary-education programs every year, the success has been extremely limited until recently. Only a small proportion of those undergoing further training complete the programs and take jobs in their own communities. Most of them return without complete skills or without much prospect of jobs. Very few of those who attempt to complete high school do so, for the distractions of life in the South, including the widespread problems with drugs and alcohol, have prevented effective completion of these courses for all but a few.

Thus the majority of young adults returning to their settlements or other places in the North are able only to work semiskilled jobs rather than displace the imported whites in running their communities. Of course an even smaller proportion manage to get on to university or other forms of higher education. To date only one or two Canadian Eskimos have actually completed university degrees, though a handful of others have successfully completed other forms of higher educational training. Of these few, some do not return to the North to take the positions for which they are qualified, having spent many years in the South and being subject to many employment opportunities. Conceivably within the next few years the picture will change radically as tens if not hundreds of Eskimos complete their training programs successfully and take over the bulk of the skilled professional employment in the North.

The Canadian government has made similarly huge efforts with respect to Eskimo health with some measurable results. In the Northwest Territories (figures from northern Quebec and Labrador are not available) the Eskimo population has grown from 9,792 in 1967 to 11,619 in 1971, a rate of increase of nearly 5 per cent per year—perhaps one of the highest in the world. The fertility rate has remained extraordinarily high to account for such a natural increase because the infant mortality rate, which has always been high among the Eskimos, has continued to remain four or five times as high as that for southern Canadians (exact figures are not available because the Northwest Territory Annual Reports do not make the breakdown among Indians, Eskimos, and whites for this statistic). Extremely high infant mortality for Eskimos is shown by the figures (for 1967–1968, the latest available) that the average age at death for Eskimos is 21 years, as opposed to 41.5 for Indians; this figure rises to 37.7 years for Eskimos when infant mortalities are excluded, and 57.3 for Indians.

It is said that the Canadian government spends over a thousand dollars per capita per year on the health of the Eskimos (including all costs such as transportation, etc.), yet in spite of this the health picture in the North, when trends are discernible, looks very poor and very different from that for the majority of Canadians. Part of this obviously results from the Indians' and Eskimos' vulnerability to such diseases as pneumonia, tuberculosis, and epidemics from which most whites recover; part may result from the cultural patterns of traditional times being carried over into the present; but a larger part results from the conditions of life in the North, which would apply to whites as well as to Eskimos and Indians pursuing the same types of occupation.

For the Northwest Territories, the morbidity figures are not broken down among Indians and Eskimos and whites, but the latter group comprises less than half the total population. The major causes of death (over the period 1967–1971) are pneumonia, 22–19 per cent; injuries, violence, and accidents, 19–24 per cent; malformation and infancy, 18–13 per cent; tumors and cancer, 9–11 per cent; cardiovascular disease, 6–10 per cent; and diseases of the nervous system, 10–7 per cent. The major features to be noted are that though the diseases of civilization such as cardiovascular disease and cancer have increased while malformation and infant mortality have decreased, causes such as pneumonia and injuries, violence, and accidents have reached levels unheard of for most populations in southern Canada. Pneumonia accounts for a large proportion of infant mortality where colds and flu lead to more serious diseases. Deaths from injuries, violence, and accidents reflect partly the life of hunting and trapping and the distance from medical facilities and for natives and whites the use of alcohol. In 1969, for instance, 25 per cent of this category of death was associated with drunkenness, and in 1970 over 40 per cent related to the "excessive use of alcohol," that is, more than 10 per cent of all the deaths in the Northwest Territories. Until recently the Eskimos of the majority of settlements have been without access to alcohol save for the home brew which was probably learned from Company officials. In the last decade government liquor stores have been opened in the larger settlements and people in more isolated areas can order by mail; the prohibition on Indians' drinking was lifted in the 1960s, and there has never been law preventing Eskimos' drinking, as they are not "wards of the government" but full citizens. A significant proportion of these alcohol-related deaths are insidious and tragic—for instance, whites have been known to get young native women drunk for sexual purposes and then shoo them out to go home, and they and other drunk people have often frozen to death by falling down and going to sleep in the snow in the middle of winter. Even more common are deaths resulting from the "spiking" of home brews with such ingredients as methyl alcohol, duplicating-machine fluid, antifreeze, etc. It does not appear that the rate of death from such causes is decreasing at all in spite of the many warnings and the familiarity of a number of disasters every winter.

In addition to the morbidity rate, other phenomena of a new and serious nature include particularly the spread of venereal disease. Gonorrhea was always common in those Eskimo settlements near military bases, but it was usually controllable by the prompt medical attention obtainable in those same settlements and the Eskimos' lack of shame or fear of getting treatment. But since dozens of young Eskimos have been flown out to secondary and higher education and back to their home settlements twice or three times a year within the last decade, gonorrhea has spread to nearly all areas, often to married or older people where medical treatment is not so convenient. The overall rate for the Northwest Territories is 288 per hundred thousand, but this figure probably represents only the small proportion of reported cases and of course the figure includes all the ethnic groups in the territory.

Owing to the vast population increase in nearly all areas, voluntary birth-control programs have been introduced by the government through their nursing stations and other agencies, but these have not always met with acceptance. Many of the older and more religious Eskimos have consciously opposed the programs or demanded the removal of their easy availability, following the Biblical edict, "Go ye forth and multiply." Their rationale has often been backed by the expression of the fact that the Eskimos constitute a very small group in the world while the whites are very many and extremely well off materially.

The very complex economic picture in the Canadian North reflects both private developments and massive government efforts. In all but a few areas there is "massive unemployment" unless hunting, trapping, and carving are considered "full-time employment." For 80 to 90 per cent of the Eskimos these three activities now provide inadequate incomes for the high cost of living and their present or desired levels of consumption. Eskimo life has become "individualized" in that most families depend on the income of their own members while community-wide or extended-family economic cooperation is a very minor factor, especially since the almost complete monetization of the economy, including hunting. Massive private-enterprise developments are on the horizon. The small nickel mine at Rankin Inlet, open between 1957 and 1963, created employment for hundreds of Eskimos and completely changed the economy and social organization of that area. This is small compared with other potential developments usually involving mineral extraction. The Asbestos Hill development at Deception Bay would be a larger and longer-term project, though probably more mechanized. Exploration for ferrous and nonferrous metals has proceeded all over the Arctic with relatively great success in finding enormous deposits, including some of the largest deposits of iron ore in the world. These will be worked, however, only when world prices rise to the point where extraction under Arctic conditions and costs of transportation can be covered sufficiently to make the enterprise profitable and competitive with poorer ores found in more temperate parts of the world. The same applies to oil and natural-gas developments. Millions of acres have been released for exploration and test drilling, especially in the high Arctic islands north of regular Eskimo habitation. These are expected to be very successful, but again the costs of such oil and gas would be far higher than present world-market prices, perhaps even higher than that from the north slope of Alaska. If Canada were heavily populated, short of energy, and isolationist or protectionist in political sentiment, these deposits might be worked, but implementation of new developments awaits massive technological breakthroughs or dramatic rise in world prices. In Canada such developments are more under government control than in Alaska and possibly there would be greater regulation concerning ecological effects and the social and economic involvement of the Eskimo people. In the meantime, huge federal and regional government programs have provided the bulk of the employment and have changed the material face of Arctic communities.

In the 1960s the Canadian government implemented a massive program to house all Eskimos in prefabricated, well-insulated, heated wooden houses. Though this started at the turn of the decade with small one-room houses slightly larger than an igloo, the housing models shipped north have become larger and more expensive. Two- and three-bedroom houses replaced the one-room models in the mid-1960s, and by the end of the decade all Canadian Eskimos were supplied at minimal cost to them with housing adequate beyond their dreams. At the same time the Eskimos' expectations have grown and the number of whites and their buildings have set new goals for the native inhabitants. Free or cheap electric power is provided to nearly all the communities, but water distribution and sewage and garbage systems are in their infancy save in the massive new community of Inuvik, in the Mackenzie Delta, with its Utilidor System.

Tourism in the Canadian North has been promoted by a few enterprising individuals but mainly through government efforts. The attractions are primarily the excellent hunting and fishing and secondarily the well-known arts and handicrafts. Both Eskimos and whites run tourist camps but for the most part only the latter are profitable. At present transportation is expensive and conditions are not "civilized" enough for the majority of potential customers, so the few who come pay a high price for an exciting, "nonplastic" vacation. The local Eskimos have not yet learned to "perform" and defer as is the case with the package tours in northwestern Alaska. Tourism may loom larger in the future with cheaper access, but it is difficult to visualize as a large-scale profitable enterprise in the more attractive but more isolated areas.

The government encouragement and subsidy of the art and handicrafts market has provided a growing income and sense of purpose for many Eskimos who can no longer rely on hunting and trapping. More important than this, these activities have formed the nucleus and inspiration for the growth of both producers' and consumers' cooperatives in many settlements. These cooperatives, started at government instigation in the late 1950s, were originally designed to market products of the North such as Arctic char fish, carvings, prints, etc., in a way that would cut out commercial middlemen and return a greater profit to the community. They were of course in competition with commercial channels in most cases and had to be heavily subsidized for the first few years. Local residents were asked to contribute token shares toward the capital but the main capital came from government and other loans. The successful producers' cooperatives soon started consumer's cooperatives in the form of general stores competing with the Hudson's Bay Company. These too have enjoyed various forms of subsidy but some of them have profited and grown into large operations. The politicoeconomic development of these cooperatives has been very uneven, and in the Northwest Territories the tendency has been for white management to run them and make policy with occasional membership involvement while Eskimos work at the lower levels. In northern Quebec, however, there is more community involvement, and all employees are Eskimos, usually monolingual leading men of the community with the assistance of more educated, bilingual, younger Eskimos. Thus in a few places Eskimos have been able through their own efforts to assume economic power and prestige comparable to that of white agents in their own communities. Such men wield great power in the community, often becoming involved in community council work and other budding political organizations.

It has been suggested that these cooperatives throughout the Canadian North form federations for economy in buying and for training and education, but this has come to fruition only in northern Quebec. This latter Federation of Indian and Eskimo Cooperatives maintains a subsidized headquarters in southern Quebec to advise them on purchasing, accounting, and production and to distribute the products. Tentative contacts have been made between cooperative members in northern Quebec and in the Northwest Territories but so far no formal organizations have emerged. The Cooperative Federation has provided a prototype organization for political consciousness and action among Eskimos. The leaders of the cooperatives parallel those in the community councils and hold conventions once or twice a year at central settlements to work on policies and aspirations that go far beyond the running of cooperative stores. This is the beginning of regional self-determination for Eskimo communities within the provincial and national political framework of Canada; the leaders of northern Quebec have recently gone so far as to propose a regional political administrative organization for their land area which they would run eventually as a separate entity, though they state that this might take one or two generations to bring to fruition given the present educational and administrative experience of most Eskimos.

GREENLAND ESKIMOS

History and Acculturation

Although the European Vikings inhabited Greenland for hundreds of years, this first major colonization has had, as far as we can determine, no significant effects on recent history. Greenland was "rediscovered" in the sixteenth century, and serious colonization started as early as 1721 when the missionary Hans Egede set up one and then a series of permanent mission colonies among the West Greenlanders. With extensive work in the Eskimo language and a relatively benign and nonexploitative attitude, these efforts met with cooperation and conversions. (It might be noted that within three decades the same organization—Unitas Fratrum, or Moravians—set up a chain of mission posts along the Atlantic coast of Labrador.) Thus the West Greenlanders became the first of their race to be subject to permanent agents of European culture.

The Protestant Church acted as an official arm of the kingdom of Denmark, the missionaries administering both the people and the land "on behalf of God and Country." Unlike most other inhabitants of the North, for centuries the Greenlanders were subject to intrusive "rulers" who came not to make profits for crown or company but who, in an unavoidably paternalistic way, implemented policies supposedly for the benefit of the natives. In addition, racial admixture led to the West Greenland Eskimos becoming distinguished as Greenlanders (much as the Atlantic coast Labrador Eskimos have become "Settlers" or "Livyers"). The missionary settlers, like the Moravians in Labrador, operated trading stores for the Greenlanders under a government monopoly ostensibly to prevent exploitation from 1774 until the 1950s. These stores stocked only what the administrators thought were beneficial to Eskimo life and any "luxuries" were in short supply and sold at very high prices; sales of tobacco and later alcohol have been allowed only in recent decades and the latter is very much controlled. At first these stores traded for Eskimo products that were not deemed essential to Eskimo life and health, so items such as sea-mammal blubber and skins were not taken. To prevent large settlements and "post living," many small stores were distributed in the best hunting areas and attempts were made not to disrupt traditional life.

At the same time, education was emphasized both for spiritual purposes and to encourage local self-government; literacy in the Eskimo language was taught using a Latin orthography. For over a century local communities have had councils for administration of law and welfare on which Eskimos have been represented, though control has usually been in the hands of Danes and more recently Danish-speaking Greenlanders.

We have already mentioned in Chapter 11 that western Greenland borders on the Subarctic and that in the last two centuries the ever-warmer climate has driven away the seals and brought huge shoals of cod and other Atlantic fish to the shores, forcing a change in both the subsistance and commercial economy. During the same period the whaling fleets had practically eliminated the baleen and some of the smaller whales upon which the Greenlanders had depended for subsistence and some trade. The introduction of firearms in the last century led to the near extinction of native caribou, thus eliminating another source of meat for consumption and hides for trade. During the nineteenth century the western Greenland population showed a marked natural increase partly due to better medical services and partly due to increased material security and end of starvation. The introduction of animal husbandry—hardy sheep and cattle—did little for the economy and, with no significant mineral extractions, commercial fishing became the principal occupation save for the northernmost part of the west coast. The majority of the Greenlanders then changed from their Eskimo-type hunting-by-kayak to European-type, small-scale line fishing. With many-hooked long lines and small wooden boats they fished in coastal waters for cod and Greenland shark. Unfortunately until recently they have been technologically behind the fleets of European motor vessels with huge nets that fish the same shoals in more open waters. Nevertheless the life of Greenlanders has become more like that of northern European peasant fishermen than that of their ancestors. As the stores began to stock many metal goods, household conveniences, and lumber, the Greenlanders, before the end of the last century, abandoned their stone and sod houses for painted, rectangular, wooden houses furnished with coal stoves, so the settlements resemble coastal villages anywhere in Scandinavia.

During the present century, although motor vessels and other forms of advanced technology have led to fish catches in the tens of thousands of tons annually, the income from exports has been far outstripped by the money that Denmark has spent on health, education, welfare, and administration for Greenland. Thus we may say that for nearly all its history Greenland has been one of the few colonies in the world that has cost its mother country far more than it has ever produced.

The two other small populations of Greenland Eskimos, the Polar Eskimos and the East Greenlanders, have had a different history. The Polar or Thule Eskimos, discovered only in the last century, led an almost undisturbed hunting existence until well into this century. They were involved in Peary's North Pole Expedition, and by the second decade a store was established at Thule by Knud Rasmussen. The profits from this small breach in the government monopoly helped finance the Thule Expeditions (see previous chapter). Later a USAF base and recently a huge BMEWS site have been established at Thule, but contact with the American military has wisely been banned. The few hundred Eskimos live in scattered hunting and trapping villages with government-operated stores and schools.

The East Greenland Eskimos centered around Ammassalik were discovered in 1884, by which time the east coast had become nearly depopulated by ecological pressures and by a drift of the inhabitants around Cape Farewell to the more hospitable west coast. This trend was halted by the construction of schools and stores, and with diminished starvation and infanticide the population grew fast. Shark fishing was encouraged but the population increase outstripped the resources, and during this century new settlements have been established along the coast to the north and south of Ammassalik, each with its schools and stores. The now near two thousand East Greenland Eskimos have partially "caught up" with the West Greenlanders through education in the west, administrative exchanges of Greenland personnel, and direct government efforts.

Present Conditions

During World War II when the Germans occupied Denmark, the Danes officially ceded temporary control of Greenland to the United States for military purposes. The Germans tried to set up bases in east Greenland but were driven off. As with certain areas in Canada, the American presence led to increased material consumption and expectation. After the war Denmark reasserted sovereignty and in a series of studies re-examined their total policies toward Greenland. As in Canada, this represented only in a small way a response to pressures of the governed indigenous peoples; it was much more a response to worldwide political events emphasizing the rights of governed peoples and a wave of liberalization in those countries having colonies. Most of the world's colonies achieved independent self-government within the next decade or so, but even though the Danes had done more in promoting education and political organization for Greenland than had the other countries with Eskimo groups, self-government was clearly not possible at that point.

The Danes took the other course—as France tried unsuccessfully in Algeria—and incorporated Greenland as a province within the kingdom of Denmark; surprisingly perhaps, only the people of Denmark were allowed to vote on the referendum deciding this matter! This major transition, implemented in 1953, was accompanied by other important changes. Local, regional, and provincial self-government was promoted and selected members were sent to the Danish parliament, as all Greenlanders became "full citizens." The government ended its trade monopoly with a policy of opening Greenland to the modern world rather than keeping it as a state of welfare-supported hunters and fishermen. Large-scale fishing enterprises were capitalized along with factories and canneries, especially for the newly discovered huge shrimp bed off western Greenland. Most importantly the Danes put additional emphasis and money into education—they introduced the teaching of Danish into elementary schools at the behest of Greenlanders, and offered more advanced education in Greenland. Successful students went on to higher education in Denmark at the rate of more than a thousand a year. Denmark also implemented massive new health programs that resulted in a rate of population increase of over 4 per cent, so that Greenland's population stood at more than 45,000 in 1972, compared with the 9,000 or so at the time of first colonization.

These programs were presented to the Greenlanders and received with apparent joy, for they foresaw this as the achievement of "equal rights" and hence access to money and material standards that seemed to make the ruling Danes so happy. The Greenlanders' self-image changed; they saw the Danes as human rather than superhuman and they felt able to make demands for rights and equality in a way that a subject colonial people rarely dreamed of. The majority of the Danes both in Denmark and Greenland took the naive but then prevalent attitude that, once legalized ethnic stratification was abolished, the Greenlander would assimilate to become a kind of Dane—much as the Americans of the last century assumed that Indians would assimilate and lose their group cohesion and distinctiveness.

Subsequent events proved both sides wrong. The vast construction and capitalization programs needed skilled labor and administration, most of which had to be supplied from Denmark. Thus many thousands of Danes worked under contract in Greenland, increasing the proportion and visibility of the ex-rulers to the resentment of the ex-colonials, and many of these Danes married Greenland women. More importantly, in order to get them to work there, the Danes received higher salaries than the Greenlanders in the same job. Even though it was pointed out that the Greenlanders did not pay the heavy income taxes that the Danes had to pay, educated and semiskilled Greenlanders looked for equal pay and better job opportunities within their own land. The educational programs were very successful and produced Greenlanders in such professions as teachers, lawyers, administrators, etc., though some of those who went to Denmark stayed there, fearing lack of advancement in their own homeland. In Greenland the Danish-speaking, educated elite wished to take the top jobs and effective power "immediately" in spite of their inexperience; in fact, many important positions are held by Greenlanders. Political parties began to compete for the votes of the mass of Greenlanders, seeking to represent them in Denmark. One party even wished to introduce the Danish income tax in order to claim equal pay for Greenlanders, but it was defeated by the mass of the poorer people.

Greenlandic identity has not disappeared, though it has been redefined by the educated leaders. Though Danes and Greenlanders live in the same apartment buildings, work at the same jobs, and speak the same language, these leaders claim to have much more in common with the more traditional monolingual Greenlanders along the coasts. And it is true that the latter consciously choose Danish speakers as their representatives even when they dislike them or distrust them personally.

A major and crucial problem, common to many ethnic minority groups around the world, is the position and future of the indigenous language vis-à-vis the majority language—that is, Greenlandic versus Danish. For a hundred years before decolonization, Danish was taught to the few in secondary schools but Greenlandic (Eskimo) continued to be used as the everyday language and in newspapers and other publications. With the increasing universality and complexity of education in the past few decades, various "tracks" were introduced allowing for more education in Danish but some secondary education in Greenlandic for the "lower achievers." After 1953 the Greenlanders, seeing that access to wealth and power depended upon a knowledge of Danish, insisted that their children be introduced to Danish in the primary grades rather than be put years behind compared with their co-citizens in Denmark. Since then 20 to 30 percent have become fluent in Danish, enjoying better jobs, more political power, and a standard of living that is a model for the aspirations of others—reinforcing the desires of the majority (for their children) to learn Danish. Thus the Greenlandic language has become more limited as the language of the home, of manual labor, and of some self-consciously "ethnic" literature.

The vast majority of Danes and Greenlanders express the sentiment that Greenlanders should never lose their mother tongue, yet some have pointed out that the dual education handicaps the majority of the bilingual young people and that eventually Greenlandic may or should be lost, especially if overpopulation leads to considerable emigration to Denmark. As with other circumpolar peoples, the burden of compulsory bilingualism for the sake of identity maintenance is proving an emotional problem with few if any satisfactory solutions. Given the experience of the United States one could say that even Danish monolingual Greenlanders will not lose, though they may change, their distinctive ethnicity. But few foresee or advocate the loss of Greenlandic for the sake of "progress and equality." In Scandinavia, by contrast, the vast majority of those of Lapp descent no longer speak Lappish or identify themselves as Samek, for the rise of ethnic consciousness and pan-Lappism came at a date too late in their history to prevent the assimilation of all but a few occupationally distinctive holdouts.

ANNOTATED BIBLIOGRAPHY

Siberian Native Peoples

Soviet policy on the national question is based in part on V. I. Lenin, *Questions of National Policy and Proletarian Internationalism* (Moscow: Progress Publishers [1913–1922], n.d.), and on J. V. Stalin, "Marxism and the National Question," in *Selections from V. I. Lenin and J. V. Stalin on National Colonial Question* (Calcutta: Calcutta Book House [1912–1913], 1970).

Some long-range historical overviews of cultural change in northern Siberia include: L. P. Potapov, "Historical-Ethnographic Survey of the Russian Population of Siberia in the Prerevolutionary Period," pp. 105–202 in M. G. Levin and L. P. Potapov (eds.), *The Peoples of Siberia* (Chicago: University of Chicago Press, 1964); Terence Armstrong, *Russian Settlement in the North* (Cambridge: Cambridge University Press, 1965); I. S. Gurvich, *Ethnic Changes in Northeastern Siberia during the Last Three Centuries*, VII International Congress of Anthropological and Ethnological Sciences (Moscow: "Nauka" Publishing House, 1964); and Marc Raeff, *Siberia and the Reforms of 1822* (Seattle: University of Washington Press, 1956).

An intelligent overview of modern conditions in Siberia written for the general reader is George St. George, *Siberia: The New Frontier* (New York: McKay, 1969). Some journalistic accounts of modern Siberia include: Dean Conger, "Siberia: Russia's Frozen Frontier," *National Geographic*, 131:3:297–347 (March 1967); and Karl Staf, *Yakutia as I Saw It* (Moscow: Foreign Languages Publishing House, 1958).

Scholarly publications by Soviet authors on the modern conditions of native Siberians include: B. A. Vasil'yev, Iu. B. Simchenko, and Z. P. Sokolova, "Problems of the Reconstruction of Daily Life among the Small Peoples of the Far North," *Soviet Anthropology and Archeology*, 5:2:11–21 (Fall 1966); I. S. Gurvich, "Directions to Be Taken in the Further Reorganization of the Economy and Culture of the Peoples of the North," *Soviet Anthropology and Archeology*, 1:2:22–30 (Fall 1962); V. B. Strakach, *National Traditions in Pre-School and School Practical Training in Taiga and Tundra Areas of Siberia*, VII International Congress of Anthropological and Ethnological Sciences (Moscow: "Nauka" Publishing House, 1964); and V. A. Tugolukov, *Development of Small Peoples of the North in Modern Conditions*, VII International Congress of Anthropological and Ethnological Sciences (Moscow: "Nauka" Publishing House, 1964). An important source of information on the Yakut, Yukagirs, Evenks, and Chukchi is M. G. Levin and L. P. Potapov (eds.), *The Peoples of Siberia* (Chicago: University of Chicago Press, 1964), in which appear S. A. Tokarev and I. S. Gurvich, "The Yakuts," especially pp. 287–304; M. V. Stepanova, I. S. Gurvich, and V. V. Khramova, "The Yukagirs," especially pp. 797–798; G. M. Vasilevich and A. V. Smolyak, "The Evenks," especially pp. 652–654; and V. V. Antropov and V. G. Kuznetsova, "The Chukchi," especially pp. 825–835. For a discussion of modern conditions of the Chukchi in Soviet ethnographic literature, see Alexander Vucinch, "Soviet Ethnographic Studies of Cultural Change," *American Anthropologist*, 62:867–877 (1960).

Some works by Western scholars on modern Siberia are Terence Armstrong, "The Administration of Northern Peoples: The USSR," pp. 57–88, and Neil C. Field, "Administrative and Constitutional Changes in Arctic Territories: The USSR," pp. 160–193, both essays in R. St. J. MacDonald (ed.), *The Arctic Frontier* (Toronto: University of Toronto Press, 1966). There is also a brief discussion of policy on the national question in Erich Thiel, *The Soviet Far East: A Survey of Its Physical and Economic Geography* (London: Methuen, 1957). A series of informative and somewhat critical articles on Soviet policy and its results in Siberia are Stephen P. and Ethel Dunn, "The Transformation of Economy and Culture in the Soviet North," *Arctic Anthropology*, 1:2:1–28 (1963); Stephen P. and Ethel Dunn, "Talks with Soviet Ethnographers and Some Reflections," *American Anthropologist*, 67:4:985–997 (1965); Ethel Dunn, "Educating the Small Peoples of the Soviet North: The Limits of Cultural Change," *Arctic Anthropology*, 5:1:1–31 (1968); and Ethel Dunn, "Education and the Native Intelligentsia in the Soviet North: Further Thoughts on the Limits of Cultural Change," *Arctic Anthropology*, 6:2:112–122 (1970).

For an account (although not a typical one) of an ethnographer working in the Siberian North under modern conditions, see Vilmos Dioszegi, *Tracing Shamans in Siberia: The Story of an Ethnographical Research Expedition* (Oosterhout: Anthropological Publications, 1968).

Alaska—General

The factual data for this section were taken mainly from: *Alaska Natives and the Land* (Washington, D.C.: U.S. Government Printing Office, 1968); Robert M. Pennington and H. P. Gazaway, *Profile of the Native People of Alaska* (Juneau: U.S. Department of the Interior, Bureau of Indian Affairs, 1967); George W. Rogers and Richard A. Cooley, *Alaska's Population and Economy: Regional Growth, Development and Future Outlook*, Vols. I and II (College: University of Alaska Press, 1963); and John R. Snodgrass, Jr., *Alaska Statistical Review 1970* (State of Alaska, Department of Economic Development, Industrial Development Division, 1970).

The theoretical discussion on the contradiction between the city and the countryside as it applies to the economy of native Americans was taken from Joseph G. Jorgensen, "Indians and the Metropolis," in Jack O. Waddell and O. Michael Watson (eds.), *The American Indian in Urban Society* (Boston: Little, Brown, 1971).

For histories of Alaska in this century, dealing with themes of monopoly, capitalism, and imposed control of the Alaskan economy, consult: Jeannette P. Nichols, *Alaska: A History of Its Administration, Exploitation and Industrial Development during Its First Half Century under the Rule of the United States* (Cleveland: Clark, 1924); Ernest Gruening, *The State of Alaska* (New York: Random House, 1968); George W. Rogers, "Change in Alaska: The 1960's and After," in George W. Rogers (ed.), *Change in Alaska: People, Petroleum and Politics* (College: University of Alaska Press, 1970); and Stuart Ramsay Tompkins, *Alaska: Promyshlennik and Sourdough* (Norman: University of Oklahoma Press, 1945).

The following works discuss Alaska native political organizations and the land-claims issue: Philip Drucker, *The Native Brotherhoods: Modern Intertribal Organizations on the Northwest Coast* (Washington, D.C.: U.S. Government Printing Office, 1958); John Borbridge, Jr., "Native Organization and Land Rights as Vehicles for Change," in George W. Rogers (ed.), *Change in Alaska: People, Petroleum and Politics* (College: University of Alaska Press, 1970); Gordon Harrison, "History of Native Organizations," *Tundra Times*, 9:14 (December 17, 1971), and "Tlingit-Haida Settlement," *ibid*. A comprehensive overview of the growth and successes of the contemporary native organization is M. Lantis, "The Current Nativistic Movement in Alaska," pp. 99–118 in G. Berg (ed.), *Circumpolar Problems* (Oxford: Pergamon, 1973).

The following government publications deal with land-claims settlements and are useful records of the views of the various groups concerned: *Alaska Native Land Claims: Hearings before the Committee on Interior and Insular Affairs* (U.S. Senate, 90th Cong., 2nd sess., 1968); *Hearings before the Subcommittee on Indian Affairs of the Committee on Interior and Insular Affairs* (U.S. House of Representatives on H. R. 11213, H. R. 15049, and H. R. 17129, 1968); *Hearings before the Committee on Interior and Insular Affairs* (U.S. Senate on S. 35 and S. 835, Parts I, II, and III, 1971); and *Hearings before the Subcommittee on Indian Affairs of the Committee on Interior and Insular Affairs* (U.S. House of Representatives on H. R. 3100, H. R. 7039, and H. R. 7432, 1971), all available from Washington, D.C.: U.S. Government Printing Office. The reference to the text of the settlement act is: *Alaska Native Claims Settlement Act* (U.S. Senate Report No. 92-581, 92nd Cong., 1st sess., 1971).

For the views of the native peoples on various issues, consult the newspaper of the Alaskan natives: *The Tundra Times*, Box 1287, Fairbanks, Alaska 99701 ($10/year). Of particular interest is the special land-claims issue—*Tundra Times*, 9:14 (December 17, 1971)—which contains a copy of the Alaska Native Claims Settlement Act Conference Report in addition to many articles on the land-claims movement.

Studies that are useful for understanding the lives of the native peoples of modern Alaska include: Diamond Jenness, *Eskimo Administration: I, Alaska* (Montreal: Arctic Institute of North America, Technical Paper No. 10, 1962); and Margaret Lantis, "The Administration of Northern Peoples: Canada and Alaska," pp. 89–119 in R. St. J. MacDonald (ed.), *The Arctic Frontier* (Toronto: University of Toronto Press, 1966).

Alaskan Eskimos

The Eskimos of Alaska have been the subject of far more research and publication than have the other native peoples, so we are able to offer a more detailed guide to the regional and local literature on them. For further references the reader should consult the extensive annotated bibliography of Arthur E. Hippler, *Eskimo Acculturation* (Fairbanks:

University of Alaska Institute of Social, Economic and Government Research, 1970), and, of course, the general introduction to traditional cultures by Wendell H. Oswalt, *Alaskan Eskimos* (San Francisco: Chandler, 1967). A number of community or regional ethnographies adequately describe the contemporary situation and problems, though they differ in emphasis and approaches: James W. Van Stone, *An Eskimo Community and the Outside World* (College: University of Alaska, Anthropological Papers, 7:1:27–38, 1958); Charles C. Hughes, *An Eskimo Village in the Modern World* (Ithaca, N.Y.: Cornell University Press, 1960); James W. Van Stone, *Point Hope: An Eskimo Village in Transition* (Seattle: University of Washington Press, 1962); Frederick A. Milan, *The Acculturation of the Contemporary Eskimo of Wainwright* (College: University of Alaska, Anthropological Papers, 11:2:1–85, 1964); Nicholas J. Gubser, *The Nunamiut Eskimos, Hunters of Caribou* (New Haven: Yale University Press, 1965); and Claire Fejes, *People of Noatak* (New York: Knopf, 1966). These may be supplemented by more extensive comparative accounts such as James W. Van Stone and Wendell H. Oswalt's *Three Eskimo Communities* (College: University of Alaska, Anthropological Papers, 9:1:17–56, 1960); Norman A. Chance, *The Eskimo of North Alaska* (New York: Holt, Rinehart and Winston, 1966); and the summaries in Don Charles Foote and Sheila K. MacBain's *A Selected Regional Bibliography for Human Geographical Studies of Native Populations in Central Alaska* (Montreal: McGill University, Department of Geography, Publication No. 12, 1964).

Works focused particularly on the problems of acculturation and social relations to the larger world include: Charles C. Hughes, "From Contest to Council: Social Change among the St. Lawrence Island Eskimos," pp. 255–263 in M. J. Swartz, V. W. Turner, and A. Tuden (eds.), *Political Anthropology* (Chicago: Aldine, 1966); Norman A. Chance, "The Changing World of Government among the North Alaskan Eskimos," *Arctic Anthropology*, 2:2:41–44; Wendell H. Oswalt, "Guiding Culture Change among Alaskan Eskimos," *American Indigena*, 21:1:65–83, "The New Alaskan Eskimo," *Americas*, 13:9:10–13, and "The Village People," *Anchorage Daily News* (1966); and, of course, the already mentioned masterful comparative works by Jenness (1962) and Hughes (1964). Other publications have concentrated on the psychological and identity aspects of acculturation, as have some of the more ethnographic accounts mentioned above; these include Seymour Parker, "Ethnic Identity and Acculturation in Two Eskimo Villages," *American Anthropologist*, 66:2:325–340 (1964); Norman .A. Chance, "Acculturation, Self-Identification and Personality Adjustment," *American Anthropologist*, 67:2:372–393 (1965); and the more personal work by Margaret Lantis, "Eskimo Childhood and Interpersonal Relationships: Nunivak Biographies and Genealogies," in Verne F. Ray (ed.), *The American Ethnological Society* (Seattle: University of Washington Press, 1960). The impact of technological innovation and the socioeconomic consequences of various adaptations are considered at length in

Margaret Lantis, "Eskimo Herdsmen," pp. 127–148 in Ed Spicer (ed.), *Human Problems in Technological Change* (New York: Russell Sage Foundation, 1952); Richard K. Nelson, *Hunters of the Northern Ice* (Chicago: University of Chicago Press, 1969); and Edwin S. Hall, Jr., "The 'Iron Dog' in Northern Alaska," *Anthropologica*, 13:1, 2:237–254 (1971). Other more specialized developments are, in the arts, Dorothy Jean Ray, *Artists of the Tundra and the Sea* (Seattle: University of Washington Press, 1961), and in education, Warren Tiffany, *Education in Northwest Alaska* (Juneau: Bureau of Indian Affairs, 1966); but the reader must consult the relevant bibliographies and journals for the mass of references to most specialized research projects and publications.

Canadian Indians and Eskimos

It has only recently become at all common for these two major northern groups to be considered together, for previously Eskimos as a whole had been considered a cultural unit and Subarctic Indians were usually included with other Indians. However, the modernization of these groups has led to an increasing social and cultural similarity as "native peoples" and an enhancement of the importance of the local and national domains within which they are found. Scattered throughout the Canadian government "Hawthorn Report" are a few basic statistical statements on the contemporary Canadian Indians—H. B. Hawthorn (ed.), *A Survey of the Contemporary Indians of Canada*, 2 vols. (Ottawa: Indian Affairs Branch, 1966–1967). Further and more up-to-date statistical data are to be found in S. M. Hodgson, *Annual Report of the Commissioner of the Northwest Territories* (Yellowknife, NWT: Department of Information, 1966–1967, 1967–1968, 1969, 1970, 1971, 1972); unfortunately in the last two or three years, this publication has failed to distinguish between Eskimos, Indians, and "others" in its presentation of much important demographic, educational, and employment data. Some shorter works on specific aspects of recent and contemporary Indian and Eskimo culture, embracing more than the Canadian north, include J. J. Honigmann, "Community Organization and Patterns of Change among North Canadian and Alaskan Indians and Eskimos," *Anthropologica*, 5:1:3–8 (1963); N. C. Field, "Administrative and Constitutional Changes in Arctic Territories," pp. 160–193, and M. Lantis, *op. cit.*, the latter two appearing in R. St. J. MacDonald (ed.), *The Arctic Frontier* (Toronto: University of Toronto Press, 1966).

The impact of particular white institutions on the Indians and Eskimos of northern Quebec appears as follows in J. Malaurie and J. Rousseau (eds.), *Le Nouveau Quebec* (Paris: Mouton, 1964); A. Cooke, "The Exploration of New Quebec," pp. 137–179; G. Carriere, OMI, "L'Oeuvre des Oblats de Marie-Immaculée Dans le Nord Canadien Oriental," pp. 395–425; and D. B. Marsh, "History of the Anglican Church in Northern Quebec and Ungava," pp. 427–437. Within this area the multiethnic community of Great Whale River has been explored by

J. J. Honigmann, *Social Networks in Great Whale River* (Ottawa: National Museum of Canada, Bulletin No. 178, Anthropological Series No. 54, 1964); A. Balikci, "Relations inter-ethniques à la Grande Rivière de la Baliene, baie d'Hudson, 1957," pp. 64–107 in *Contributions to Anthropology, 1959* (Ottawa: National Museum of Canada, Bulletin No. 173, 1961).

In the western Arctic, the Mackenzie Delta region has long been inhabited by both Indians and Eskimos whose descendants now constitute mixed populations in the modern communities. A useful overview of the recent history and "social development" of the new town of Inuvik is J. J. and I. Honigmann, *Arctic Townsmen: Ethnic Backgrounds and Modernization* (Ottawa: Canadian Research Centre for Anthropology, St. Paul University, 1970); some problems in the twin community of Aklavik are described and analyzed in D. H. J. Clairmont, *Notes on the Drinking Behavior of the Eskimos and Indians in the Aklavik Area* (Ottawa: Northern Co-ordination and Research Centre, 62-4, 1962), and *Deviance among Indians and Eskimos in Aklavik, NWT* (Ottawa: Northern Co-ordination and Research Centre, 63-9, 1963). Further intensive research on most sociological and material aspects of the Mackenzie Delta region appear in the many volumes of the *Mackenzie Delta Research Project* (1967–present), obtainable from the Northern Science Research Group, Department of Indian Affairs and Northern Development, Ottawa.

Canadian Subarctic Indians

The Canadian Subarctic Indians have received less attention both from anthropologists and the government than have the Eskimos. Chapter 9 has covered the majority Indian population of the Mackenzie Delta; other references appear in Chapter 10 and in the section on Canadian Indians and Eskimos above. There are few overviews of the history of the Subarctic Indians as such, but Chapter 17, "Interaction of Indians and Whites," in D. Jenness, *The Indians of Canada* (Ottawa: National Museum of Canada, Bulletin No. 65, 6th ed., 1963) may serve as a useful if pessimistic introduction, and J. Helm and E. Leacock, "The Hunting Tribes of Sub-Arctic Canada," Chapter 12 in E. B. Leacock and N. O. Lurie (eds.), *North American Indians in Historical Perspective* (New York: Random House, 1972) provides an overview by two of the leading experts in the field.

For the views of scholars on more specialized aspects of Indian life in modern Canada, see G. C. Monture et al., *Indians and the Law* (Ottawa: Queens Printer, Canadian Corrections Association, 1967); R. Poppe, "Where Will All the Natives Go?" and J. Hodgkinson, "Is Northern Education Meaningful?" both in *Western Canadian Journal of Anthropology* (Special Issue on Athabascan Studies), 1:1 (1970), 150–155 and 164–175 respectively; and J. W. Van Stone, "Changing Patterns of Indian Trapping in the Canadian Subarctic," *Arctic*, 16:3:159–174 (1963).

Regional and community studies are more common, at least for certain areas. (All bulletins and papers listed in this paragraph are published by the National Museum of Canada in Ottawa.) The Cree surrounding James Bay and Lake Mistassini have received considerable attention, especially from E. S. Rogers: *Subsistence Areas of the Cree-Ojibwa of the Eastern Subarctic: A Preliminary Study* (Bulletin No. 204, 1966, pp. 87–118), "Band Organization among the Indians of Eastern Subarctic Canada," pp. 21–50 in *Contributions to Anthropology: Band Societies* (Bulletin No. 228, 1969), *The Material Culture of the Mistassini* (Bulletin No. 190, 1960). See also R. Knight, *Ecological Factors in Changing Economy and Social Organization among the Rupert House Cree* (Anthropological Papers, No. 15, 1968); and L. Mason, *The Swampy Cree: A Study of Acculturation* (Anthropological Papers, No. 13, 1967).

For discussions of the social, economic, political, and ecological impact of the James Bay Project, see "La Baie James des Amerindiens," in a special issue of *Bulletin d'Information Recherches Amérindiennes au Québec* (Montreal), 1:4,5 (1971).

The McGill University Cree Developmental Change Project, based on research among the eastern James Bay and central Quebec Cree, has so far published one volume of collected essays, N. A. Chance (ed.), *Conflict in Culture: Problems of Developmental Change among the Cree* (Ottawa: St. Paul University, Canadian Research Centre for Anthropology, 1968), and other works are expected. The few northeasternmost Algonquians have been the subject of research by members of the Institute of Social and Economic Research at Memorial University of Newfoundland; G. Henriksen's "Moshwa'w Inno: The Barren Ground People," concerning the Davis Inlet Naskapi, is in press, but may appear with a modified title. E. Leacock's "The Montagnais-Naskapi Band," pp. 1–17 in *Contributions to Anthropology: Band Societies* (Ottawa: National Museum of Canada, Bulletin No. 228, 1969) summarizes our information of the social organization of the eastern and northeastern Algonquians and complements her previous work on these people.

The northern Athabascan peoples have been subject to less intensive historical contact and relatively fewer research projects than the Algonquians. (See also the bibliographies of Chapters 7 and 9.) Ethnography of contact-traditional Athabascan culture around the Great Lakes of the Northwest Territories have been described by J. J. Honigmann, *Ethnology and Acculturation of the Fort Nelson Slave*, Yale University Publications in Anthropology, No. 51 (New Haven: Yale University Press, 1946), and *Foodways in a Muskeg Community* (Ottawa: Northern Co-ordination and Research Centre, 62-1, 1962); by C. Osgood, *The Ethnography of the Great Bear Lake Indians* (Ottawa: National Museum of Canada, Bulletin No. 70, 1932, pp. 31–34; and by J. A. Mason, *Notes on the Indians of the Great Slave Lake Area*, Yale University Publications in Anthropology, No. 34 (New Haven: Yale University Press, 1946).

Much of the recent work on the Dogrib and other Athabascan groups has been published by J. Helm, "The Dogrib Indians," Chap. 2 in M. Bicchieri (ed.), *Hunting-Gathering Societies* (New York: Holt, Rinehart and Winston, 1972); with N. O. Lurie, *The Subsistence Economy of the Dogrib Indians of Lac la Martre in the Mackenzie District of the Northwest Territories* (Ottawa: Northern Co-ordination and Research Centre, 1961); with D. Damas, "The Contact-Traditional All-Native Community of the Canadian North: The Upper Mackenzie 'Bush' Athapaskans and the Igluligmiut," *Anthropologica*, 5:9–22 (1963); and with June MacNeish, "Leadership among the Northeastern Athabascans," *Anthropologica*, 2:131–163 (1956), and "Bilaterality in the Socio-Territorial Organization of the Arctic Drainage Dene," *Ethnology*, 4:361–385 (1965).

Some more recent publications touching on more contemporary problems of these groups include R. Slobodin, *The Metis of the Mackenzie District* (Ottawa: St. Paul University, Canadian Research Centre of Anthropology, 1966); A. R. King, *The School at Mopass: A Problem in Identity* (New York: Holt, Rinehart and Winston, 1967); and B. Cox, "Land Rights of the Slavey Indians at Hay River, NWT," *Western Canadian Journal of Anthropology*, 1:1:150–155 (1970). Articles and issues in the journal *Recherches Amérindiennes au Québec* have paid particular attention to the contemporary problems of the Ungava and James Bay areas, and have been diligent in presenting the Indians' points of view on such matters as the James Bay Project. It is expected that increasing Euro-Canadian penetration and exploitation of this huge Subarctic area will provoke considerably more research and publication in the near future.

Eskimos—General

The outstanding work on the recent history and sociopolitical changes of all Eskimos is C. C. Hughes, "Under Four Flags: Recent Culture Change among the Eskimos," *Current Anthropology*, 6:1:3–73 (1965); this work and D. Jenness's four volumes on *Eskimo Administration* have contributed much to the relevant sections of this chapter. D. Jenness, "The Administration of Northern Peoples: America's Eskimos—Pawns of History," pp. 120–129 in MacDonald, *op. cit.*, is a shorter summary of the recent history of contact of the North American Eskimos. Other short works touching upon limited aspects of the contemporary Eskimos include M. Lantis, "Problems of Human Ecology in the North American Arctic," *Arctic*, 7:3, 4:307–320 (1954); E. H. Ackerknecht, "Medicine and Disease among Eskimos," *CIBA Symposium*, 10:916–921 (July–August 1948); C. W. Hobart, "Eskimo Education, Danish and Canadian: A Comparison," *Canadian Review of Sociology and Anthropology*, 3:2:47–66 (1966), and contributions to the special issue of *The Beaver* on Eskimo art (Outfit 298, Autumn 1967). For a more thorough listing of relevant works, see the annotated bibliography of A. E. Hippler, *Eskimo Acculturation* (College, Alaska: Institute of Social, Economic and Government Research, No. 28, 1970).

As with the literature on traditional Eskimo culture, there is probably more published research on the relatively fewer Eskimos of Canada
than on those of either Alaska or Greenland. We have relied heavily
on D. Jenness, *Eskimo Administration: II, Canada* (Montreal: Arctic
Institute of North America, Technical Paper No. 14, 1964); and for
a selection of essays on aspects of contemporary Eskimo culture, the
reader should also consult M. van Steensel (ed.), *People of Light and
Dark* (Ottawa: Department of Indian Affairs and Northern Development, 1966); and V. F. Valentine and F. G. Vallee (eds.), *Eskimo of
the Canadian Arctic* (Princeton, N.J.: Van Nostrand, 1968), especially
Part II.

In a number of monographs that analyze general sociocultural developments regionally or comparatively, the principles elucidated may be
applied to other Eskimo groups, even beyond the bounds of Canada.
A. Balikci, *Development of Basic Socio-Economic Units in Two Eskimo
Communities* (Ottawa: National Museum of Canada, Bulletin No. 202,
1964) is a detailed analysis of sociological, economic, and technological
change; N. H. H. Graburn, *Eskimos without Igloos* (Boston: Little,
Brown, 1969) attempts to cover the total range of social, economic,
and political changes up to urbanization; F. G. Vallee, *Kabloona and
Eskimo in the Central Keewatin* (Ottawa: St. Paul University, Canadian
Research Centre for Anthropology, 1967) concentrates on changing life
styles and the growing intra-Eskimo social stratification.

The Northern Co-ordination and Research Centre (now the Northern Science Research Group, see above) has supported much research
and many publications on contemporary Eskimo community since
1958: J. W. Van Stone and W. H. Oswalt, Eskimo Point, 1959; W. E.
Willmott, Port Harrison P.Q., 1961; R. C. and L. A. Dailey, Rankin
Inlet, 1961; J. D. Ferguson, Tuktoyaktuk, NWT, 1961; T. Yatsushiro,
Frobisher Bay, 1963; N. H. H. Graburn, Lake Harbour, NWT, 1963;
and Sugluk and environs, 1964, etc. The extreme cases of the urbanization of Canadian Eskimos and resultant sociopsychological problems
are considered in J. J. and I. Honigmann, *Eskimo Townsmen* (Ottawa:
Canadian Research Centre for Anthropology, University of Ottawa,
1965) and in those works on the Mackenzie Delta described above.

Among the significant recent developments in Canadian Eskimo
culture, artistic endeavors set them off from other Eskimos and have
been subject to a number of important publications: the historical archeological background is best seen in C. A. Martijn, "Canadian Eskimo
Carving in Historical Perspective," *Anthropos*, 59:546–596 (1964), and
in the issue of *The Beaver* mentioned above; for a short introduction
see N. H. H. Graburn, "The Eskimos and 'Airport Art'," *Trans-action*,
4:10:28–33 (1967); and for two opposing views, see G. Swinton, *Sculpture of the Eskimo* (New York: New York Graphic Society, 1972) and
E. Carpenter, *Eskimo Realities* (New York: Holt, Rinehart and Winston,
1973). The growing cooperative-political movement stemming from
these artistic developments is described in: F. G. Vallee, *The Eskimo*

Cooperative at Povungnituk (Ottawa: NCRC, 1967); N. H. H. Graburn, "The Marketing of Canadian Eskimo Art," Northeastern Anthropological Association, Annual Meetings, 1970; and other publications already mentioned in the bibliography of this chapter and Chapter 12.

Though many of the above works touch upon the delivery of health care and the state of Eskimo health, O. Shaefer's "When the Eskimo Comes to Town," *Nutrition Today*, 6:6:8–16 (1971) presents a fairly reliable summary of the present trend toward the "diseases of civilization" correlating with changing diet and life style. For a lay presentation of the major developments in the Canadian North, told in a breezy, anecdotal style, D. Iglauer's *The New People: the Eskimo's Journey into Our Time* (Garden City, N.Y.: Doubleday, 1966) is an excellent introduction.

Recent developments in Labrador where Eskimo history differed from that of the rest of Canada have been the subject of little research and brief mention in this book. By far the best reference work and description is D. Jenness, *Eskimo Administration: III, Labrador* (Montreal: AINA, Technical Paper No. 16, 1965); and for a description of a typical community in this atypical area, see S. Ben-Dor, *Makkovik: Eskimos and Settlers in a Labrador Community* (St. Johns: Newfoundland Social and Economic Studies, No. 4, 1966). Until well into this century, the overwhelming outside influence in Labrador was the string of Moravian missions, well described in F. W. Peacock, "The Cultural Changes among the Labrador Eskimos Incident to the Coming of the Moravian Mission," pp. 439–456 in J. Malaurie (ed.), *op. cit.*

Greenlanders

There is very little literature in English on the modern conditions of the Greenlanders, but, as with other "Eskimo" areas, the authors and readers have to rely on C. C. Hughes, "Under Four Flags: Recent Culture Change among the Eskimos," *loc. cit.*, and D. Jenness's excellent *Eskimo Administration: IV, Greenland* (Montreal: AINA, Technical Paper No. 19, 1967). The special situation of the Polar Eskimos is described in J. Malaurie, *The Last Kings of Thule* (New York: Crowell, 1966) but, as C. Hughes noted, there have been very few community studies in Greenland compared with Alaska or Canada.

Artistic production in Greenland is described in the special issue of *The Beaver* (see above) and in J. Meldgaard, *Eskimo Sculpture* (London: Methuen, 1960), although by comparison the production is less important and less noteworthy than in Canada or even in Alaska. For special problems in self-government and in Greenlandic identity and bilingualism, the authors have relied heavily on the excellent thematic articles of I. Kleivan, "Language and Ethnic Identity: Language Policy and Debate in Greenland," *Folk* (Copenhagen) 11–12:235–285 (1969–1970), and H. Kleivan, "Culture and Ethnic Identity," *Folk*, 11–12: 209–234 (1969–1970).

APPENDIX

SUPPLEMENTARY BIBLIOGRAPHY

This section contains general references, additional materials on peoples less thoroughly covered in the body of the text, and guides to specialized journals and ethnographic films. For an intelligent introduction to social anthropological theory at the level of band and tribal societies which characterize all Arctic and Subarctic peoples, the reader may consult Elman R. Service, *The Hunters* (Englewood Cliffs, N.J.: Prentice-Hall, 1966), and Marshall D. Sahlins, *Tribesmen* (Englewood Cliffs, N.J.: Prentice-Hall, 1968).

The serious scholar should consult the extensive annotated *Arctic Bibliography*, Vols. 1–14, prepared by the Arctic Institute of North America and edited by Marie Tremaine (Montreal and London: McGill—Queen's University Press, 1953–1969), for the most complete compilation of materials concerning all aspects of the Arctic and its people. A particularly interesting historical overview of European exploration of all areas of the Arctic is that of Jeannette Mirsky, *To the Arctic: The Story of Northern Exploration from Earliest Times to the Present* (Chicago: University of Chicago Press, 1970).

GUIDE TO ADDITIONAL BIBLIOGRAPHY

Siberian Peoples

Selected works not listed in Chapters 3–6, 8, and 13 on Siberia are included here, beginning with the basic ethnographies. Asiatic Eskimo: Waldemar Bogoras, *The Eskimo of Siberia* (Memoirs of the American Museum of Natural History, Vol. 12, 1913). Koryak: Waldemar Jochelson, *The Koryak*, Parts I and II (Memoirs of the American Museum of Natural History, Vol. 10, 1901). Nanays: Lattimore Owen, *The Gold Tribe, "Fish Skin Tarters" of the Lower Sungari* (Memoir of the American Anthropological Association, No. 40, 1933). Samoyeds (general): Peter Hajdu, *The Samoyed Peoples and Languages* (Bloomington: Indiana University Publications, Uralic and Altaic Series, No. 14, 1968). Nganasan: A. A. Popov, *The Nganasan: The Material Culture of the Tavgi Samoyeds* (Bloomington: Indiana University Publications, Uralic and Altaic Series, Vol. 56, 1966). Sel'kups: Kai Donner, *Among the Samoyed in Siberia* (New Haven: Human Relations Area Files, 1954). Needless to say, M. G. Levin and L. P. Potapov (eds.), *The Peoples of Siberia* (Chicago: University of Chicago Press, 1964) is a basic reference on all Siberian peoples.

Problems in ethnogenesis and archeology: H. N. Michael (ed.), *Studies in Siberian Ethnogenesis* (Toronto: Arctic Institute of North America, Anthropology of the North, Translations from Russian Sources, No. 2, 1962), and *The Archaeology and Geomorphology of Northern Asia: Selected Works* (Toronto: AINA, Anthropology of the North, Translations from the Russian Sources, No. 5, 1964); M. G. Levin in H. N. Michael (ed.), *Ethnic Origins of the Peoples of Northeastern Asia* (Toronto: AINA, Anthropology of the North, Translations from the Russian Sources, No. 3, 1963); S. I. Rudenko, *The Ancient Culture of the Bering Sea and the Eskimo Problem* (Toronto: AINA, Anthropology of the North, Translations from the Russian Sources, No. 1, 1961); A. P. Okladnikov, *The Soviet Far East in Antiquity: An Archaeological and Historical Study of the Maritime Region of the USSR* (Toronto: AINA, Anthropology of the North, Translations from the Russian Sources, No. 6, 1965).

Special studies in Siberian folklore include the following works of Waldemar Bogoras: *Chukchee Mythology* (Memoirs of the American Museum of Natural History, Vol. 12, Part 1, 1910), *Koryak Texts* (Publications of the American Ethnological Society, Vol. 5, 1917), and *Tales of Yukaghir, Lamut, and Russianized Natives of Eastern Siberia* (New York: Anthropological Papers of the American Museum of Natural History, Vol. 20, Part 1, 1918).

For a collection of articles on Siberian religion, consult the works of V. Dioszegi (ed.), *Popular Beliefs and Folklore Tradition in Siberia* (Bloomington: Indiana University Publications, Uralic and Altaic Series, Vol. 57, 1968), and Henry N. Michael (ed.), *Studies in Siberian Shamanism* (Toronto: AINA, Anthropology of the North, Translations from the Russian Sources, No. 4, 1963).

For some rather dated overviews of the Siberian peoples refer to M. A. Czaplicka, *Aboriginal Siberia: A Study in Social Anthropology* (Oxford: Clarendon Press, 1914), and Waldemar Jochelson, *Peoples of Asiatic Russia* (The American Museum of Natural History, 1928).

For an account of an anthropologist's fieldwork in Siberia in prerevolutionary times, refer to M. A. Czaplicka, *My Siberian Year* (London: Mill and Boom [1915], n.d.), and for a useful overview of the Siberian geography and ecology refer to L. S. Berg, *Natural Regions of the USSR*, trans. by Olga A. Titelbaum (New York: Macmillan, 1950).

For a useful bibliography of English-language sources on Siberia (including a number of journal articles not given here), consult Sylvia

H. Forman, "The Siberian Peoples: Annotated Bibliography of English Language Sources," *Kroeber Anthropological Society Papers*, 36 (Spring 1967).

Northern Athabascans

A number of works concerning northern Athabascans which have not been listed in the references to Chapters 7–9 are listed here. We start with standard ethnographies. Chippewyan: Kaj Birket-Smith, *Contributions to Chipewyan Ethnology* (Report of the Fifth Thule Expedition 1921–1924, Vol. 6, No. 3, 1930); James W. Van Stone, *The Economy of a Frontier Community: A Preliminary Statement* (Ottawa: Northern Co-ordination and Research Centre, 61-4, 1961), *The Snowdrift Chipewyan* (Ottawa: Northern Co-ordination and Research Centre, 63-4, 1963), and *The Changing Culture of the Snowdrift Chipewyan* (Ottawa: National Museum of Canada, 1965). Dogrib: June Helm and Nancy O. Lurie, *The Subsistence Economy of the Dogrib Indians of Lac La Martre in the Mackenzie District of NWT* (Ottawa: Northern Co-ordination and Research Centre, 61-3, 1961). Eyak: Kaj Birket-Smith and F. de Laguna, *The Eyak Indians of the Copper River Delta* (København, 1938). Great Bear Lake: C. Osgood, *The Ethnography of the Great Bear Lake Indians* (Ottawa: Bulletin of the Canada Department of Mines, National Museum of Canada, Vol. 70, 1931). Han: J. R. Lotz, *The Dawson Area: A Regional Monograph* (Ottawa: Yukon Research Project—2, 1965). Hare: Janice Harlbert, *Age as a Factor in the Social Organization of the Hare Indians of Fort Good Hope, NWT* (Ottawa: Northern Co-ordination and Research Centre, 62-5, 1962); and Hiroko Sue, *Pre-School Children of the Hare Indians* (Ottawa: Northern Co-ordination and Research Centre, 65-1, 1965). Southern Ingalik: Edward H. Hasley, *The McGrath Ingalik* (Anthropological Papers of the University of Alaska, Vol. 9, No. 2, 1961). Kaska: J. J. Honigmann, *Culture and Ethos of Kaski Society* (New Haven: Yale University Publications in Anthropology, Vol. 40, 1949), and *The Kaska Indians* (New Haven: Yale University Publications in Anthropology, Vol. 51, 1954). Sarcee: Diamond Jenness, *The Sarcee Indians of Alberta* (Ottawa: Bulletin of the Canada Department of Mines, National Museum of Canada, Vol. 90, 1938). Sekani: Diamond Jenness, *The Sekani Indians of British Columbia* (Ottawa: Bulletin of the Canada Department of Mines, National Museum of Canada, Vol. 84, 1937). Slave: J. J. Honigmann, *Ethnography and Acculturation of the Fort Nelson Slave* (New Haven: Yale University Publications in Anthropology, Vol. 33, 1946); J. Alden Mason, *Notes on the Indians of the Great Slave Lake Area* (New Haven: Yale University Publications in Anthropology, Vol. 34, 1946); and June Helm, *The Lynx Point People: the Dynamics of a Northern Athapaskan Band* (Ottawa: National Museum of Canada, Bulletin No. 176, 1961).

For general overviews, special surveys, or studies of special topics consult Diamond Jenness, *The Indians of Canada* (Ottawa: National

Museum of Canada, Bulletin 65, Anthro. No. 15, 1963); Ronald Cohen, *An Anthropological Survey of Communities in the Mackenzie-Slave Lake Region of Canada* (Ottawa: Northern Co-ordination and Research Centre, 62-3, 1962); L. S. Bourne, *Yellowknife, NWT: A Study of Its Urban and Regional Economy* (Ottawa: Northern Co-ordination and Research Centre, 63-8, 1963); and R. A. Jenness, *Great Slave Lake Fishing Industry* (Ottawa: Northern Co-ordination and Research Centre, 63-10, 1963).

Bibliographies which are particularly useful in a study of Athabascans and other northern peoples include George Peter Murdock, *Ethnographic Bibliography of North America*, 3rd ed. (New Haven: Human Relations Area Files, 1960); Mary Jane Jones, *Mackenzie Delta Bibliography* (Ottawa: Mackenzie Delta Research Project—6, n.d.); J. R. Lotz, *Yukon Bibliography* (Ottawa: Yukon Research Project—1, 1964); and Anonymous, *Social Science Research Abstracts, 1959–1965* (Ottawa: Northern Co-ordination and Research Centre, 1966).

GUIDE TO JOURNALS

Acta Arctica Irregular publication; English, French, or German; humanistic/natural sciences. Arktisk Institut, L. E. Bruunsvej 10, Charlottenlund, Denmark.

Alaska Medicine 1959– ; quarterly; $6; book reviews, advertising, index. Dr. Arndt Von Hippel (ed.), 519 West Eighth Street, Anchorage, Alaska 99501.

Alaska Review of Business and Economic Conditions Published monthly May 1964 to January 1965, then irregularly; 8-page issues; statistics and analyses of income, exports, industry, population, etc. College, Alaska.

Alaska's Health and Welfare 1943– ; bimonthly; free. Ruth Anderson (ed.), Alaska Department of Health and Welfare, Information Section, Juneau, Alaska 99801.

Anthropologica Published by University of Ottawa, Canadian Research Center for Anthropology, n.s., Vols. 1–5; formerly by University of Ottawa, Research Center for Amerindian Anthropology, Nos. 1–8.

Anthropological Journal of Canada Bulletin of Anthropological Association of Canada, organ of Guild of American Prehistorians, Ottawa, Ontario, Canada.

Arctic 1948– ; abstracts in English, French, and Russian, bibliography, book reviews, charts, illustrations, maps, index. Anna Monson (ed.), Arctic Institute of North America, 3458 Redpath Street, Montreal 109, Canada.

Arctic Anthropology Chester S. Chard (ed.), University of Wisconsin Press, Madison, Wisconsin.

Arctic Circular 1948– ; quarterly (approx.); $1/vol.; charts, index. Mrs. G. W. Rowley (ed.), Arctic Circle, Box 68, Postal Station D, Ottawa, Ontario, Canada.

Beaver   Published quarterly by the Hudson's Bay Company, Hudson's Bay House, Winnipeg 1, Canada.

Canadian Historical Review   1920–   ; quarterly. R. Craig Brown (ed.), University of Toronto Press.

Habitat   Bimonthly; free; English and French, book reviews, illustrations. E. H. Q. Smith (ed.), Central Mortgage and Housing Corp., Montreal Road, Ottawa, Ontario, Canada.

Musk-Ox   Published by the Musk-Ox Circle, Saskatoon, Canada. University of Saskatchewan. Institute for Northern Studies

North   Journal of information and opinion; 1954–   ; bimonthly; $3; book reviews. Jane Pequegnat (ed.), Canada Department of Indian Affairs and Northern Development, Information Services, Ottawa, Ontario, Canada.

Recherches Amérindiennes au Québec   Articles and bibliography in French and English; 1971–   ; quarterly and special issues; $8/year. Société des Recherches Amérindiennes au Québec, c.p. 123, succ. g., Montréal 130, P.Q., Canada.

Samefolket   Journal of Samek affairs (in Swedish). Uppsala, Sweden.

Sentinal   (Supersedes *Roundel*) Canadian Armed Forces; French and English; 1965–   ; 10/year; $2.50/Can.; book reviews, charts, illustrations. Queen's Printer, Ottawa, Ontario, Canada.

Soviet Anthropology and Archeology   A journal of translations; 1962–   ; quarterly; $15. Stephen P. Dunn (ed.), International Arts and Sciences Press, Inc., 901 North Broadway, White Plains, New York 10603.

Soviet Union   An illustrated monthly; 1949–   ; 17 languages besides Russian. 8 Ulitsa Moskvina, Moscow K-9, USSR.

Tundra Times $10/year; weekly, Wednesdays. Owned, controlled, and edited by Eskimo, Indian, Aleut Publishing Company, a Corporation of Alaska Natives. Box 1287, Fairbanks, Alaska 99707.

GUIDE TO ETHNOGRAPHIC FILMS

B/W   Black and white
EBF   Encyclopaedia Britannica Films
EDC   Educational Development Center
FCE   Film Classic Exchange
IFB   International Film Board
M-H   McGraw-Hill
NFBC   National Film Board of Canada

General

Age of the Beaver   B/W; 17 min.; NFBC
1952–53—Documentary introduction to the history of the Canadian fur trade.

Peoples of the Arctic   B/W; 10 min.; Knowledge Builders
Introductory human geography of northern lands.

Comparative development of northern Canada and Siberia; TV documentary style with political overtones.

Trappers and Traders Color; 11 min.; sound; Crawley Films Ltd. and Canadian Geographic Society; IFB
Dramatized the role of the fur trader in Canadian history. (Is the same as the first half of *Portage.*)

Samek (Lapps)

Bear and the Hunter B/W; 11 min.; English; EBF
Romantic story of Lapp bear hunt; "natural man in the raw."

Forgotten Ancestors Color; 45 min.
1950s

Laplanders 9 min.; EBF
1952—Family moves from summer fishing grounds to highland reindeer pastures; slaughtering and preparing the year's food supply; reindeer for food, clothing, shelter, and transportation.

The Living North 70 min.; FCE
Romantic narrative of semitraditional Lapp reindeer herding.

People of the Reindeer (The Wind from the West) B/W; 18 min.; English narration; EBF
1956—Juvenile daydream of Swedish schoolboy; very little Lapp ethnography.

Samoyeds

Deer Tracks B/W; 25 min.; English subtitles, Russian narration; Moscow
The reindeer-herding Dolgans of the Tamyr Peninsula.

Evenks

Reindeer Tungus—The Lindgren Expedition to Northern Manchuria B/W; 60 min.; silent; Lowie Museum—Oscar Mamen
Excellent, rare Tungus ethnography; no acting, no "plastic."

Northern Athabascans

The People at Dipper Color; 18 min.; M-H
Chippewyans in northern Saskatchewan where "new ways of living do not conflict with the traditional activities"; pictures life of Moise MacIntyre who could leave but does not and why; emphasizes feeling of community.

Powwow at Duck Lake B/W; 15 min.; M-H
Indian-Metis problems discussed in gathering: schooling, limitations of education.

Northern Algonquians

Attiuk Color or B/W; 17 min.; Crawley
Contemporary Montagnais Indian caribou hunt and rituals.

Ka Ke Ki Ku B/W; Crawley
Poetic story of educational problems of young Montagnais Indians.
Land of the Cree B/W; 10 min.; FCE
Life of the Indians near Hudson Bay; bad commentary.
Trout Lake Cree B/W; 20 min.; University of Alberta, Edmonton
Technology and life of modern Cree.

Eskimos, Including Greenland

Alaska, USA Color; 30 min.; sound; Alaska Development Board
Survey of Alaska—geography, people, resources, industries; activities of Eskimos including ivory carving, sewing, dancing; shows logging, fishing, mining, farming; brief discussion of statehood.
Angotee Color; 32 min.; English voice; NFBC
1953—Account of Eskimo boy's life, birth to marriage, in contact-traditional period.
The Annanacks 60 min.; Crawley for Canadian Broadcasting Corp.
1962—Sociological account of history of a group of Eskimos from the George River district; deals with founding of Eskimo cooperative and life in the 1950s and 1960s.
Arctic Seal Hunt B/W; 11 min.; Bailey
1955—How Eskimo solves basic needs for food, shelter, and clothing.
Eskimo B/W; 55 min.; English and Eskimo sound; MGM
Good "acted" documentary made in the 1930s; story of traditional Eskimo life and first contacts with stereotypic whalers and police.
Eskimo Arts and Crafts Color; 21 min.; sound; NFBC
1945—Bone and ivory crafts; clothes and hunting equipment; community life.
Eskimo Children B/W; 11 min.; sound; Erpi, EBF
Activities of Eskimo family on Nunivak Island; changes resulting from contact.
Eskimo Family Color; 17 min.; sound; EBF
Eskimo family en route to and in spring camp; trading post; contact with industry/military; emphasis on acculturation.
Eskimo Hunters (Northwestern Alaska) B/W; 21 min.; sound
1949—Life conditioned by climate that is cold year round; hunting, fishing, trapping, details of life in the home.
Eskimo in Life and Legend (Living Stone) Color; 21 min.; English and Eskimo voice; EBF
1959—Picturesque but nonethnographic; Eskimo life and "traditional" soapstone carving; spirit world. A sales effort.
Eskimo River Village Color; 12 min.; Northern
1962—Life and living conditions of inland Eskimos of Alaska; typical village of Sleetmute, showing home, school, church, and social and business activities.
Eskimos (Winter in Western Alaska) Color; 11 min.; sound; EBF
Family life; women fishing through ice, men trapping fish, preparing for seal hunt; transportation, eating raw meat, Eskimo dance.

Eskimo Trails   B/W; 11 min.; sound; Twentieth Century Fox
   Shows Father Hubbard's Alaskan trip to study ethnological similarities of Eskimos; illustrates boat and home building, dancing, playing.

Fishing Arctic Style   12 min.; Bailey
   1955—Hand-made seines used for catching humpback salmon in Kobuk River; fish wheels operating on Yukon; Eskimo fishing through ice with barbless hooks and gill nets.

Hunters of the North Pole   10 min.; Sterling
   1951—Eskimo life in Greenland; scenes of walrus, seal, and polar-bear hunt.

Kenojuak—Eskimo Artist   Color; 20 min.; English and Eskimo sound; NFBC
   1964—Romantic semidocumentary of Eskimo artist and print making at Cape Dorset.

Kuma the Sleepy Hunter   13 min.; New York University
   Eskimo legend.

Land of the Long Day   Color; 2 parts @ 19 min.; sound; NFBC
   Semitraditional ethnographic: Part I, winter and spring; Part II, summer and fall; Baffin Island.

Life in Cold Lands (Eskimo Village)   Color or B/W; 11 min.; sound; Coronet
   Common family life in Unalakleet, Alaska; main concerns of food, warmth; shopping, games, trapping.

Nanook of the North   B/W; 54 min.; 2 reels; English commentary; Robert Flaherty; M-H/Contemporary Films
   Classic; authentic, humorous, and at times dramatic portrayal of contact-traditional Eskimo life.

Netsilik Eskimos   Series of films with Netsilik reenacting their past:
   Autumn River Camp   2 parts @ 30 min.; EDC
   Part I—snow, *karmaks* in river valley, toys, women gather moss, fishing, family eats cooked fish; Part II—igloo, move, making sled, woman making parka, children play, family travels down river.
   Fishing at the Stone Weir   Color; 57 min.; 2 parts; EDC
   Summer camp life; fishing and recreation.
   Winter Sea-Ice Camp   4 parts @ 30 min.; EDC
   Trekking across ice, igloo, hunting seal, liver sharing, play of women and children, etc., trials of strength, cooking, clothing repair, making stone pot, seal-meat sharing, visiting, story telling, juggling, drum dance.

Next Door to Siberia   11 min.; Bailey
   1955—Life in the community of Diomede in the Bering Strait.

Nomads of the North   12 min.; Bailey
   1955—Life at herder's camp; killing of ptarmigan; gathering firewood; fishing through the ice; children at play; rounding up the reindeer; living conditions during –70° weather.

Tigeria: Ageless City of the Arctic   11 min.; Bailey
   1955—Archeological remains; comparison of living conditions three

thousand years ago with the present; construction of igloos, walrus-skin boats, sled pulled by huskies.

The Wedding of Palo B/W; 72 min.; Eskimo dialogue; Palladium Films (The Museum of Modern Art) by Knud Rasmussen
1937—Broad portrayal of Ammassalik social life, through the story of the rivalry of two men over a girl, portraying a "song contest" and subsequent violence; excellent "acted" documentary.

INDEX